Managing Equally and Legally

For being *with* me:
Wayne and Jenny, Joey and Ben,
Bill and Mom and Dad

For support above and beyond:
Doug and Ken and Dawn

Managing Equally and Legally

A Practical Business Guide to Preventing Discrimination Complaints and Termination Lawsuits

by

Lynne Curry-Swann

with a foreword by
DOUGLAS S. PARKER

McFarland & Company, Inc., Publishers
Jefferson, North Carolina, and London

British Library Cataloguing-in-Publication data are available

Library of Congress Cataloguing-in-Publication Data

Curry-Swann, Lynne, 1951–
Managing equally and legally : a practical business guide to preventing discrimination complaints and termination lawsuits / by Lynne Curry-Swann.
p. cm.
[Includes index.]
Includes bibliographical references.
ISBN 0-89950-520-1 (sewn softcover : 50# alk. paper) ∞
1. Discrimination in employment—Law and legislation—United States—Popular works. 2. Employees—Dismissal of—Law and legislation—United States—Popular works. 3. Executives—United States—Handbooks, manuals, etc. I. Title.
KF3464.Z9C88 1990
344.73'01133—dc20
[347.3041133] 89-43685
CIP

Manufactured in the United States of America

McFarland & Company, Inc., Publishers
Box 611, Jefferson, North Carolina 28640

Contents

Foreword

The rights of nonunion employees have increased dramatically in the past decade, both nationally and in my own state. Alaska's supreme court, its trial courts, and state administrative agencies have kept pace with other more liberal jurisdictions in increasing the rights of private-sector employees. The most profound developments have been in the areas of employment due process—in other words, in the erosion of the traditional "employment-at-will" principle.

It used to be that a nonunion, private-sector employment relationship could be terminated at any time without notice and for any reason. Unlike their public-sector counterparts, employees in the private sector had very little protection against an employer's unilateral decision to terminate their employment. The employment-at-will doctrine has come under sweeping attack by state and federal courts in recent years. A large number of the states now recognize numerous contract and tort legal theories that require that termination and discipline be only for "just cause."

The various legal protections now available to unrepresented employees have been created by legislative bodies and the courts. Statutory enactments include "whistleblower" protection, including antiretaliation statutes for employees who foster unionism or file worker's-compensation, health-and-safety, discrimination, wage-and-hour, and other kinds of statutory claims. Several states have enacted statutes that provide that employees can be terminated only for "just cause." The statutory enactments of state legislatures have been overlaid with various federal laws enacted by Congress. The result is an ever-increasing and somewhat complicated safety net of statutory protections for employees. These new statutes complement the increasingly strengthened civil-rights laws first enacted a quarter century ago.

Judicially created theories that now protect employees include express and implied contract theories and intentional and negligent tort remedies. Contractual protections are being implied from employee handbooks, personnel policies, promises of "permanent" employment, promissory-estoppel theories, promises to employ for a specified duration, and the implied covenant of good faith and fair dealing. Tort theories recognized in various jurisdictions include tortious interference with contract, wrongful discharge, misrepresentation, intentional or negligent infliction of emotional distress, defamation, negligent performance evaluation, negligent personnel-files maintenance, negligent maintenance of work conditions, negligent supervision, and so on. A new theory beginning to gain some momentum in various states is so-called defamation by compelled self-publication. Under this theory, an employer is culpable for defamation when the employee discloses in subsequent job interviews to unemployment agencies or others the reasons given by the employer for termination. Other theories that may now show up in wrongful-discharge cases include loss of spousal consortium and a new hedonistic remedy ("loss of enjoyment of life").

Unfortunately for employers, the explosion in legal remedies protecting employees is not merely the grist for law-classroom instruction or ivory-tower musing. These legal principles are being embraced by the courts and applied against employers on a daily basis. The price tag for industry is mounting. Jury verdicts for hundreds of thousands, occasionally millions, of dollars are being rendered in wrongful-death cases. Although some states, including heretofore liberal California and Alaska, have in the past year begun limiting the instances where a jury can award punitive damages, the litigation floodgates remain quite open for discharged workers.

It has become imperative that every employer view every contemplated instance of discipline and discharge as potentially ending in a lawsuit. It is critical that employers understand as best they can the increasing number of personnel pitfalls that might result in adverse decisions by judges or juries.

The materials prepared by the author provide a good commonsense approach to personnel administration. Lynne Curry-Swann has made a considerable effort to demystify and uncomplicate the many legal theories that confront employers. This book will review practical approaches for dealing with the many unexpected events that occur daily in the workplace. It provides a strong personnel-training format for management at most levels, including first-line supervisors, personnel directors, and upper management.

Douglas S. Parker
Anchorage, Alaska
March 13, 1989

1

This Book's Purpose

YOU'RE IN CHARGE

Equal employment opportunity, just cause, employment at will, employee rights, and affirmative action affect each manager and supervisor. They raise questions you need answers for:

You believe one of your employees is drunk. Can you give him a sobriety test?

You want to fire someone for having a bad attitude. Can you?

Can an employer use arrest records as a criterion for denying employment?

Will you be found guilty of discrimination if you always give the women on your shift or in your department the easiest jobs?

Recently you were passed over for a promotion. The job went to a person with less seniority and, in your opinion, fewer qualifications than you have. Because he was a member of a minority group, you feel there was reverse discrimination. What are your rights?

You'd like to hire honest employees. Can you give applicants polygraph tests?

Can women be fired after they are eight months pregnant, even if they are still physically able to perform their jobs?

One of your employees is moonlighting. Can you fire her for that?

Can an employer lawfully refuse to hire women who have small children at home?

You want to fire an employee who's been sick a lot, but you haven't given him written notice. Can you fire him now?

Can a company lawfully recruit new workers by word-of-mouth referrals if most of its employees are white?

This book answers these questions. Even more, *it teaches you to answer questions like these before they cause problems for you* and translates the complexity of legislation into what each manager and supervisor needs to know to make daily personnel decisions.

In this training manual, you'll get a working understanding of the law as it might be applied in actual situations and in day-to-day dealings with employees. You'll learn practical guidelines and will have a chance to test your understanding of them in actual cases.

The training materials you'll be given have been tested by hundreds of participants in equal-employment-opportunity, discipline, and termination training workshops held by major organizations. The guidelines were written by a business owner and management consultant to offer you a practical business approach to understanding and handling your requirements under the law.

Employee employment grievances, discrimination complaints, and lawsuits are costly in both time and money. These costs can be avoided. Learning and following the guidelines presented in this book will reduce the number of complaints that will be filed against you. You'll learn the specific kinds of action that you must avoid in daily dealings with subordinates and job applicants. You'll learn your legal rights as well as the rights of all employees, particularly those who are minority, handicapped, female, or a member of another "protected" class.

You'll learn by having your skills tested. We'll present the reasoning behind the law, the specific guidelines you need to follow, and then ask you to test your judgment in specific cases that represent the types of situations you might face on the job today or tomorrow.

HOW MUCH CAN YOU RELY ON THIS BOOK?

This book will help you recognize, prevent, and handle problematic situations. This book covers a multitude of areas and is current through January 1990.

The author is a management consultant who has presented training seminars to thousands of managers and company officials, including attorneys. Companies, including law firms, have hired the author to advise them on issues related to employment law. Two attorneys reviewed the book for accuracy.

However, do not use this book to replace an attorney. The law is constantly evolving. Many cases involve complex issues and gray areas. There is no substitute for an attorney in legal areas.

STEPS YOU SHOULD TAKE

Stay educated. After reading this book, call your state human rights and municipal equal rights commissions for a copy of your state and city laws and regulations. Contact your state's Department of Labor for a copy of applicable labor laws in your state. Read your company's personnel policies.

Use resources. If a situation becomes a problem, contact the resources your company offers: your personnel manager, your labor-relations specialist. If your company has no resources, your state may offer free information and assistance. If not, seek out legal advice. An attorney is less expensive and more effective than going it alone.

2

Terms Defined So They Make Sense: Discrimination; Equal Employment Opportunity; Affirmative Action; Just Cause; Employment at Will; Employee Rights

DISCRIMINATION

Although it is legal to think prejudiced thoughts privately, prejudice that becomes discrimination is illegal. Discrimination means that due to our conscious or unconscious biases, stereotypes, prejudices, or assumptions, we deny certain categories of people equal employment opportunities. The effect is that a person may be unfairly categorized, often unintentionally, without any of our assumptions being true. Discrimination is prejudice brought into the job market.

Prejudices are natural. They grow from a strength—the ability to learn from past experiences. The problem comes when your prejudice about an individual person, due to his or her being a member of a category, denies the person equal employment opportunity. Maybe that mother of six young children is willing to work overtime and never to miss a day of work.

When prejudice enters the employment situation and denies individuals equal opportunities, it becomes illegal discrimination. We each have the right to be considered on the basis of our individual abilities rather than to be stereotyped because of our "category."

You Need to Discriminate (Sometimes)

Some kinds of discrimination are part of a manager's or supervisor's job and are legal. You make discriminations constantly in terms of an individual's abilities or a job's requirements. Without this ability, you couldn't decide which person to hire, promote, or discipline. Also, it may be legal to discriminate against "nonprotected" categories of people, such as smokers. However, you cannot discriminate against anyone in a "protected" category because of a characteristic related to that category. It is unlawful to discriminate against someone on the basis of her

age,
sex,
race,
color,
national origin, or
religion.

Depending on whether or not your company is a federal contractor, you may also be restricted from discriminating against a person who is handicapped.

In some states, other discrimination is unlawful, such as discrimination against someone due to her pregnancy, parenthood (whether she is the parent of small children), marital status (whether someone is divorced, single, or married), or changes in marital status.

EQUAL EMPLOYMENT OPPORTUNITY

Equal employment opportunity means that each individual has a right to be fully considered for any job for which he is qualified. It means that each employee has the right to be treated equally in all job-related matters and that all decisions should be based on the abilities of the individual and the requirements of the job. It does not mean that every individual has the right to a job—simply that each person merits equal treatment.

AA ≠ EEO

Affirmative action goes beyond equal opportunity and at the same time makes equal employment opportunity possible. Affirmative action is a remedy or antidote to counter past discrimination. Larger companies and companies that have federal contracts must have affirmative-action programs. Though there are guidelines and standards for affirmative-action plans, the specifics of a plan are developed by the individual company.

AFFIRMATIVE ACTION

Affirmative action means that individuals who belong to a category of people that have in the past suffered from the effects of discrimination are given a chance to "catch up." Qualified groups, minorities, and women—and in some cases the handicapped or veterans of the Vietnam era—must be actively recruited and fully considered on the basis of their qualifications.

Affirmative action does not necessarily mean that unqualified and untrainable people are hired. If applicants cannot meet a job's minimum qualifications, you need not hire them. However, affirmative action does give "preferential" treatment; job candidates who are minorities, women, or in other "protected categories" are sought out (and sometimes hired preferentially over someone more qualified) or are eligible for special trainee programs.

It's a Race

If you consider that getting a job is a contest, it was a rigged contest before affirmative action. Before affirmative action, it was normal to see white men (and usually those younger than 55) get most jobs. Often, these applicants were the most qualified for any individual job. Because of past discrimination, many women and minority applicants did not have the chance to accumulate the past employment experiences that would make them the most qualified applicants. Also, reports of past or probable discrimination kept many female, older, and minority applicants from applying for certain jobs and to certain organizations.

Another reason for affirmative action is that it is standard in both the past and present to use word-of-mouth recruiting. If an employer's work force is largely white, members of other races may not have had access to the word-of-mouth information about available jobs. Affirmative action is thus intended to correct inequities.

Is It Fair?

Before you say that this is not fair or equal, consider what "equal" means. If the race was rigged in the past, doesn't a temporary set of regulations help rebalance the odds?

A doctor gives equal treatment when each person gets the medicine she needs. The concept of equal does not mean that every person gets equal doses of the same medicine. "Equal" is true balance. Affirmative action is intended to even things out.

Surprise—A New Job

This gives managers and supervisors in midsize to large organizations a new responsibility. Before affirmative action, managers made hiring decisions solely on the basis of productivity: "Who is the most qualified for this job?" With the introduction of affirmative action, a manager's responsibility has changed. Until the work force becomes more balanced in its racial and sex makeup, the manager's responsibility is to balance productivity with affirmative action.

Table 2.1 (see p. 8) explains this in concrete terms. Imagine that this chart categorizes the job candidates you generally face. If you are faced with a choice of an *O* in the (a) or (b) position and an *X* in the (d) or (e) position, you'll probably want to hire the *O*. And, you'll be able to—you're not discriminating by saying that an applicant needs to meet all the minimum job requirements to get a job. Obviously, how you define the job's minimum requirements is key (see Chapter 17). In the past, people who have hired minority applicants without the needed qualifications as tokens have done equal employment opportunity a disservice by creating a backlash of resentment and setting up job applicants for failure.

In any case, you are not forced by affirmative-action legislation to hire someone unqualified or untrainable. If you don't have any *X* candidates in the (a), (b), or (c) positions, that is a recruiting problem, not a hiring problem. Affirmative action does require you to make a concerted effort to seek out qualified minority applicants; if there are none, you can't hire them. And in some cases, your company's affirmative-action plan may state that you will hire some partially qualified applicants for special trainee positions. If there are no qualified minority candidates, yet you've made an effort to recruit them and have conducted your hiring interviews in a nondiscriminatory manner, you have complied with the intent of the legislation.

The decision points come when you're faced with a choice of an *O* in the (a) position and an *X* in the (a), (b), or (c) positions. If you have a predominantly nonminority, male work force, you'll probably hire the *X* in the (a) or (b) position over the *O*. In these two cases, you're choosing a candidate who more than meets the job requirements *and* who also furthers your chances of meeting your affirmative-action goals.

The real gray area comes with the decision between the *O* in the (a) position and the *X* in the (c) position. In this case, the composition of your work force is key. Do you have a relatively balanced work force, with minorities and women represented in similar proportions to their representation in your community's work force? If so, you will probably hire the *O* candidate because of his or her outstanding qualifications. On the other hand, if your work force is predominantly nonminority and male, you'll do a better job of meeting both your productivity and your affirmative-action goals by hiring the *X*.

TABLE 2.1

(a)	*X*	*O*
(b)	*X*	*O*
(c)	*X*	*O*
(d)	--------*X*------------*O*--------(line of minimum qualifications)	
(e)	*X*	*O*

X = minority, older, handicapped, other "protected" categories of applicants.
O = applicants of nonprotected categories, often nonminority, male applicants.

JUST CAUSE AND FIRING

Many personnel policies state that a supervisor can fire an employee for cause if the supervisor has followed standard procedures. "Cause" often includes an employee's incompetence, misconduct, poor work performance, or excessive absenteeism. "Just cause" means that termination is warranted.

When an employee doesn't believe that the firing decision is fair, a lawsuit may be filed. You'll increase your chances of winning the suit if your firing decision complies with these seven "just-cause" principles:

1. The reason for the termination was a job-related or work-performance problem. The rule violated was directly related to safe, efficient, or orderly business operation.
2. The employee had foreknowledge that the problem could result in discipline and possibly in termination.
3. The employer fairly and impartially conducted an investigation to see if the misperformance happened. Documentation was kept.
4. Substantial evidence indicates that firing was justified.
5. Firing was not an unusually harsh action because of the severity of work-performance problem(s).
6. This work-performance problem was handled evenhandedly; the employer's actions were consistent with how the employer has handled similar disciplinary problems with other employees.
7. No discrimination took place.

Ex-employees may bring suit protesting termination on a number of grounds, including the following:

- Abusive or wrongful discharge,
- Bad-faith denial of the existence of a contract,
- Defamation by libel or slander,
- Economic injury or duress,
- Fraud,
- Implied covenant of good faith and fair dealing,
- Violation of public policy ("whistleblowing"),
- The intentional and negligent infliction of emotional distress (outrage),
- Interference with contract or breach of contract,
- Loss of consortium,
- Malicious termination of contract,
- Privacy invasion, and
- Trespass.

EMPLOYMENT AT WILL

It used to be that most employer/employee contracts, including unwritten ones, were "at will." This meant that employees could resign when they wanted to, often without notice. It meant that employers could terminate the employee "at will," even without notice.

Increasingly, however, employers are being regulated. Courts in 30 states have ruled that an implied contract exists in the words "you're hired." This implied contract is that the employee will have his job indefinitely unless there is a specific reason for the firing. Employees are suing ex-employers, and winning, when they are fired unjustly, wrongfully, abusively, or without notice. The costs of losing, or even winning but suffering through the lawsuit, warrant a full understanding of the term "at will."

"At will" means that an employer can terminate an employee at its "will" or choice and that the employee can leave employment at his will or choice. Legal actions by employees protesting at-will terminations have convinced many employers to fire an employee only if the employee has been given "reasonable" notice of the expected termination and is fired for just cause.

What is "reasonable" depends on factors such as an employee's length and positive record of employment, standard industry practices, and an employer's verbal assurances of continued employment. Verbal assurances may create a binding contract under special circumstances. Also, the new federal plant-closing law restricts employers of 100 or more employees who intend to lay off or terminate employees for economic reasons.

To protect themselves, many employers are declaring themselves "at will" employers in written personnel policies. "At will" means that an employer can discharge or lay off an employee when termination is in the employer's best interest. Similarly, an employee may quit at any time.

EMPLOYEE RIGHTS

Increasingly, even nonunion private- and public-sector employers are having to ensure that their actions are obviously fair and equitable. The courts are acting to protect public policy and employee rights.

Employee rights include rights

- to privacy;
- to off-the-job associations;
- to access to information that concerns themselves;
- to free expression;
- to protest unsafe working conditions;
- to protest discrimination;
- to self-organize and form unions;
- to fair treatment;
- to file worker's-compensation claims;
- to pursue wage-and-hour claims.

Privacy. Laws and regulations in the area of privacy include laws

- limiting the use of polygraph tests for job applicants or as a condition of continued employment (23 states as well as the federal government have specific laws);[1]
- restricting the use of arrest records in the hiring process (11 states);[2]
- setting limits on the data that the government can disclose to employers about individuals (10 states and the Federal Privacy Act of 1974);
- setting limits on the information a supervisor or employer can release about an employee, so that confidential or sensitive information is released only appropriately.

[1]These states include (as of the date of writing) Alaska, Arkansas, California, Connecticut, Delaware, Hawaii, Idaho, Iowa, Maryland, Massachusetts, Michigan, Minnesota, Montana, New Jersey, New York, Oregon, Pennsylvania, Rhode Island, Vermont, Virginia, Washington, West Virginia, and Wisconsin.

[2]These states include (as of date of writing) California, Colorado, Florida, Hawaii, Illinois, Massachusetts, Michigan, New York, Ohio, Oklahoma, and Virginia.

Off-the-job associations. Except in special instances, employers have no right to curtail an employee's off-the-job associations.

Access to information. Laws in 20 states and the District of Columbia[3] grant public-sector and often private-sector employees access to their personnel files.

Twenty-five states have "right-to-know" laws requiring companies to divulge information concerning hazardous substances used in the workplace. A new federal law and laws in three states require that employers provide notice of plant shutdowns and severance pay for affected workers.

Free expression. Except in special instances, employees have the right to speak freely. Courts in 24 states[4] have specific laws protecting employees who report legal violations by their employer or who refuse to violate a public policy such as an environmental law. Employee rights are, however, balanced by employer rights. For example, an employment relationship may require accuracy in employee statements in matters of public concern, an unusual degree of confidentiality, or discretion and avoidance of public criticism. In *Pickering v. Board of Education* (1972), the U.S. Supreme Court devised a "balancing" test to measure an employee's right to free speech versus the employer's rights.

To protest unsafe working conditions. Employees have the right to protest unsafe working conditions without needing to fear reprisals. Specific federal laws include the Toxic Substances Control Act, the Resource Environmental Conservation Act, and the Occupational Safety and Health Act (OSHA).

To protest discrimination. Employees who protest discrimination are protected against retaliation.

To self-organize and form unions. Employees are protected in their rights to self-organize, form unions, and bargain collectively.

To fair treatment. A number of federal and state laws, such as the

[3]These states include (as of the date of writing) Alaska, California, Connecticut, Delaware, District of Columbia, Illinois, Maine, Massachusetts, Michigan, New Hampshire, New Jersey, Oregon, Pennsylvania, Rhode Island, South Carolina, South Dakota, Tennessee, Utah, Vermont, Washington, and Wisconsin.

[4]These states include (as of the time of writing) Arizona, Colorado, Connecticut, Delaware, Florida, Hawaii, Illinois, Indiana, Iowa, Kansas, Kentucky, Louisiana, Maine, Minnesota, Michigan, New Hampshire, New Jersey, New York, Ohio, Pennsylvania, Rhode Island, South Carolina, Texas, and Utah.

- Fair Labor Standards Act,
- Employee Retirement Income Security Act,
- Tax Equity and Fiscal Responsibility Act, and
- Workers' Compensation laws,

protect employees' rights to fair treatment.

3

The Bottom Line: A Practical Description of the Laws Governing You

EQUAL EMPLOYMENT OPPORTUNITY AND AFFIRMATIVE ACTION

Every business or organization that has 15 or more employees must comply with the federal equal-employment-opportunity laws. Additionally, businesses and organizations that contract with the federal government or participate in a federally subsidized program may need to comply with both the federal equal-employment-opportunity and the affirmative-action laws. Depending on where your business is located, you also must comply with state and city regulations on discrimination.

The employment discrimination laws apply to

- recruiting, advertising for, and processing job applicants;
- hiring, promoting, demoting, transferring, laying off, upgrading, and firing employees;
- awarding employees tenure;
- rates of pay or compensation, changes in compensation;
- job assignment and classification;
- organizational structure, position descriptions;
- lines of progression and seniority;
- leaves of absence; sick, vacation, and other leaves such as maternity leave;
- fringe benefits;
- training, selection for training;
- employer-sponsored activities, including social and recreational activities, professional meetings and conferences;
- any other terms, conditions, or privileges of employment.

In short, the employment-discrimination laws apply to everything affecting employment.

These laws are intended to reduce the effect of prejudice on a person's employment opportunities. Three federal laws affect all employers with more than 15 (or in the case of age discrimination, 20) employees:

- the Civil Rights Act of 1964 (Title VII);
- the Age Discrimination in Employment Act of 1976;
- the Equal Pay Act of 1963.

Two laws affect employers who have federal contracts:

- the Rehabilitation Act of 1973;
- the Vietnam Era Readjustment Act of 1974.

Federal employers or organizations that contract with the federal government may also need to comply with applicable executive orders (see Table 3.1, p. 15).

THE CIVIL RIGHTS ACT OF 1964 (TITLE VII)

This law (as amended by the Equal Opportunity Employment Act of 1972) bans discrimination in employment on the basis of race, color, religion, sex, or national origin by employers, unions, and employment agencies. The Equal Employment Opportunity Commission (EEOC) administers the act.

Employers can't legally discriminate or deny anyone an equal opportunity in hiring, firing, wages, or any terms, conditions, or privileges of employment. Employers can't legally limit, segregate, or classify employees or applicants by race, color, religion, sex, or national origin in any way that would negatively affect their employment status. Want ads must be written without discriminatory words.

Employment agencies cannot legally discriminate in referring applicants.

Unions cannot legally discriminate in membership or in referral for jobs. Discrimination in apprenticeship and training programs is banned.

Title VII has been broadly interpreted by the courts. "Intent" to discriminate is often irrelevant since it can be neither proved nor disproved. Employment practices that deny opportunities to persons protected by Title VII are illegal, no matter what the manager's or organization's intent.

TABLE 3.1 Chart of Laws*

Equal Employment Opportunity and Affirmative Action	Employee Rights and Labor Laws
Civil Rights Act of 1964, Title VII (as amended by the Equal Employment Opportunity Act of 1972)	National Labor Relations Act (NLRA) of 1935
Executive Order #11246 (1965) (as amended by #11375 (1967)	Fair Labor Standards Act of 1938
Pregnancy Discrimination Act of 1968	Welfare and Pension Plans Disclosure Act of 1958
Equal Pay Act of 1963	Employee Retirement Income Security Act (ERISA)
Age Discrimination in Employment Act of 1967	Landrum Griffin Labor Management Reporting and Disclosure Act of 1959
Rehabilitation Act of 1973	Labor Management Relations Act
Vietnam Era Readjustment Act of 1972 and Reemployment of Veteran's Provisions of the Selective Service Act of 1967	Occupational Safety and Health Act of 1970 (OSHA)
Civil Rights Restoration Act of 1988	Federal Privacy Act of 1974
State laws and Municipal codes	Federal Mine Safety and Health Act of 1977
42 United States Code 1981, 1983, and 1985	1978 Uniform Guidelines on Employee Selection Procedures
	Civil Service Reform Act of 1978
	Tax Equity and Fiscal Responsibility Act of 1982 (TEFRA)
	Immigration Reform and Control Act of 1986
	Railway Labor Act
	Consumer Credit Protection Act
	Right-to-work laws
	Court rulings and public policy
	Worker's Compensation laws

*Your state and municipal laws and regulations may be more stringent than the federal laws and regulations.

When Title VII was first passed, it was viewed by Congress as a prohibition against unequal treatment of women and minorities. However, subsequent interpretation by the court has extended the law to cover additional areas.

First, "disparate" (essentially different) treatment of persons based on race, religion, color, age, sex, handicap, veteran's status, or national origin is unlawful.

Second, an ostensibly neutral employment practice that has disparate impact on minority or female employees or applicants is unlawful unless it is compelled by "business necessity" or job-relatedness. The employer has the burden of proof in establishing the "business necessity" of an employment practice. The plaintiff must show that an alternative practice that serves the employer's needs equally well would have a less drastic impact on the affected group. Recent Supreme Court rulings in this area may shift the burden of proof.

Third, unequal treatment is not always a necessary ingredient for a finding of discrimination. Equal application of the same rules, standards, or policies to all employees or applicants may have a discriminatory impact. For example, if requiring a high school diploma for certain jobs has an adverse impact on black applicants, it will be unlawful unless it is justified by business necessity.

Fourth, an ostensibly neutral policy that perpetuates past employer discrimination is unlawful unless compelled by "business necessity." An important exception is that a bona fide seniority system that perpetuates pre–1965 discrimination is lawful under Title VII.

When the courts find the effect of a basically neutral employment practice to be discriminatory against a member or members of a group protected under Title VII, the employer is ordered to provide remedies for the results of discrimination. Action to eliminate discrimination usually applies to all members of the "affected class" to which an individual complainant belongs.

There are very few exceptions to Title VII, and the exceptions that do exist have been interpreted narrowly by the courts. Justifying any practice or policy that has a disparate effect on groups protected by the law requires the employer to demonstrate a compelling business necessity and to show that no alternative nondiscriminatory practice can achieve the required purposes.

"Business necessity" has been narrowly interpreted to mean that the employer must show overriding evidence that a discriminatory practice is essential to the safe and efficient operation of the business. The employer must prove extreme adverse financial impact unless allowed to discriminate.

The following groups are subject to Title VII:

- All private employers with 15 or more employees;
- All educational institutions, public and private;
- State and local governments;
- All employment agencies, public and private;
- Labor unions with 15 or more members;
- Joint labor-management committees for apprenticeship and training.

Collective-bargaining agreements are no defense to unlawful discrimination or to practices that cause underutilization of minorities or women, except for a bona fide seniority system.

In 1980, the Equal Employment Opportunity Commission took the unequivocal stand that any action that interferes with an individual's job performance or "creates an intimidating, hostile, or offensive work environment" can be viewed as an illegal act.

EQUAL PAY ACT OF 1963

This law requires employers to provide equal pay for men and women performing work requiring equal skill, effort, and responsibility. The actual content of the job is important under the act, which is aimed at situations in which employees doing substantially similar work under similar conditions are paid differently because of their sex.

A difference in wages is permitted only if it is based on a merit or seniority system or on a system that measures earnings by quantity or quality of production. Pay differences must be justified by real job differences. The courts will not allow employers to pay male employees for "extra duties" if some male employees get the extra pay without doing the extra work or some females do the extra work without the extra pay or the extra duties are minor (don't exist or don't consume much time) or qualified females are not given the chance to perform the extra duties.

Records documenting each employee's wages and her hours worked must be kept for three years.

PREGNANCY DISCRIMINATION ACT OF 1968

This act forbids discrimination against women due to pregnancy.

AFFIRMATIVE ACTION: EXECUTIVE ORDER #11246 AS AMENDED BY #11375 (1967)

This order bans discrimination in federal employment and federal contracts or subcontracts in the areas of race, color, creed, religion, or national origin. It requires that employers promote the full realization of equal employment opportunity through affirmative-action programs. Not only are affirmative-action programs mandatory, but each affirmative action plan must include an upward-mobility program to increase the chances that those hired will not be limited to entry-level jobs.

Any employer or contractor who has a government contract in excess of $10,000 must demonstrate that it has made every reasonable effort to secure and promote minority and other specified applicants based on an appropriate recruitment policy.

Contractors with 50 or more employees holding contracts of $50,000 or more must develop a written affirmative-action program.

The Secretary of Labor created the Office of Federal Contract Compliance Programs (OFCCP) to implement the powers and responsibilities of this act.

AGE DISCRIMINATION IN EMPLOYMENT ACT OF 1967

This law bans employers of 20 or more persons from discriminating against persons older than 40 because of age. Many state laws specifically protect employment opportunities for employees over the age of 40. Employers in these states are forced to abandon mandatory retirement as a practical matter. Minnesota, Maine, and Alaska are other states with more restrictive age statutes than the federal law.

REHABILITATION ACT OF 1973

This act prohibits discrimination in the employment of handicapped persons if an employer has federal contracts of $2,500 or more. The act requires employers to develop affirmative-action programs in recruiting and hiring to improve the chances for handicapped applicants. Written affirmative-action programs must be developed if the contract or subcontract exceeds $50,000 and the contractor has 50 or more employees.

More than 30 states have amended their fair-employment laws to prohibit discrimination based on physical handicap.

VIETNAM ERA READJUSTMENT ACT OF 1974

This act bans discrimination in employment against veterans and disabled veterans of the Vietnam era. The act requires that every employer who has federal contracts of $10,000 or more must take affirmative action in recruiting and hiring to improve the employment opportunities for veterans. Written affirmative-action programs are required if the contract or subcontract exceeds $50,000 and the contractor has 50 or more employees.

REEMPLOYMENT-OF-VETERANS PROVISIONS OF THE SELECTIVE SERVICE ACT OF 1967

This act grants reemployment rights to anyone who is required to have other than a temporary job for military service or training if two conditions are true. First, the employee must seek reemployment within 90 days after termination of his military duty or hospitalization (with certain exceptions). Second, he must still be qualified to perform the duties of his old profession.

If the veteran is still qualified to perform the duties of his old position, he must be restored to that position or to a like position with the same seniority, status, and pay. If he is not qualified by reason of disability sustained during service, the employer must restore the veteran to another position for which he or she is qualified.

Alternatively, a returning veteran is entitled to severance pay. The act forbids discharging or denying promotion to any person because of any pending military obligation.

Employees have the burden of proving that their old jobs were not temporary. Employees are entitled to have a U.S. district attorney represent them in their suits.

THE CIVIL RIGHTS RESTORATION ACT OF 1988

This legislation expands protection for women, minorities, the elderly, and the handicapped against discrimination in federally funded programs.

It reverses a Supreme Court decision that narrowed the interpretation of earlier laws intended to guarantee the protection.

STATE LAWS AND MUNICIPAL CODES

Many states and municipalities have laws that are even stricter than are the federal laws. Organizations and small businesses that are not covered by certain federal laws may be covered by more stringent local or state regulations.

42 U.S. CODE 1981, 1983, AND 1985

These civil-rights acts, primarily focused on public-sector employers, protect applicants against discrimination related to race, national origin, citizenship, religion, sex, and color. Section 1981 also applies to private-sector employers and relates only to race, citizenship, and, in some cases, national origin.

EMPLOYEE RIGHTS AND LABOR LAWS

A multitude of laws cover employer/employee relations. The laws listed on the following pages cover only situations related to employee rights and to termination-related areas.

National Labor Relations Act (NLRA) of 1935

This act vests the National Labor Relations Board with broad powers. These powers include the right to investigate and remedy labor disputes and unfair labor practices and to monitor representation elections.

The National Labor Relations Act is concerned primarily with the protection of individuals' rights to engage in, or refrain from, concerted activities vis-a-vis their employer.

Unfair labor practices may include such things as

- discharging employees because they urged other employees to join a union;
- refusing to reinstate employees when jobs they are qualified for are open because they took part in a union's lawful strike;
- demoting employees because they circulated a union petition;
- refusing to hire qualified applicants for jobs because they belong to a union;
- interfering with employee rights by threats or promises;
- dominating a union by financial support;
- discriminating against union members;
- refusing to bargain in good faith.

National Labor Relations Board decisions in unfair-labor-practice cases are enforceable in U.S. courts of appeal. Each year, the U.S. courts of appeals handle approximately 350 cases.

Fair Labor Standards Act of 1938

This act sets a national minimum wage, a 40-hour workweek for regular pay, overtime, and other working conditions. In essence, employees have the right to be paid fairly according to certain guidelines.

The only businesses that are specifically exempted from compliance with this act are those in which *all* of the employees are of the owner's immediate family.

The act exempts certain types of employees from the wage-and-hour rules. The following listing gives you an indication of employees who might be excluded. To answer specific questions, you will want to consult both the federal act and your local state and municipal laws, which may be more strict.

- bona fide executives, administrators, and professionals;
- certain outside or commissioned salespeople;
- employees of newspapers with less that a 4,000 daily circulation in a localized area; and
- independent contractors (exempted under the statutory definition of "employee").

Some employers have been faced with double-damage back-pay orders and suits of staggering size under this act because there was no cutoff date for liability. Consequently, the Portal-to-Portal Act of 1947 was adopted as a statute of limitations on claims for unpaid minimum wages, unpaid overtime compensation, or liquidated damages.

As amended in 1966, the act requires an employee to bring a claim for back pay within two years after it accrues or within three years for willful violations of the law. A separate claim "accrues" on each separate payday. This limits an employer's liability to two years of back pay plus an equal liquidated sum. Employers who knowingly underpay an employee are guilty of a willful violation and have their exposure increased an extra year.

Nearly every state has some form of fair-labor or minimum-wage and overtime-pay law. Some states set a higher minimum wage than the FLSA or may require time-and-a-half pay for hours worked over 8 in one day or more than 40 in one week. Employers must check both federal and state requirements because state law applies where it is more generous to employees than federal law. Also, state laws may impose wage-related requirements, such as prompt-payment rules.

The act prohibits retaliatory firing of an employee who exercises rights guaranteed by this statute.

Labor Management Relations Act – Landrum Griffin Labor Management Reporting and Disclosure Act of 1959

This act protects employees from discharge for union activity. This statute was enacted as a bill of rights for union members. Any employer who

- makes payments or loans to any labor organization;
- makes payments to or reimburses the expenses of any employee to cause him to influence other employees with respect to their right to organize;

- makes expenditures with the intent of interfering with employees' rights or to obtain information concerning organizational activities, *except* for use in conjunction with certain proceedings; or
- hires a labor-relations consultant to persuade employees with respect to their organization and bargaining rights, *except* in conjunction with certain proceedings,

must report to the Secretary of Labor.

Employee Retirement Income Security Act (ERISA)

This act sets regulations for pension and other employee-benefit plans. The act prohibits employer reprisals against employees who exercise rights guaranteed by ERISA.

Welfare and Pension Plans Disclosure Act of 1958

All employers engaged in or affecting interstate commerce are required to register and report information concerning employee welfare and pension-benefit plans if the plan covers more than 25 people.

Occupational Safety and Health Act of 1970 (OSHA)

This act was established to ensure safe and healthful working conditions. The act gives the Secretary of Labor the responsibility for instituting regulations related to toxic materials or harmful physical agents.

In a Supreme Court decision related to this act, Justice Potter Stewart wrote, "The Act does not wait for an employee to die or become injured." An employee has the right to refuse to do a job when "a reasonable person would conclude that there is a real danger of death or serious injury and there is insufficient time, due to the urgency of the situation, to eliminate the danger through resort to statutory enforcement channels."

This act prohibits adverse personnel actions, including the firing of employees who exercise their rights under this statute.

A number of states have additional regulations to protect the health and safety of employees. These include regulations related to sanitary facilities, ventilation, heating, and seating.

Federal Privacy Act of 1974

This act limits the amounts and types of data that the government can disclose to employers.

The act outlaws requiring an applicant to take a lie-detector test.

California, Michigan, and other states have laws or court decisions forbidding requiring applicants and employees to take a polygraph or lie-detector test as a condition of employment or continued employment.

Michigan, Washington, and other states have laws requiring employers to give employees access to their own personnel files. Employees are entitled to commence a legal action if the employer has placed false information in the file.

Federal Mine Safety and Health Act of 1977

This act sets standards for safe and healthful conditions in mines.

1978 Uniform Guidelines on Employee Selection Procedures

These guidelines cover the major federal equal-employment-opportunity statutes and orders. The guidelines emphasize that any measure or test used as the basis for any employment decision must be nondiscriminatory.

The guidelines stress the necessity of avoiding adverse impact against a protected group. There is no adverse impact if the worst-performing group is achieving at a rate of 80 percent as well as the best-performing group. These groups include

- blacks;
- American Indians and Alaskan natives;
- Asians and Pacific Islanders;
- Hispanics (Mexicans, Puerto Ricans, Cubans, Central and South Americans, and others of Spanish culture or origin);
- females; and
- males.

Civil Service Reform Act of 1978

This statute protects federal-sector employees against dismissal at will. Public-sector employees may be protected by state statutes. Also, an employee against whom action is taken is entitled to

- 30 days' advance written notice unless there is reason to believe that the employee has committed a crime for which a sentence of imprisonment would be appropriate;
- reasonable time of at least seven days to file an answer to the charges;
- representation by an attorney or other representative;
- a written decision, with specific reasons.

Tax Equity and Fiscal Responsibility Act of 1982 (TEFRA)

This act contains an amendment to the Age Discrimination in Employment Act of 1967. Employers are required to offer employees aged 65 to 69 the same health benefits they offer to their younger employees.

Immigration Reform and Control Act of 1987

The act affects employers of four or more employees. An employer can no longer hire an illegal alien without facing a $250 to $10,000 fine for *each* illegal alien hired.

The law requires that employers get proof of citizenship or work-authorization documents on all new employees within three working days of hire.

Employers may apply for a 21-day extension if they have proof they've requested the necessary documentation.

It is unlawful to continue to employ the alien, "knowing the alien is, or has become, an unauthorized alien."

Aliens who have applied for amnesty during the legalization period may verify their right to work in the United States by showing their amnesty-application-fee receipts.

The I-9 forms that employers must keep to show that new employees are legally eligible to work can be inspected by government agents without warning. Even though Immigration and Naturalization Service inspectors have to give companies 3 days' notice of an inspection visit, officials from the Wage and Hour Division can drop in at any time and demand to see these documents.

In 1988, the Immigration and Naturalization Service (INS) began fining employers who either hired illegal aliens or failed to keep adequate records. Fines range from $250 to $10,000 for each illegal alien, depending on the number of citations the employer has already received. Employers who show a "pattern or practice" of violating the law face criminal sanctions and up to 6 months in jail.

While most managers assume that they are exempt from fines unless they hire illegal aliens, they also face fines for paperwork violations. Even employers of regularly scheduled babysitters and maids who work regularly must comply with the regulations.

Railway Labor Act

This act prohibits discriminating against employees in certain transportation industries such as railroads and airlines on the basis of union activity.

Consumer Credit Protection Act

This act prohibits firing an employee for wage garnishment except in certain instances where other factors apply.

Right-to-Work Laws

At least 20 states have enacted right-to-work laws prohibiting employers from denying work based on an applicant's or employee's refusal to join a union.

COURT RULINGS AND PUBLIC POLICY

Recent court decisions in the areas of employee rights and employment at will have created new precedents.

If an employer violates employee rights, the courts may rule in favor of the ex-employee, even though no specific law prohibits the employer's actions. This has happened regularly where an employer has asked an employee to commit illegal acts or perjury. These court rulings are intended to protect public policy.

Similarly, courts are deciding in favor of ex-employees who have been terminated without just cause. Cleveland Board of Education v. Loudermill, 105 S.Ct. 1487 (1985), holds that public sector employees have a "property" interest in their job and are entitled to notice. In some cases, this property right extends to instances in which employees are temporarily suspended while a supervisor investigates allegations of gross misconduct (violence, drunkenness, and so on). In these cases, suspension with pay is a safer route than suspension without pay.

A number of states have specific statutes prohibiting firing an employee for

- refusing to commit perjury, illegal acts, or sexual acts;
- blowing the whistle on unsafe or defective products or procedures; or
- filing workers'-compensation claims.

These states include California, Connecticut, Idaho, Illinois, Indiana, Kansas, Maryland, Massachusetts, Michigan, Missouri, Montana, New Hampshire, New Jersey, New York, Oregon, Pennsylvania, Texas, Washington, and West Virginia.

4

This Is to Scare You: The Obvious and Hidden Costs of Discrimination, Unlawful Termination, and Violations of Employee Rights

TIME AND MONEY

The costs for violating discrimination, termination, and employee rights laws and regulations are extremely high. There are costs to you as soon as a complaint is filed, whether the charges are proved true or false.

The first cost to the company is time and energy—your own, the legal department's, and the time of other managers. Regardless of the suit's merit, you will spend time complying with the investigation and meeting with government officials.

If you don't have a legal department, you need to get, use, and pay an attorney.

Even if just one employee of one facility of a company files a complaint, the entire organization may be investigated. You pay the time and legal costs, regardless of the complaint's merit.

As an example, one Denver lawsuit consumed the time and effort of the managerial staff for a two-year period. The company eventually lost the suit and paid an additional $500,000.

If the complainant (plaintiff) prevails, the employer may be liable for

- lost wages,
- lost benefits,
- the reduction in the value of the pension,
- reasonable and other costs,
- interest on the back wages and benefits.

The employer may have to pay the plaintiff's legal fees. The employer may be assessed special punitive damages or other damages for pain, suffering, and humiliation.

In *Eide v. Kelsey-Hayes,* the court awarded damages to the spouse of a discrimination victim, stating that the discrimination created emotional distress, so that the victim no longer provided the spouse an expected level of companionship. While this issue was not covered by federal laws, it is a part of some state statutes (in this case, Michigan).

The courts may order the employer to reinstate the employee or to provide three to five years of front pay if the working relationship is irreparably damaged.

HIDDEN COSTS

Some costs for illegal treatment are not immediately obvious and yet are possibly the worst personal costs to a supervisor. A fired employee who proves that the firing was discriminatory or unlawful may be reinstated. An applicant whom a manager refuses to hire may be granted the job. The supervisor who discriminatorily or unfairly disciplines an employee may face an injunction against further harassment of the employee. These hidden costs can hurt a supervisor's effectiveness or damage a career.

SPECIAL COSTS FOR ILLEGAL DISCRIMINATION

The 1972 amendment to Title VII of the Civil Rights Act gave the EEOC authority to take civil action against an organization that is using discriminatory employment practices. As a result, legal actions by the EEOC against organizations have increased substantially.

If the employee or applicant proves discrimination or the employer cannot prove nondiscrimination, the employer may have to pay wages, lost benefits, reasonable costs, interest on the back wages and benefits, and attorney fees to the employee.

In a class-action suit, if even one employee proves discrimination, the courts may offer compensation for denied wages, opportunities, and benefits to the suing party and to all other members of similar categories of workers. Back pay for every affected member of a given category can lead to extremely high costs:

- AT&T paid in excess of $100 million dollars.
- A jury in Colorado awarded more that $15 million to a 33-year employee of Sears, Roebuck and Company who was discharged because of his age.
- $100,000 was awarded to a female chemistry professor in compensatory damages in a sex-discrimination suit brought against the University of Minnesota.

- Nine steel companies and unions paid $31 million in back pay in another settlement.
- The Ford Motor Company was ordered to pay $23 million to make up for past discrimination against women and minorities.
- Many organizations have had to pay between $500,000 and $1 million in back pay for violations of the Equal Pay Act.

TIGHTER REGULATIONS AND SCRUTINY

Employers who are found to have discriminated face increased costs in meeting new restrictions that are often more stringent than those placed on other employers. The courts may order them to comply with new and more stringent regulations, policies, and affirmative-action guidelines. For example, a company that might previously have set its own voluntary affirmative-action goals might be ordered to comply with mandatory affirmative-action goals. Not only will the company be ordered to stop discrimination, it will be ordered to make specific changes to increase its hiring from the affected class of applicants to erase the present effects of past discrimination. The courts may also require more stringent reporting or self-monitoring procedures.

INTANGIBLE COSTS

The artificial barriers we create in discrimination act against us. They prevent us from making the best possible use of the available labor market. Some of the potentially most productive and loyal workers are the ones our unconscious or outmoded biases prevent us from considering. Discrimination not only denies opportunities to the people we don't hire or promote but also creates artificial arrangements—schools in which only women work, companies in which all 450 employees above the level of management trainees are men. If the most valuable asset to a strong organization is the best human resources available, discrimination is our largest barrier to strength.

VIOLATING THE EMPLOYEE'S RIGHT TO SAFETY

The Occupational Safety and Health Administration recently issued some of the largest fines in its history. It levied a record fine of just over $1.5 million against a car manufacturer for safety violations and a fine of $615,000 against a defense contractor for accident-reporting violations. OSHA says the fines should be a "clear signal to all employers that we mean what we say."

5

Where the Rubber Meets the Road: What Discrimination Laws and Employee Protection Mean to Each Manager and Supervisor

Despite the complexity of discrimination legislation, there are only two main responsibilities for the supervisor or manager to have in mind: (1) prevention: preventing complaints from occurring; (2) being legal: being legally in compliance to enable your company to be on the winning side of any complaint or lawsuit filed. Several basic guidelines will help you manage to do both at the same time.

Acting to prevent problems and to remain in legal compliance also helps to protect you, the individual manager or supervisor. In cases of sexual harassment and other areas of supervisor-employee relations, individuals may bring a private suit alleging discrimination or the tort of outrage against an individual supervisor or manager.

PREVENTING COMPLAINTS AND LAWSUITS FROM BEING FILED

As you learned in Chapter 4, complaints and lawsuits are costly in time and money. It's totally to a company's advantage to reduce the number of complaints. This does not mean that managers need be so afraid of a potential complaint or suit that they feel their hands are tied when they want to discipline an employee.

A manager has the right to hire only qualified or trainable employees, to expect a full day's work from each employee, to insist on employees meeting stated performance standards, and to use standard disciplinary measures.

You can prevent complaints by being

- obviously fair,

· aware, and
· legally in compliance.

Be Obviously Fair

Complaints are usually not filed when it is clearly visible to both the supervisor and the employee or applicant that a hiring, firing, promotion, or disciplinary decision was based on an objective assessment of the individual's ability and the job's requirements.

Most complaints are filed because of a perception of unfairness. The employee or applicant believes the supervisor was prejudiced, that the decision was biased. Typical complaints are

"I was more qualified, but someone else got the promotion."
"I was given a bad performance review after only one warning, but John has had three warnings, and his performance review was okay."
"I was late to work—so are most of the guys, off and on. But I got fired."

It's the perception of bias that results in discrimination complaints.

Often, it's clear to the manager why one person was fired, hired, or promoted. A problem results when these reasons aren't visible to others. If the manager can't clearly explain a decision, he leaves his company open to a complaint or suit.

You can eliminate many complaints and suits by protecting your company in 3 trouble areas:

· Lack of perceived fairness: let employees and applicants know that decisions were based solely on job-related reasons.
· Differential treatment: consistently apply standards to all individuals and have logical and legal reasons for any exceptions.
· Inability to explain decisions: Nothing increases the chance of a complaint or suit being filed faster than a manager's inability to give a reason. If an applicant asks, you should be able to say, "The successful applicant was the most qualified when measured against relevant criteria."

Be Aware

As a supervisor or manager, you're used to the fact that your position entails responsiblity for your employees' productivity. You are also responsible for your employees' behavior if the behavior of one employee denies employment opportunity to another. No one expects you to hear every remark spoken by one employee to another or to observe every interchange. However, if a complaint arises in the workplace, you are responsible to investigate. And if a lawsuit is filed and it is later found that there was a pattern or practice of sex harassment; religious, race, or other discrimination; or other violations of employee rights, the court will likely conclude that as a supervisor, you either knew or *should* have been aware.

These issues are not new to supervisors and managers; they are part of following sound management practices. It has always been important to have job-related reasons for decisions and to be fair and consistent. The new issue here is the importance of having one's fairness and consistency be obvious. The bonus is that following fair and consistent decision-making principles tends to lift morale among nonminority as well as minority workers. All employees tend to function best when clear job standards are set, when it is clear what decisions are based on, and when workers are treated fairly and consistently.

Legal—Being in Compliance

The same standard management practices that prevent complaints and suits from being filed will also help organizations win lawsuits. If managers are able to state, "This is what the job standards are; this is what the employees are paid to do; this is what the decision was based on," in clear, nondiscriminatory terms the suit will generally have no basis and be easily defended.

Managers must be able to logically justify decisions and actions regarding work assignments, discipline, promotion, and hiring.

Being in legal compliance means having objective job standards and requirements and objectively made decisions. It's tough to defend an overly subjective decision. In some cases, the courts have found discrimination because an employer could point to no objective standards for making promotions and other employment decisions.

As a manager, you can also ask yourself, "Would an investigator find a 'pattern of discrimination' in our company?" In one large organization, 90 percent of the minority workers fired during a three-year period had "attitude" problems. No nonminority employees were fired for that reason. Employers who use the subjective and vague term "attitude" when describing attitude problems keep lawyers busy. As a manager, consider "attitude" a general description. What are the *tangible specifics* you want changed?

YOU'RE ON

To prevent complaints and lawsuits from being filed and to be legally in compliance, each supervisor and manager needs a basic understanding of employment laws and a working understanding of how the laws apply in specific areas.

Most supervisors and managers will learn after reviewing the guidelines in this book that they've been guilty of illegal actions. While most charges are brought against a company rather than an individual manager or supervisor, it is the individual who goes one-on-one with the government in explaining why an individual decision was made. It is the individual who needs to know the law and how it applies.

6

Age Discrimination: He's Too Old, She's Too Young, They're Too Middle-Aged

We grow up with age discrimination. How often do you remember being told you were too young? Sometimes a person is too young to have accumulated enough experience to handle a new responsibility. However, some of us are old enough at 15 to do things other people haven't learned to do at 30. The idea of eliminating age discrimination in employment opportunities is that some of the stereotypes are not accurate.

Remember the cliché "You can't teach an old dog new tricks"? Consider the effect of that when applied to an older person's employment opportunities. Does it mean that a person who is 45 should not have a chance at a new job, promotion, or training opportunity? Or that a person of 57 should just curl up and die because he can't learn anymore? Discrimination causes hardships, and stereotypes get in the way of employers' making use of a valuable labor resource, the older employee. Stereotypes deny an older person who's willing to work hard a chance to show it.

Some of us can't imagine staying at a job past 65; some of us can't imagine leaving our jobs. Because of inflation or the enjoyment of work, many older Americans went to work past age 65.

The federal Age Discrimination in Employment Act of 1967 (ADEA) bans discrimination against older employees and applicants.

In 1987, the federal Equal Employment Opportunity Commission approved a policy giving employers the responsibility of maintaining a work environment free from age harassment. This policy obligates employers to take "positive steps" to eliminate insults and intimidation relating to a person's age.

As a means of testing your knowledge on age discrimination, what are your decisions in these situations?

1. A supervisor, forced to lay off workers, tends to lay off first those employees who are within a few years of retirement.
   Discrimination? Yes__ No__ Don't know__
   Why?
2. Because of the youth of most of the employees in the summer program the manager wants to hire a "young, aggressive" person who can relate to youthful workers as a supervisor.
   Discrimination? Yes__ No__ Don't know__
   Why?
3. Company X has an informal policy of placing only individuals under 40 years of age in management-trainee programs.
   Discrimination? Yes__ No__ Don't know__
   Why?
4. A manager, Jack, has an opening in his section and already knows the person he wants to fill it with. However, John, who is being laid off from another department, has slightly better qualifications and asks to be considered for the position. John is 53. The manager chooses his 30-year-old friend, in part because the friend could be groomed to take his position should he be promoted. After all, John might retire in 2 years under the company's early-retirement program.
   Discrimination? Yes__ No Don't know__
   Why?
5. Although no employee is required to retire at 65, after 65, employees no longer accrue additional retirement benefits.
   Discrimination? Yes__ No__ Don't know__
   Why?
6. All of the 50 employees laid off during the past 3 months were over age 50.
   Discrimination? Yes__ No__ Don't know__
   Why?
7. None of the employees above age 62 are sent to training programs.
   Discrimination? Yes__ No__ Don't know__
   Why?
8. Airplane pilots who are responsible for flying are asked to retire at age 60.
   Discrimination? Yes__ No__ Don't know__
   Why?

If you checked Yes in situations 1 through 7 and No in situation 8, you're batting 100 percent. Let's take a look at the guidelines you need to handle these and harder case situations.

AGE-DISCRIMINATION GUIDELINES

· It is unlawful to discriminate against persons above the age of 40 on the basis of their age.

In New York, the protected age group is 18 to 65. In Alaska, individuals of all ages are protected *as long as they are of working age* (which can be as young as 14, with a permit). In Alaska, California, Connecticut, Delaware, Hawaii, Illinois, Iowa, Maine, Maryland, Montana, Nevada, New Jersey, South Carolina, and West Virginia, there is no upper limit on the protected age group.

· You may not apply an assumption or stereotype about "older workers" as a group to a decision affecting an individual. This includes assumptions about

- Physical ability—"She's too old to stand on her feet all day."
- Learning ability—"When they get that old, they can't pick up new knowledge too well."
- Mental alertness—"I knew an older guy who just couldn't keep up with the pace."
- The cost of training—"He might retire in a year; it's just not worth it to train him."
- The possibility of illness or turnover—"At her age, she'll probably be sick a lot."
- Motivation—"I'm not sure he'd be willing to keep up with the amount of work the job requires."

Each of the above assumptions denies an individual a chance.

· Age harassment is not allowed. Age-harassment examples include a supervisor's characterizations that an older employee is rigid or accident-prone, constructive discharge through harassment that a reasonable person would find intolerable, or the assignment of less desirable jobs to an older worker to force the employee to resign.

· Comments such as "recent" college graduate or "lack of energy" may be seen as evidence of age discrimination.

· Employment decisions must be based on functional ability (Can this person do this job?) rather than on chronological age. Watch for the difference between someone's "real" versus his or her "assumed" ability.

· EEO guidelines and court decisions have established general guidelines for factors that are reasonable for an employer to ask for if they are job-related. These include physical-fitness requirements, production quantity and quality, and hours to be worked.

· As a general rule, group comparisons about performance ability or costs related to workers of a certain age may not be used in making employment decisions about individuals.

Also, the decision to terminate a number of employees based on productivity measured in terms of output related to salary was not seen as age discrimination in *Donnelly v. Exxon Research and Engineering* (1975), despite the relationship between age and salary.

· Considerations of age may not be used in decisions regarding pay and benefits. As a result of the Tax Equity and Fiscal Responsibility Act of 1982 (TEFRA), employers must offer employees aged 65 to 69 the same health benefits they offer younger employees.

· Compulsory retirement is prohibited. (*Note:* This rule may be modified in certain states for some federal agencies.) Further, the use of threats or intimidation to force early retirement is unlawful.

However, age considerations may be used as the basis for forced retirement if dangers to the public's safety exist.

For example, pilots of carrier planes and helicopters and drivers of carrier buses are required to retire at the age of 60. Although some older drivers and pilots might be safe, the increased risk of accidents and the potential of danger to the public justify their forced retirement. However, the employer's justification may be subject to considerable second-guessing in a subsequent legal action.

Similarly, in *Usery v. Tamiami Trail Tours* the court upheld a company rule stating that job applicants for bus driver must be under age 40. The company defended its policy by showing that it took years to attain bus-driver proficiency and that physiological degeneration with age would affect performance and safety.

Unfortunately, there is no test accurate enough to predict which drivers or pilots might have enough physical deterioration due to age to make them an increased risk in certain conditions. If there were, the guideline of functional ability rather than chronological age could be used.

In *Aaron v. Davis* and *Rodriguez v. Taylor,* in which companies attempted to terminate firemen who reached age 62 and refused to consider applicants of 40 or more years for security jobs, the court found discrimination.

· Beware of situations in which you terminate or lay off employees, "cutting costs where it hurts the most." This will usually lead to disparate treatment of older employees. If you terminate employees at the high end of the pay scale, make sure that terminations are directly related to specific job and organizatonal needs such as

· relevance of skills;
· need for physical strength;

· specific education levels needed for certain jobs;
· performance.

· Selected layoffs and terminations that appear to be directed at older employees as a category create the presumption of unlawful age discrimination. This presumption is hard to rebut.

· There are six main exemptions to age discrimination:

1. Where age is a bona fide occupational qualification (BFOQ) (a qualification absolutely needed to do the job right—for example, only an actor or actress of a certain age can play some parts).

Legitimate BFOQs normally relate to the gradual deterioration of most individuals' strength, nervous system, and stamina with advancing age. These defenses are often difficult to counter.

An employer must establish that there is a "factual basis of believing that substantially all applicants" over a certain age limit would be unable to meet the job's qualifications or that the physical and mental qualifications of applicants or employees over a certain limit cannot practically be determined, and so automatic exclusion is necessary.

A BFOQ involving Greyhound Lines was upheld. Greyhound refused to consider driver applicants over 35. According to the Seventh Circuit Court of Appeals, because the body undergoes "degenerative changes due to the aging process" and because of the strenuous work of a bus driver (some driving days total 12 hours), age was seen as a BFOQ, an issue of public safety, and as "reasonably necessary to normal business operation."

Conversely, the Fifth Circuit (1986) held that a Mississippi statute requiring game wardens to retire at 60 was not a BFOQ.

2. Where legitimate business needs justify an age BFOQ. For example, certain executives and "high policy-making" employees are still subject to involuntary retirement.

3. Where differential treatment relates to a bona fide seniority system.

4. When an employment action is made for good cause, such as the inability to do the job. However, the use of contrived arguments to justify unwarranted terminations due to age reasons is illegal.

In a 1988 case, the U.S. Supreme Court left intact a Third Circuit U.S. Court of Appeals ruling that direct evidence of age bias is not necessary to prove that an employer's non-age-related reason is pretextual. Though the plaintiff could prove no direct evidence of age discrimination, the court held for the plaintiff: because the reason the employer gave for firing the employee wasn't legitimate.

5. When danger to the public safety is involved.

6. Where differential treatment is based on factors other than age.

CASES

With the age-discrimination guidelines in mind, please make two decisions in the following cases: (1) Is there a possible case of discrimination? (2) Which guidelines apply?

Case 1: Sam Smith

Sam Smith, an equipment specialist for Automotive Service Company (ASC), is due to retire in three years. One of his strengths as an employee has been in helping new employees learn their jobs.

Recently, much of the equipment information for ASC was computerized. A new position was created for an individual who would be responsible for educating the other specialists in the many uses they could make of the system.

Sam applied for the position and because of his past work in educating new employees, thought he had a good chance of getting it. He was upset when it went to a younger person, one he had helped greatly during the past three years. When he asked the manager why, the manager said that the younger person had learned his job quickly and had committed to be with the firm for at least five years.

Sam thought this over and the next week went to the state's Human Rights Commission to file a complaint.

Case 2: Martha Johnson

Ms. Martha Johnson has worked for the Training Department for nine years. She is called a secretary but informally is responsible for keeping all of the company's training records and has attended workshops in record keeping. On her sixtieth birthday, she learns that a new position, "records administrator," has been created. This position formalizes the duties that Ms. Johnson has handled for the past three years.

Though she applied for the position, she didn't get it. According to the personnel officer, the position went to a woman in her early thirties who was hired because she has a college degree. Ms. Johnson has an A.A. degree in secretarial science. The other woman has a B.A. in English.

Case 3: John Rodrick

Bell Company began to experience financial problems due to a decline in the demand for its products. As a result, the company president decided to temporarily close the plant John Rodrick managed.

John, 54, has worked for Bell for 27 years and was one of its highest-paid employees.

Although the plant was reopened after several months, Rodrick was fired and replaced by a 43-year-old manager. The president cited business reasons for the decision, saying that the new manager was paid only half Rodrick's salary.

Rodrick brought suit. Will he win?

Case 4: Bonuses

Although Youngess Company management clearly understood the illegality of age discrimination and forced retirement, they encouraged early retirement by offering individuals from age 62 to 64 a bonus for "early retirement." Employees called the offer intimidating because they were given only five days to make a decision.

Decisions

Sam Smith has a possible case under the age-discrimination law. It appears he has strong qualifications for the position, as does the other applicant. The decision point comes in the reasosn the manager gave for hiring the other employee: The other employee has committed to be with the job for at least five years; Sam, due to retire in three years, was probably not going to be around that long. However, other qualifications, not the factor of possible retirement, should have been the reason for giving the other employee the job over Sam.

This case violates not only the age-discrimination legislation but practical business sense. A younger employee, even one who "commits" to stay for five years, will not necessarily stay with a job as long as an older employee due to retire in three years. The older employee is likely to be there for those three years; the younger employee may become dissatisfied or find a better job offer elsewhere and leave.

Martha Johnson has a possible case under the age-discrimination law. The reason given for why she didn't get the job was very weak: The other woman had a B.A. However, the B.A. was in a field less related to the job than Martha's A.A. in secretarial science and workshops in record keeping. Further, Ms. Johnson has been keeping the records for 3 years and thus has strong past experience. No mention was made of the other candidate's work experience.

In this case, too, because the reason for the younger employee's getting the job is weak and because of the ages of the two candidates, there is at least a possible case for age discrimination. Also, the B.A., of itself, may be discriminating against older employees and thus would need to be proved a necessary job requirement.

John Rodrick may win. This case falls into an obviously gray area.

In a similar case, *Metzu Transit Mix* (1987), the Seventh Circuit addressed the question of whether salary savings were nondiscriminatory justification.

The court said no, basing its ruling on a two-part test created by the Sixth Circuit. Part one concerns whether the necessity for a cost reduction is real; part two asks that forced retirement be the least detrimental alternative to reduce costs.

In this case, the court determined that the company was not in serious enough financial straits to use the cost issue. Second, the court suggested that the company could have pursued less drastic remedies such as offering the plaintiff a lower salary or a lesser position.

In *Gelof v. Papineau* (1986), the First Circuit held that an employer's use of high salary as a criterion for termination did not violate age discrimination. In this case, the plaintiff claimed his former employer had discriminated on the basis of age when it terminated several high salaries to reduce its payroll by half a million dollars. According to the court, "...the fact that the employer used high salary as a reason for discharge does not necessarily discriminate against older employees; the plaintiff did not present evidence showing that choosing higher salaried people had a disparate impact on older workers; the plaintiff offered no statistics to show that age is significantly related to salary."

The court also rejected the plaintiff's request that the employer offer him a demotion, because of the impact on potentially "bumped" lower-level employees.

In *Bonuses,* The Youngess Company management is in trouble. Their "five days to make a decision" places undue pressure on the older employees. Their bonus program was seen by some employees as a subtle threat and constituted a practice of "forcing" early retirement.

COSTS

With age discrimination, stereotypes, assumptions, and bias are expensive "habits." Because of the hardships suffered by older employees, penalties under the age-discrimination law are sometimes even more severe than under the civil-rights law.

In one settlement, an oil company charged with age discrimination for laying off employees over 40, paid $2 million in back wages to the discharged employees and reinstated 120 employees.

In 1982, over $20 million was awarded to plaintiffs in EEOC-monitored discrimination suits. In 1985, more than $30 million was awarded. In 1987, the EEOC received 20,000 discrimination complaints. In one of them, Pan Am was assessed $17.2 million in damages.

Interestingly, most age-discrimination suits are brought by individuals in their fifties, not sixties, and most stem from the perception of bias when employees are passed over for promotions.

7

Do You Want a Boy or a Girl? The Realities of Sex Discrimination

SEX DISCRIMINATION

Sexual discrimination often starts before we're born. Our parents are rarely neutral; most would prefer a boy or a girl. And not only are there real biological differences between men and women, but each of us has been conditioned to treat men and women in different ways.

Employment discrimination occurs when our personal preferences or conditioning denies someone a job opportunity or when we allow biological differences to categorize a job as available only to men or only to women, regardless of an individual's talents, strengths, or abilities.

Most of us are unaware of how strong our assumptions are about what is man's work or woman's work. As a short experiment, after you read each word in the following list, make a mental image of a person who fits the word:

- postman
- senator
- scientist
- diplomat
- business owner
- lawyer
- accountant

If you're like most of us, each of the persons you imagined was a man. In our world, many of the recognized professionals in each of the above fields are men, which subtly conditions us to stereotype jobs. Avoiding sex discrimination means choosing individuals for jobs solely on the basis of their ability, regardless of their sex, and whether or not you personally are accustomed to that job as a man's or a woman's.

Sex discrimination exists and shows up in dollars. In a 1985 study by the National Research Council, more than one-third of the disparity in earnings between men and women was attributable to sex discrimination.

Avoiding sex discrimination means applying the same standards to men and women. If a family picture on a man's desk means he's a "responsible family man," why does a child's picture on a woman's desk mean "her family will come before her career"? If a man has lunch with his supervisor, you probably assume they're friends or discussing business. Then why assume a woman lunching with a male supervisor is having an affair? Even if one woman employee of yours has had a hard time taking criticism, don't assume all women will. If one man can't handle criticism, do you assume the same is true of all men? If a woman employee tells you she's getting married, don't assume she'll then get pregnant and leave when you assume a male employee will become more "settled" after marriage. If you assign a woman a business trip, don't ask her what her husband will say if you wouldn't ask a man the same question.

A record number of lawsuits have been won by women. In one of the most famous, in 1983, television anchorwoman Christine Craft won $500,000 against a television station whose executives demoted her, she claimed, for being "too old, unattractive, and not deferential to men." In 1986, women won a $2.6 million lawsuit against Sunitomo's for widespread sex discrimination.

In 1988, some 1,100 women denied jobs as State Farm Insurance Company agents received individual awards of up to $420,000, costing State Farm over $300 million. In 1988, the Alaska Pulp Corporation paid $200,000 to 32 women discriminated against by mill hiring practices in the late 1970s; 20 of these women will receive seniority and pay benefits dating from the time they first applied for employment. The suit also cost Alaska Pulp 5 years of legal wrangling.

Sex discrimination, of course, works both ways. For example, it is illegal to assign heavy work to men and lighter work to women. In one company, the manager hired a female for its packing and shipping department and said that the woman would have to handle the heavier boxes. The men filed suit. The arbitrator ruled for the men.

As a means of testing your knowledge of sex discrimination, what are your decisions in these six situations? Assume the related facts you need to make a decision.

1. To hire a male accountant of a quality comparable to the female accountants, the company found it had to offer a higher salary.
   Discrimination? Yes__ No__ Don't know__
   Why?

2. Ann Smith was transferred to a position in personnel because the men working for her in maintenance would not take orders from a woman. She received a slight increase in pay.
   Discrimination? Yes__ No__ Don't know__
   Why?
3. A woman with small children missed 1 to 2 hours of work every day for 8 weeks. She was counseled after 4 weeks, given written notice after 6 weeks, and fired after 8 weeks.
   Discrimination? Yes__ No__ Don't know__
   Why?
4. A supervisor privately asks the manager if Joanne Watson, who was recently recommended for the management-trainee program, plans on having kids. If so, he doesn't want to okay the recommendation as the program is 2 years long and costs $15,000 per employee.
   Discrimination? Yes__ No__ Don't know__
   Why?
5. Supervisor X doesn't want a visibly pregnant woman on his shift. He doesn't doubt her ability, but he knows his men will spend too much time helping her.
   Discrimination? Yes__ No__ Don't know__
   Why?
6. Due to a limited number of washroom facilities for women employees, they were not hired for the first 6 months of the project.
   Discrimination? Yes__ No__ Don't know__
   Why?

If you checked Yes in every case except 3, you were right. Case 3 involves a person who misses work and is disciplined according to standard procedures. In the other cases, an issue related to sexual characteristics biases other decisions. If case 1 stumped you initially, you might want to reread it. Why pay more money for an accountant of comparable quality unless you specifically want a male accountant? Let's take a look at the guidelines relating to sex discrimination.

SEX DISCRIMINATION AND SEXUAL PROPRIETY GUIDELINES

· As a supervisor, you are supervising employees rather than members of the same or opposite sex. Your employee's ability to do the job and not his or her gender is important.

Each applicant must be judged on the basis of his individual abilities. Using generalizations such as "most women" or "many men" is illegal. It's unlawful to classify jobs as "heavy" or "light" and to limit women to the "light."

Job requirements such as the ability to lift 35 pounds may be used. However, no assumptions about a woman's inability to lift 35 pounds may be used.

· Assumptions about women such as "They can't handle difficult men," "They'll leave to have babies," "They will stay home when their children are sick," "They're not aggressive," are not allowed.

For example, an employer who failed to promote a female personnel representative because "there was no way a woman could stand up to a union" was found guilty of sex discrimination (*Thomas v. Cooper Industries,* 1986).

· Rules and standards of conduct must be applied to men and women equally, so that neither sex is denied employment opportunities. Decisions relating to travel, business entertainment, and shift or job assignment may not be based on sex considerations.

For example, a decision not to ask women to work nights may result in denied opportunities if a later promotion hinges on experience they could have gotten only by working a night shift. Similarly travel, business entertainment, and certain job assignments are crucial to an employee's job and career development, and may not be denied.

· An employer cannot refuse to hire women because of a lack of separate toilet facilities. An employer who has only one restroom can either buy a portable toilet or hang a co-ed sign on the one restroom door. Sleeping facilities can become co-ed by hanging a blanket down the center of the room.

· In handling a relationship between two employees, any discipline must be applied equally to both parties. If the relationship affects the work performance either both individuals must be disciplined or neither, or the individuals concerned should decide between themselves who should look for new employment.

· Any policy related to unwed pregnancy, employee affairs or the parenthood of employees must be applied to both sexes. However, these categories (pregnancy and parenthood) are protected categories in some states.

· The non-work-related and private activities of employees are protected *unless* the employer can *prove* these activities adversely affect job performance.

· Standards of conduct must apply equally to both sexes. In 1987, a federal court ruled (*EEOC v. FLC and Brothers Rebel*) that a woman fired for using "unladylike" language was held to higher standards than male employees and was thus a victim of sex discrimination.

In *Hopkins v. Price Waterhouse* (1987), the "Big Eight" accounting firm was found guilty of sexual stereotyping when it denied the plaintiff a partnership because of her "abrasive personality." The court concluded that the male partners reviewed the plaintiff's qualifications against criteria that they did not apply to male candidates. Although the plaintiff had brought more revenue to the firm than the male candidates, the firm's partners said she lacked "interpersonal skills" and "social graces." She was advised to "talk more femininely." Price Waterhouse contended that unconscious sexual stereotyping does not amount to intentional disparate treatment. The court disagreed and found that discrimination existed.

· Dress-code appearance restrictions must be reasonable and consistently applied to both sexes. In *O'Donnell v. Burlington Coat Factory* (1987), the courts struck down a dress code requiring only women to wear smocks.

· Customer, client, or co-worker preferences are not reasons for discrimination. In *Morris v. Bianchini* (1987) the court ruled that promoting a man and not a woman to athletic director because customers preferred a "male macho" image was illegal.

CASES

With these guidelines in mind, please make two decisions in the following cases: (1) Is there a possible case of discrimination? (2) Which guidelines apply?

Case 1: Lynn Swanson

Lynn Swanson applied for a sales-trainee position with Stereo Systems, Inc. She had responded to an ad that read: "Sales trainee, m/f, no experience needed, looking for an aggressive, career-minded person."

Lynn filed a complaint after she did not get the job, stating that she was asked several questions that indicated sex discrimination, such as "Do you plan to get married and have children?" "Do you really want a career?"

The company responded to the complaint by saying that they hired a more qualified person who had taken an electronics course in high school. They also said that all applicants were asked questions relating to their career attitudes. They said that Lynn was marked down for not being willing to answer these questions.

Stereo said that they had turned down several male applicants and that if the EEOC would send them a qualified female, they would hire her.

In investigating, you learn that out of 11 positions, Stereo has no women employed as sales trainees. Also, 3 of the 11 had no electronics background when hired. Stereo has a very extensive one-year training program in electronics for its sales trainees.

Case 2: Joyce Hasquel

Joyce Hasquel filed a sex-discrimination complaint. She claimed that she applied unsuccessfully for three years to get summer employment as a meter maid. She stated that the reason all the meter maids were male was that the police chief who hired favored students he knew from the all-male college at which he taught.

The police chief could prove that for the third summer in question he had hired a more qualified applicant. However, he couldn't justify the questions he had asked Joyce, such as whether she thought she could make an unassisted arrest or help in a stakeout, as job-related.

Case 3: Jim Dawson

Jim Dawson was denied a job as a kindergarten teacher, even though he had more student-teaching experience and higher grades in his education classes than the female applicant who won the position.

He filed suit, charging that he was subjectively denied the job.

Under questioning, the hiring panel gave these reasons for choosing the female candidate:

- She had a number of younger brothers and sisters, so had years of experience with children.
- Her approach to children was gentle and caring, in contrast to Jim's, which they characterized as matter-of-fact.
- She had a team attitude, in contrast to Jim who seemed much more independent.
- They pay little attention to grades since they do not seem related to actual job performance.
- She and Jim both had an acceptable period of student-teaching experience.

Will Jim prevail?

Decisions

Lynn Swanson's case indicates a pattern of discrimination. The company

- advertised that no experience was needed;
- hired several people with the same experience Lynn had;

- had no women sales trainees;
- asked questions that indicate potential discrimination.

It is the "pattern" in this case, the accumulation of pieces of evidence, that indicates discrimination and gives Lynn Swanson a good case.

Joyce Hasquel has a case for discrimination. The police chief asked her questions that were not job-related for a meter maid. It is allowable to hire the most qualified candidate; however, when the questioning process indicates possible discrimination, the employer is making a case against his reasoning and hiring process.

Jim Dawson is right. Many of the reasons were subjective and potentially discriminatory. For example, it's an opinion whether "gentle" or "matter-of-fact" approaches work best with children.

The hiring panel may have had a tough choice, between two comparably qualified applicants. In this case, they may have legitimately chosen either applicant for valid reasons. In many ways, the female candidate was stronger. Unfortunately, they undercut their defense by giving two subjective reasons. Jim may prevail.

8

What to Say When She Says She's Expecting: Pregnancy and Maternity Leave

You thought she was putting on weight; instead, she's pregnant. If she's your employee, what do you say after "congratulations"? What are your responsibilities and your rights?

If you haven't yet faced this issue, you will. Almost half of the U.S. labor force is female, and 90 percent of working women have had or will have children during their careers.

For an employer, the prospect of an employee announcing "I'm pregnant" is other than joyous. It means the company may lose an employee and will face maternity and possibly other leave, resulting in work disruption.

THE LAWS IN SUMMARY

The Pregnancy Discrimination Act of 1978 outlaws discrimination against women due to pregnancy, childbirth, or related medical conditions. Women may not be fired or refused jobs (other than short-term temporary jobs) or promotions because of pregnancy or abortion. While the law stops short of dealing with the issue of job protection, it covers both written and unwritten employment practices.

A number of states (Montana, Connecticut, California, Massachusetts) have laws specifically protecting the jobs of women who have babies. New York, New Jersey, and other states require employers to provide temporary disability-insurance benefits for childbirth. California law requires employers to provide pregnant women up to four months' disability leave with the guarantee of a job after their return to work. This law has been challenged by employers and upheld by the U.S. Supreme Court.

Congress is considering the Family and Medical Leave Act (H.R. 925), a bill governing medical and child-care absences. This parental-leave bill would require employers of 50 or more employees to provide at least 10 weeks of unpaid leave to parents of newborn or seriously ill children. The bill also safeguards the employees' job security. This bill has enormous support; it could become law in the early 1990s. Employers may want to ready plans to raise employee contributions to medical-insurance premiums.

Minnesota and Oregon have recently passed laws guaranteeing employees who become natural or adoptive parents up to 6 (Minnesota) or 12 (Oregon) weeks' unpaid leave.

PREGNANCY GUIDELINES

· Treat pregnant women and women recovering from childbirth exactly as you treat other applicants and employees. Make management, supervisory, and employment decisions on the basis of their ability or inability to work.

· You may not fire or refuse a job or a promotion to a woman merely because she is pregnant or has had an abortion.

· An employer cannot refuse to hire a woman because of her pregnancy-related condition if she is able to perform the major functions of the job. An employer cannot refuse to hire a pregnant woman because of the preferences of co-workers, clients, or customers.

· If a woman employee needs to stop work because of pregnancy, treat her like other employees who have a medical condition or temporary disability. Pregnancy is *just another medical condition*.

· In hiring interviews, do not question whether a job applicant has small children at home, anticipates a pregnancy, or is pregnant. Avoid asking questions about child-care provisions. Even if you think a woman with small children or a pregnancy will be sick or absent frequently, this is not sufficient reason for a no-hire decision.

· Do not let stereotypes about maternal obligations deny employment opportunities to a pregnant woman.

· Do not single out pregnancy by creating special procedures for determining an employee's ability to work. Instead, use the same procedures you would use to determine the ability of any employee.

· Women cannot be forced to go on leave as long as they are able to work. The exception to this is with airlines, which must maintain stringent safety standards for passenger protection (*Conduit v. United Airlines*). Otherwise, mandatory departure and return dates for maternity leave are generally unlawful.

· In some cases, business necessity and safety may justify mandatory maternity leave or refusal to hire a worker. For example, if you supervise a remote construction camp where travel is by plane and the weather is often poor, you might be able to give mandatory leave to a woman who is eight months pregnant on the grounds that getting her to the hospital in time would be difficult. If you're hiring to fill a five to seven week vacancy, you'll probably be excused from having to hire a woman who's eight months pregnant. However, don't arbitrarily bypass her for a permanent position unless another applicant is more qualified or there are other legitimate nondiscriminatory reasons.

· A woman who is unable to perform certain aspects of her job because of pregnancy must be accommodated to the same extent that the company accommodates other temporarily disabled employees.

GUIDELINES RELATED TO MEDICAL AND EMPLOYEE BENEFITS

· Benefits regarding pregnancy or raising children cannot be based on the sex of the employee.

· Any medical- or disability-insurance programs must cover pregnancy to the extent that other "disabilities" and medical conditions are covered. If an employer provides leaves of absence for other illnesses or disabilities, these benefits must be available to an equal extent to pregnant women.

· Generally, if benefits or leave privileges are restricted—for example, available only to employees who have been with the company for at least a year—these same restrictions may also apply to pregnant women. The requirement is that the restrictions be nondiscriminatory. Also, except in certain states, employers are not required to pay for or grant extended leaves of absence for pregnancy or birth-related incapacity unless they provide similar disability leave for other illnesses such as heart attacks or hernias.

However, the federal Equal Employment Opportunity Commission has stated that pregnant employees must be given "reasonable" leave, even if inadequate leave is otherwise provided to other disabled employees. Their reasoning is that both men and women may have disabilities, but only women become pregnant. Inadequate sick leave for pregnant women, they argue, thus constitutes sex discrimination.

· This principle of equal treatment extends to employees' spouses; if health-insurance benefits are available for male employees' spouses, the same benefits must be available to female employees' spouses. However, an organization may provide one level of pregnancy-related coverage to female employees and another to employees' spouses or dependents.

· If an employer allows its employees to take leave without pay or to use accrued annual leave for travel or non-job-related education, this same type of leave must be granted to those who wish to remain on leave for infant care, even though they are medically able to return to work.

· There is no legal requirement that an employer must grant a female an additional leave of absence after she has fully recovered from the delivery. However, such a bill could become law in the 1990s and would apply to both mothers and fathers.

CASES

With these guidelines in mind, please make two decisions in the following cases: (1) Is there a possible case of discrimination? (2) Which guidelines apply?

Case 1: Linda Anderson

Linda Anderson worked for Advance Bank as a receptionist. After her daughter was born, she took two months of unpaid leave. As a result, she lost her job. Because Advance Bank is headquartered in California and California law requires that women who take up to four months' disability leave for childbirth be guaranteed their jobs, Linda filed a suit.

Advance Bank management contended that it is difficult to run a business while holding jobs open for employees on disability leave. Also, they stated that the California law is discriminatory and that a male employee who lost his job after being out two months for a heart attack could sue for reverse or handicap discrimination.

This case eventually went to the Supreme Court. Who prevailed?

Case 2: Betty Sanders

Thompson Architects fired Betty Sanders, an architect with a master's degree and two years' work experience, for "work not up to the caliber of the office." This shocked Betty, who had received a voluntary merit raise four months earlier, following her six-month performance review.

Because her dismissal came less than a month after she'd told a senior partner she was three months pregnant and that she wasn't sure how long she'd be out after the birth, Betty felt the firing was pregnancy-related. She then looked at the personnel policies and learned that her maternity leave would be fully covered, once she was a one-year employee. She was a 10-month employee at the time of the firing.

What do you think the courts will say?

Decisions

Linda Anderson won. First, California law guaranteed her four months' unpaid leave; she took only two months. Second, the court refuted Advance's claim that finding a temporary replacement for a bank receptionist was difficult.

Finally, the court said that the law is not discriminatory but instead corrects an imbalance caused by the fact that only women have babies. Justice Thurgood Marshall wrote, "California's law" promotes equal employment opportunity by allowing "women, as well as men, to have families without losing their jobs."

In *Betty Sanders's* case, the decision will rest on whether the termination was for job-related work-performance problems and whether standard disciplinary procedures were followed.

The circumstantial evidence suggests that this termination *was* related to the pregnancy; however, if there were serious questions about the quality of her architectural work that had surfaced in the four months after the six-month review and if Betty had received verbal and written counseling, the firing might be defensible.

9

They're Dating: Sexual Propriety, Conduct, Affairs; and Marital Discrimination

What do you do when an employee's conduct or personal situation creates a problem in the office? Do you hope the problem will fade? Do you intervene? How do you avoid jumping in with both feet and creating a worse problem?

How do you handle two employees having an affair? What if one of your employees is dating a competitor? What if one of your supervisors marries an employee?

SEXUAL PROPRIETY, CONDUCT, AFFAIRS, AND MARITAL-DISCRIMINATION GUIDELINES

· In handling a relationship or affair between two employees, any approach or discipline must be applied equally to both parties. If the relationship negatively affects the work environment, either both individuals must be disciplined or neither, or the individuals concerned should decide between themselves how to resolve the situation.

Make sure all your policy statements are gender-neutral.

· You may not use concerns about propriety or potential misconduct to deny opportunities related to business travel, entertainment, shift assignments, or other job assignments.

· You are responsible for an employee's sexual misconduct if it results in denied or threatened employment opportunities for another employee.

· Any policy related to unwed pregnancy or an employee affair must be applied to both sexes. In Alaska and other states that consider marital status a "protected category," such policies themselves are illegal.

· Unless "morality" is related to job performance, you cannot refuse to hire or dismiss an unwed mother. (In some cases, the courts have allowed dismissal when unmarried fathers were also dismissed, but these are a minority.)

· Work-related standards and expectations must apply equally to both sexes. In 1987, a federal court ruled that a woman fired for using "unladylike" language was held to higher standards than male employees and was thus a victim of sex discrimination (*EEOC v. FLC and Brothers Rebel*).

In *Hopkins v. Price Waterhouse* (1987), the accounting firm was found guilty of sexual stereotyping when it denied the plaintiff a partnership because of her "abrasive personality" and lack of "interpersonal skills" and "social graces." The court concluded that the male partners reviewed the plaintiff's qualifications against criteria they did not apply to male candidates.

· Rules and standards of conduct must be applied to men and women equally. Decisions relating to travel, business entertainment, and shift or job assignment may not be based on sexual considerations. As an example of this, you cannot use a stereotyped assumption about women's domestic duties as a reason for rejecting women for a job.

· Dress-code and appearance restrictions must be reasonable and consistently applied to both sexes. In *O'Donnell v. Burlington Coat Factory* (1987), the courts struck down a dress code requiring only women to wear smocks.

· In some states, you can set standards regarding marital status and supervisor-reporting relationships (that spouses may not work for the same company). Beware of any situation in which primarily one sex is denied employment opportunities because of the nepotism rule.

In many states, antinepotism policies (policies banning the employment of spouses in the same company) have been the focus of numerous lawsuits. Unless an employer can defend its policy on the basis of "business necessity," the employer may lose.

In a nepotism situation, "business necessity" would relate to a definite conflict of interest. In general, conflict of interest is easiest to prove when one spouse would be supervising another. The courts sustained nepotism rules in *Harper v. TransWorld Airlines* and in *Smith v. Mutual Benefit Life Insurance.* In both situations, the company refused to employ spouses in one department.

· If there are strong business reasons, such as the conflict of interest that occurs when one spouse supervises another, you may dismiss after the marriage one member of a husband-wife team. It is best if you allow them time to select who will leave. If they refuse to choose, you may terminate the one with less seniority. Offering one spouse a transfer is a more defensible decision than terminating either spouse.

· Marital-status regulations have been the focus of many lawsuits. The regulations of the airline industry have generally been held to be discriminatory. In *Inda v. United Airlines* and *Sprogis v. United Airlines,* the courts held that discharging a married stewardess upon marriage was illegal.

· You cannot refuse to hire someone on the basis that she is married to someone who is a member of a specific ethnic, religious, racial, or other protected group.

· You cannot insist on hiring husband-wife teams for certain jobs.

· In some cases, you may terminate a woman or man whose husband or wife goes to work for a competitor, provided this rule is applied equally to both sexes, unless your state, like Alaska, considers marital status a protected category.

· In one case, the court held that a no-spouse rule may be applied to couples living together.

· In states where marital status is a protected category (18 states at the most recent count), no discrimination is allowed based on marital status or changes in marital status.

· In general, avoid questions relating to marital status in a hiring interview.

This means that you cannot ask questions such as "What does your spouse do?" "Have you been maried long?" "What impact has your divorce had on your work?"

You want to avoid assumptions about marital status. If you hear information concerning marital status, disregard it to avoid a charge related to sex discrimination.

CASES

With the sex discrimination guidelines in mind, please make two decisions in the following cases: (1) Is there a possible case of discrimination? (2) Which guidelines apply?

Case 1: Cindy States

Cindy, a 19-year-old college student, was fired from her summer job because she allegedly distracted a male employee she was dating. Cindy and the male employee worked at a shoe store.

Store management contended that Cindy's presence affected the sales efficiency of the male employee and that they terminated her because she was selling fewer shoes per week.

Cindy filed a suit. How will this case turn out?

Case 2: Living Together

(In this scenario, please decide what the supervisor should do and whether discrimination exists.)

"Two of my employees recently began living together. Until now, both have been quality employees. Now one of them seems preoccupied with the other, to the point where his work performance has suffered.

"I'm afraid the other employee's work performance will also begin to falter if this keeps up. What should I do? My common sense says that I should talk to both employees together. Would this be discrimination? What should I do?"

Case 3: Sun Oil

Sun Oil Inc.'s corporate policy against married couples working in the same unit has been included in its personnel policy handbook for six years. Despite this, two years ago, when one of the company's three pilots (John Warren) married one of the seven flight attendants (Chelsea Bentson), nothing was said.

Last year, the company plane had an emergency landing due to engine trouble. Warren and Bentson each received a special commendation for handling the troubled situation professionally and averting a disaster. Both Warren and Bentson received excellent performance reviews for their four and three years of company service.

Recently, however, Sun Oil management decided to enforce the company's policy against married couples working in the same unit. As a first step, the company personnel office notified all employees, including Warren and Bentson, that the policy would be enforced. The memo said that the company had previously been "liberal" in interpreting the policy but would strictly enforce it in the future.

A subsequent memo went directly to Warren and Bentson. This memo said that pilots and flight attendants must be able to place passenger safety above their own. "Not only are spouses working together a poor business practice, but having them work together on an airplane could lead to a significant safety problem. Were a plane's crew member unable to control, even briefly, the natural tendency to think first of his or her spouse, lost lives and enormous property damage might be the cost."

In the final paragraph of this memo, the company gave Warren and Bentson two weeks to decide which spouse would elect to be transferred or to resign. Warren and Bentson drafted a reply that said that since the policy hadn't previously been enforced and the policy discriminated against them because of their marital status, they would both stay where they were.

Two weeks after this memo, Bentson received a notice giving her the choice of two other company jobs or being terminated. The couple has filed a complaint with the state's Human Rights Commission. What do you think the outcome will be?

Case 4: Bill Williams

Last week, Bill Williams made out work assignments for his crew. This was particularly difficult because his crew includes two sets of technicians who are involved in living-together relationships.

Although Bill has not changed his attitude or treatment toward any of the four technicians, he believes that their cohabitation could cause problems should an emergency, disciplinary, or other work-performance problem adversely impact one member of either couple.

The technician couple living together longest gives no indication at work that they live together.

However, one member of the other technician couple gives a number of indications of that relationship. In several cases, one member of the duo called the other "honey." When his partner looked embarrassed and ignored him, he became upset and later blew up at another technician. On another occasion, this man became angry at a third technician when that technician had a loud disagreement with his partner. Bill had to intervene.

What is your advice for Bill?

Decisions

Cindy States won a similar case in 1986. Cindy won back pay. Store management should have worked with both employees, particularly the man, on the work-performance issue, and should have left the personal relationship out of the picture.

In *Living Together,* the supervisor can best handle the situation as a work-performance problem. By ignoring the personal aspects, he will avoid discriminatory issues.

A good answer to the supervisor is:

You're facing a work-performance problem with one employee. If you handle this situation with verbal counseling and discipline focused on tangible work-related issues, you have the opportunity to regain a productive employee.

If the other employee also begins to have problems, then you can counsel her—about work-related issues.

If, instead, you bring both employees in together, the employee with no problem may ask you why she is being included. If you then say, "Well, because you two live together," you'll be giving both employees the impression that their private lives are the subject of your concern.

In fact, when you counsel the man, leave unspoken your belief that his private life has affected his work performance. His relationship with your other employee is not the issue; his work and behavior at work are.

While you have every right to be concerned about every aspect of work performance, the non-work-related and outside activities of your employees are none of your affair.

The *Sun Oil* case is based on a 1988 case involving a major oil company. Marital status is a protected category in this state. The court's decision is pending. The oil company will probably lose because the termination-transfer would be discrimination against Bentson due to her marital status.

While the company has a strong argument related to safety, the argument is an opinion that is not substantiated by past experience involving the pilot and flight attendant, who in fact recently received commendations for work in emergency situations. Further, the company could schedule so that the two pilot-flight-attendant couples employed with them don't work the same shifts or flights.

Bill Williams should handle each situation on an individual yet consistent basis. He should disregard the private life or relationship status of the technician couples. He should deal directly with the behaviors causing job-performance problems.

The relevant issues are these.

Concerns about propriety or possible misconduct may not be used to deny opportunities.

Non-work-related private activities of employees are protected unless they can be shown to affect work performance adversely.

10

The Hint of Sex – Legal Hot Water: Sexual Harassment

A HOT ISSUE

Thousands of times each year, managers and supervisors find themselves in legal hot water: Complaints have been filed against them for sexual harassment. An increasing number of these complaints read like *Peyton Place* stories.

Sexual harassment involves subtle behaviors as well as blatant sexual acts. In some instances, harassment is simply one employee being the constant butt of sexually oriented jokes. In other cases, harassment includes unwelcome touches or advances.

A *Redbook Magazine* survey (November 1986) found that 88 percent of the 900 female respondents felt they had experienced some form of visual, verbal, or physical harassment.

A survey of 8,523 federal workers completed in 1987 by the Merit Systems Protection Board concluded that 42 percent of women (and 1 out of every 7 men) working for the federal government had been sexually harassed within the prior two years. This pattern and frequency have existed unchanged since a 1980 report.

Daniel Levinson, chairman of the U.S. Merit Systems Protection Board, estimated the cost to the federal government of sexual harassment at $134 million per year. This study factored in reduced productivity, job turnover, emotional stress, and absenteeism. A similar study showed that sex harassment costs a typical *Fortune* 500 company $6.7 million per year. Nearly 90 percent of *Fortune* 500 companies have received complaints of sexual harassment. Over one-third have been sued.

Sexual harassment is an issue because some work situations were so intolerable that women and men could not work in them, even if the women or men were highly qualified for the job. Legislative and court actions are intended to protect both men and women from situations in which they are subjected to undesired advances. The guidelines in this chapter are based on the Civil Rights Act of 1964, the Equal Employment Opportunity Commission guidelines, and recent court decisions.

It makes economic sense for you as a supervisor to understand the law. Ignorance could cost you thousands of dollars in legal fees and hundreds of thousands of dollars in monetary awards. Suits and complaints cost you the loss of production time by you and others in your company who find yourselves in court or preparing a defense.

Damages paid by companies who have lost sex-harassment suits have ranged from $2,000 to $2 million. A plaintiff can recover compensatory damages of back pay, reinstatement, attorney's fees, and punitive damages related to assault, battery, invasion of privacy, and intentional infliction of emotional or mental distress. In 1987, K Mart Corporation paid $3.2 million to settle a single case.

There are costs beyond the monetary. Sexual-harassment charges are damaging to employee morale and company image, even when accusations are false. Also, harassed employees may leave, resulting in turnover costs and the loss of good employees. Harassed employees may avoid work, resulting in excessive absenteeism.

A manager's and company's best defense is stating a position very clearly in a company policy manual. This sends a message to all employees. If company management is both sensitive and quick to investigate potentially dangerous situations, most situations can easily be resolved.

As a means of testing your knowledge on sexual harassment, consider the following situations:

1. After Anne asked her supervisor not to use the term "the girls," he stopped. He began to keep a close eye on her and to watch himself around her. Because of this close scrutiny, he began to notice a series of frequent but minor performance problems. After 6 weeks, he called her in for verbal counseling. In the interval, he told her that the frequency of some of the minor problems would result in a written reprimand and possibly a termination. Anne said, "You're building a case against me."
   Discrimination? Yes__ No__ Don't know__
   Why?
2. John was the first and is the only male clerk in a mortgage company. Many of the women managers have teased him about having a nice smile and "nice legs." He has politely rebuffed his immediate manager several times; however, she continues to make joking comments.
   Discrimination? Yes__ No__ Don't know__
   Why?

The answers: Both situations involve sexual harassment.

In situation 1, Anne's request that her supervisor not use "the girls" and similar remarks led her supervisor to keep a "close eye" on her. Because he closely monitored her after that, his scrutiny amounted to harassment or retaliation for her comment. Because Anne apparently has some job-performance problems, this case gets into a gray area. However, the "bottom line" is that her co-workers were not subjected to the close scrutiny.

In situation 2, the manager continues to make jokes, despite John's rebuffs. The teasing situation affects John's job and is a "condition of employment." The employer's liability is even greater because the supervisor takes part in the teasing.

The courts decide sexual-harassment cases on the basis of "prima facie" evidence: Would the facts presented by both parties lead a reasonable person to decide that harassment exists? While it's hard to make a decision in a situation where one person's word directly contradicts another's, in sexual-harassment cases, this is rarely true. Generally, witnesses have seen or heard evidence or have themselves been the victims of harassment.

SEXUAL HARASSMENT GUIDELINES

· You are not responsible for what employees think. However, if actions of yours and other employees' result in diminished employment opportunities, you are responsible.

· Sexual harassment is

- a form of discrimination relating to a different treatment of the sexes leading to different job-related outcomes:
  - explicitly or implicitly a term or condition of employment (i.e., a job situation that the "victim" must put up with);
  - a situation in which the plaintiff's employment is adversely affected or in which the submission or rejection to the advances is the basis of an employment decision affecting the individual;
  - a situation in which employees of the opposite sex are not affected;

- an intimidating, hostile, unreasonably interfering, or offensive work environment, including:
  - unwanted sexual attention, invitations, or pressure for dates;
    sexual remarks, verbal abuse, slurs, or insults;
    job-related awards or punishments;
    suggestive comments or off-color jokes;

- comments on appearance;
- sex-oriented insults;
- displaying sexist cartoons, pictures, or magazines;
- leering, sexual or abusive tones of voice;
- touching, pinching, patting, bumping, cornering, mauling, nudging, kissing, or unwanted physical contact;
- leaving notes;
- implied threat of firing or loss of promotion or raise;
- threats of punishment;
- insulting forms of address.

An example of clear harassment was the $100,000 award to a former Silicon Valley saleswoman who accused her boss of crude sexual jokes for 2½ years. The plaintiff complained to her boss, who laughed. As a result, she left her job and (a single mother) was without work for four months.

According to California's Fair Employment Commission's unanimous decision, "Language, humor and related activities that may be acceptable in the locker room do not belong in the workplace." The sales manager's conduct created a work environment that was "offensive, oppressive, hostile and intimidating."

The U.S. Supreme Court stated (In *Meritor Savings Bank v. Vinson*) that sexual harassment that is either severe or pervasive creates a hostile or abusive work environment and thus is illegal.

· Where employment opportunities or benefits are granted because of an employee's submission to the employer's sexual advances or requests for sexual favors, the employer may be held liable for unlawful sex discrimination regarding *other* persons who were qualified for but denied that employment opportunity or benefit. For example, in 1983 (*Toscano v. Nimmo*) a woman who did not get a promotion because it went to an employee having an affair with the supervisor won pay compensation and damages.

· In harassment cases, the victim may be the same sex as the harasser.

· You must maintain a working environment free of bias or abuse. If you allow it, it is assumed that you have given your okay. Ask yourself: Is this "sexually neutral?" If not, you may want to make a change.

Your role is the same as that of any other person in charge when a group begins to pick on or harass one person. A supervisor's job is to maintain a neutral environment in which all employees can work. Once you are notified of a harassment problem, it is your responsibility to investigate and take immediate action to correct the problem if there is one.

· There's nothing wrong with an employee saying, "Hey, pretty lady" or even "You dumb ______" if it doesn't offend the person you're speaking with or others around you. What a manager or supervisor needs to notice is how are these remarks given, and how are they taken? Also, a supervisor should never make such remarks, because the superior-subordinate relationship makes them "conditions of employment."

· Some work environments are different. You would expect the workers in a construction camp to talk differently than employees in a church school. Regardless of the work environment, however, employees should not be forced to listen regularly to unwelcome jokes, curse words, and insults directed toward members of their sex.

The Supreme Court (summer 1986) ruled that a terminated woman employee who claimed (and had corroborating evidence of) sexual harassment had a right to sue her former employer, even without proof that she had been economically harmed. It was enough that she was treated differently because of her sex and that the climate at work was "hostile."

· As a supervisor, you must work to prevent employees from making repeated sexual advances or comments. It is even more important for you to do nothing that might be construed as a sexual advance. Sexual advances *are* harassment if the woman (or man) cannot freely say "yes" or "no" without potentially damaging her economic livelihood. When this fear of economic loss and/or repeated advances becomes a term or condition of employment affecting only the members of one sex, harassment exists.

· It is never allowable for a supervisor to make the advance, as a request by a supervisor may be seen as a demand by an employee.

Advances also become harassment when even polite requests are repeated often enough that they make the job intolerable or when there is the perceived (not necessarily real) threat of a loss of a promotion, raise, supervisor's liking, or job.

· An employer, employment agency, joint apprenticeship committee, or labor organization is responsible for its acts and those of its agents and supervisory employees, regardless of whether the specific acts complained of were authorized or even forbidden by the employer and whether the employer knew or should have known of their occurrence.

· A supervisor should

- avoid physical contacts (even the most innocent hug or pat can be used against you);
- show no favoritism, such as repeatedly inviting the same worker for lunch or drinks;
- think before speaking when complimenting an employee on her appearance;

- avoid asking a subordinate to do favors such as gift wrapping or making personal phone calls.

· With respect to conduct between fellow employees, an employer is responsible for acts of sexual harassment in the workplace where the employer (or its agents or supervisory employees) knows or should have known of the conduct unless the employer can show that it took immediate and appropriate corrective action.

· An employer is responsible for the acts of nonemployees if the employer knew or should have known of the conduct and failed to take immediate action. In reviewing these cases, the commissions or courts consider both the extent of the employer's control and any other legal authority or responsibility that the employer has with respect to nonemployees' conduct.

· A recent Supreme Court ruling holds companies strictly liable for a supervisor's actions, even if management is unaware of the offending behavior.

· To avoid liability, an employer must show that

- it had no knowledge of the situation;
- it discourages such behavior by supervisors;
- the employee failed to make a complaint to the company.

· An employer's first obligations are to provide an avenue for grievance and to investigate *any* complaint.

As an example of a court's decision, in *Barrett v. Omaha National Bank* (1984), an employee complained to her superiors that she was repeatedly sexually harassed by a co-worker while both were attending an out-of-town seminar. The superiors' corrective action was taken within four days. The court said that because the employer acted within a reasonable period of time and took a remedial action responsive to the harassing actions, it was not liable.

· Improper handling of sexual-harassment allegations leaves a company open to litigation.

· Men can also be harassed. A number of men have prevailed in sexual-harassment suits. A Wisconsin state employee won $196,500 for being demoted after ending an affair with a supervisor.

SAMPLE SEX-HARASSMENT POLICY

As an employer you should have a written policy. A policy communicates to all employees that harassment is not allowed and increases the likelihood that a complainant will first raise the issue internally and not in court.

Dear Employee:

As an Equal Opportunity Employer, it is our company's policy to prohibit discrimination with regard to national origin, race, color, sex, age, religious practice, handicap, veteran status, marital status, pregnancy, or parenthood.

Our company has established an Equal Employment opportunity policy that includes maintaining a working environment free of sexual harassment. There are basically two types of sexual harassment.

Sexual harassment exists when an employee is subjected to unwelcome sexual advances or overtones as a term or condition of employment. Examples of this type of sexual harassment are unwelcome sexual advances, requests for sexual favors, and other verbal or physical conduct of a sexual nature.

Sexual harassment also exists when a person is forced or required to work in an intimidating, hostile, or offensive environment when such environment is caused as a result of gender and has the effect of interfering with an individual's work performance.

Persons who feel they have been sexually harassed should immediately contact their supervisor or the Human Resources section of Employee Relations. Such contact will remain confidential and will protect the employee from fear of reprisal for valid complaints.

We are firmly committed to maintaining a working environment free of sexual harassment. We expect all employees to be equally committed and to endeavor to maintain a working environment free of all forms of discrimination and harassment.

HOW DOES THE COMMISSION OR COURT DECIDE?

Often, people assume that a harassment case is one person's word against another. That is rarely the case. Often, others have been harassed, or other information exists.

In determining whether the alleged conduct constitutes sexual harassment, the commissions and courts look at the record as a whole and at the totality of the circumstances, such as the nature of the sexual advances and the context in which the alleged incidents occurred.

The courts consider the severity of the offense, the frequency of the conduct, and the probability that the conduct occurred.

The court considers how the employer handled the harasser: Was the penalty sufficient? The employer is not obligated to terminate the harasser; however, this is a possible action in some cases.

In *Meritor Savings Bank v. Vinson,* the Supreme Court stated that the conduct of the victim is relevant to a decision on whether the advances were welcome. For example, the court stated that the plaintiff's provocative dress and speech were relevant to the issue of whether the advances were unwelcome.

However, the court held that the fact that a plaintiff voluntarily acquiesced in sex-related conduct does not constitute a defense; the advances may still have been "unwelcomed." Also, the court held the employer liable despite an antidiscrimination policy and a grievance process (unused by the plaintiff). The policy did not specifically mention sex harassment. The grievance process required the plaintiff to appeal first to her supervisor, who was the harasser.

There are always facts. The court's determination is based on the facts.

PRACTICAL RECOMMENDATIONS FOR CONDUCTING AN INVESTIGATION

1. Begin the investigation immediately.
2. Investigate thoroughly.
3. Take written statements from the employee, the accused, and all witnesses who are interviewed.
4. A detailed written statement should describe the conduct complained of and should include dates, times, places, persons present, and witnesses with respect to each incident reported.
5. Note what steps the plaintiff has taken independently to resolve the situation.
6. Ask the accused to admit, deny, or explain each incident.
7. Obtain relevant materials (such as the plaintiff's performance evaluations and any written documentation kept concerning the harassment).
8. Handle the investigation in a confidential manner, taking reasonable safeguards to protect the privacy of the complainant and the accused.
9. If the investigation establishes that the accused harassed the plaintiff, take appropriate disciplinary action. Base the level of discipline on the severity of the offense and the frequency of the conduct. The discipline should be sufficiently harsh to indicate that sexual harassment is not condoned.
10. Discuss with the complainant the results of the investigation and the proposed action before taking final action. If the investigation or the proposed action is not acceptable to him, again review your decision.
11. If the investigation neither proves not disproves the harassment, post a notice restating the company's policy on harassment and the ramifications of such conduct. Also, periodically contact the complainant to ensure that the conduct complained of has stopped.
12. Do not penalize the complainant in any way.

CASES

With the above guidelines in mind, what would you decide in each of the following cases: (1) Is there harassment? (2) Which guidelines apply?

Case 1: Anne Murphy

Anne Murphy is an equipment operator. Her company transferred her from one construction camp to another six months ago. She is the only woman on her shift. Most of her fellow crew members tease her when they are assigned to work together, and she jokes with them. However, two people on the crew do not like to work with her and have made comments to her such as "Women should be at home," "Construction work isn't for women," or "Women shouldn't take a man's job."

Although Anne tried to ignore her co-workers' comments, the remarks became increasingly personal and insulting. One of the workers told her in front of the rest of the crew that he wasn't going to work with a "detestable bitch." The rest of the crew is now beginning to treat her poorly.

Anne complained to her supervisor. He had never heard any of the remarks and thought she was being "thin-skinned." He told her she would need to learn to deal with remarks like these if she wanted to work in a construction environment.

Is the supervisor correct in his handling of the situation?

Case 2: Sally Jones

Sally Jones told Sam Clemons, the boss of Clemons Construction, that her immediate supervisor, Jack Forth, had made advances to her. According to her, he propositioned her, and they argued. She said John had ended it by saying she should be a little more friendly.

Sam called Jack to check this out, and Jack told him not to worry. Jack said he had been teasing, and Sally apparently hadn't been able to take a joke.

A month later, at a work party, Jack got a little drunk and sexually roughed Sally up. Sam was out of town, so Sally filed charges with the state equal rights office.

What is the likely outcome of this case? Will the company, as well as Jack, be found at fault?

Case 3: Janet Adman

Janet Adman began working as a technician in 1978 and was promoted twice. In 1983, she was fired for taking excessive leave.

She sued the company and her immediate supervisor, saying she had been constantly subjected to sexual harassment by the supervisor.

She said that her supervisor had called her at home and that some of her leave was taken because she wanted to avoid the supervisor.

The supervisor said that she was retaliating for being fired. However, he admitted calling her at home. Another employee said that the supervisor had also asked her out but had done it politely.

Case 4: Sue Brown

John Doe Corporation, an international company, was constructing a $55-million corporate center. Sue Brown was hired on the project as a secretary for a high company official. She was outstanding in her job performance and was eventually promoted to project manager in charge of Interior Design.

About nine months after she started, her immediate supervisor, Joe Dougs, made sexual advances toward her. Dougs's sexual advances became more frequent and more insistent over the following two years. In the meantime, Sue began an affair with the son of a member of the board of directors, and she complained to him about her supervisor's advances. The son passed this information on to his mother. Sue also complained directly to the board member and to another high official of the company.

Finally, Dougs called Sue into his office and told her that she was to have an affair with him or be fired. When Sue refused, she was given notice that her employment would be terminated. After her termination, Sue complained again to a member of the board of directors and to another high company official, alleging that she had been terminated because of her refusal to have sexual relations with Dougs.

The company official questioned Dougs, who denied any wrongdoing. No further action was taken by the company. Plaintiff brought an action for sex discrimination under Title VII.

The Findings

In *Anne Murphy,* the supervisor handled the situation poorly. He should have listened to Anne and investigated or taken other action. Not only was Anne harassed but she had a record of being able to take a normal level of teasing. She notified her supervisor when the remarks continued, began to affect her working situation, and became a "condition of employment."

Had the supervisor investigated and taken some action, whether that involved counseling with Anne or her co-workers or making a policy statement followed by disciplinary action, he would have acted responsibly.

Sally Jones has a case. According to her, her supervisor made sexual advances on at least two occasions, the second time in view of others. Since he was an immediate supervisor, the fact that she refused the advances could be seen as potentially damaging to her work life.

The company as well as the supervisor can be sued in this instance because they were notified and made an inadequate investigation. It is not enough to check out a complaint with the party involved and to drop it. Sam should have talked to Sally and Jack further or checked with other workers to learn if harassment was going on.

In a related case won by a complainant in 1981, the woman won despite the fact that she complained to the supervisor only once during a long period of harassment. Since the company did nothing when she complained, the court found that the employee had tried to resolve the problem within the company and that the company was at fault.

Janet Adman has a possible case. She can defend her absences by claiming that the stress of having to turn her supervisor down for dates led her to miss work. Even though the superior was "polite" in other advances and separated his request from work by calling at home, he is still her supervisor, and thus his advances may be seen as demands.

Sue Brown prevailed. She established a prima facie case of sex discrimination by proving that (1) submission to sexual advances of her supervisor was a term or condition of employment, (2) this fact substantially affected her employment, and (3) employees of the opposite sex were not affected in the same way by the supervisor's actions.

John Doe Company might have lessened its liability had it established that it had no knowledge of the activities of the supervisor and that it had a policy discouraging sexual harassment. However, the company would still retain some liability.

John Doe, through its director and corporate officer, knew of discriminatory activity and failed to take appropriate action to correct it. Therefore, the company was liable for the discriminatory acts of its employee. The investigation consisted only of questioning the accused supervisor and was wholly inadequate.

The plaintiff received damages of back pay and lost employment benefits, and was awarded attorney fees. This case was based on *Heelen v. Johns-Manvill Corp.,* 451 F.Supp. 1382 (D.Colo. 1978).

11

"He Makes More Than I Do, and It's Not Fair": Equal Pay

The concept of equal pay puts employers on notice that equal treatment extends to money. The liability for employers who violate the Equal Pay Act is enormous. In recent cases involving state employees in Washington and California, potential settlement amounts have been quoted at $500 million (Washington) and $1 billion (California).

EQUAL PAY GUIDELINES

· The Equal Pay Act of 1963 prohibits sex-biased discrimination in salary for employees who perform substantially similar work under similar working conditions. Employers must give equal pay for equal work. For example, the courts concluded that both the boys' and the girls' track and tennis coaches in a school district should get the same wages because the two spent roughly equal time performing their duties, despite the fact that the boys' team had more students and played in more events.

Two jobs need not be identical to be equal, and different job titles alone do not justify a difference. Actual job content is crucial. Also, two employees with similar work, or similar work for 90 percent of their work hours, should be paid the same.

· When making comparisons to determine comparable wages, an employer must make a comparison between the person who formerly held the job and her replacement. Employers must avoid either giving unequal credit for prior experience or using a willingness to work at a lower rate as justification for pay inequities.

· An employer may not lower wages to correct an equal-pay problem. Transfers to new jobs or job titles cannot be used to circumvent equal pay.

· Employers may pay men and women differently, however, if the quality or quantity of production *is* substantially different.

· Employers have the burden of proof in explaining pay differences in an equal-pay dispute.

· When investigators receive an equal-pay complaint, they look for

- what the job descriptions say;
- what the actual content of both jobs is;
- what the exact wage information is for men and women;
- whether jobs that are not identical are in fact equal;
- whether formal and informal benefits are equal;
- whether breaks, rest periods, holidays, and other forms of compensation (such as job titles) are equal.

· In evaluating jobs and pay, investigators consider

- the job's entry level and responsibilities;
- the job's physical effort and additional duties;
- the person's seniority or tenure;
- the training or skill required.

· A company can defend a wage differential by showing

- that the skills in the two jobs are different;
- that the responsibility or effort involved in the two jobs is different;
- that there is a difference in the longevity of the personnel in the two jobs.

· A difference in wages is permitted if it is paid because of

- a seniority system;
- a merit system;
- a system that measures earnings by quantity or quality of production;
- a differential based on a factor other than sex.

· The courts will not allow the employer to pay males for "extra duties" if

- some male employees get higher pay without doing extra work;
- some females do extra work without higher pay;
- qualified females are not given the chance to perform extra duties;

- extra duties do not actually exist;
- extra duties are minor or do not consume much time.

CASES

With the equal-pay guidelines in mind, please make two decisions in the following cases: (1) Is there a possible case of discrimination? (2) Which guidelines apply?

Case 1: Janice Nye

The Division of Economic and Community Development has two employees doing the same task. Jim Greenough is a Planner I, range 17, and Ms. Janice Nye is an Administrative Assistant I, range 12. Both employees have similar backgrounds in planning. They both applied for the Planner I position, but Ms. Nye was also on the register for the Administrative Assistant I position. At the same time, the division was advertising for the planner, they also advertised for an Administrative Assistant I. Ms. Nye was the third person on that register.

After they started working, Ms. Nye realized that she was doing the same tasks as Mr. Greenough. When she discussed the discrepancy with her immediate supervisor, she was told that Mr. Greenough needed the money more than she did and "had" to have that starting salary. He said that he couldn't go into the reasons without breaching confidentiality.

Would Ms. Nye win an equal-pay dispute?

Case 2: Bookkeeper

A woman bookkeeper was paid $5.00 an hour. Her work was closely supervised, and she was not required to exercise any self-directed judgment. A man who was an assistant to the office manager and was somewhat more experienced than the woman received $6.00 an hour. In addition to bookkeeping, he had to know accounting; he received and disbursed cash on hand; and he used independent judgment in spending large sums.

Is there discrimination?

Case 3: Super Value

Super Value Stores, Inc., pays one rate, $6.00 per hour, to the women clerks who handle the health and beauty aids. It pays clerks who handle perishable foods, all men, $6.50 per hour because they have to alert management to the need for markdowns in price.

Is there job discrimination? What criteria would you use in making your decision?

Case 4: Linda

Linda and Craig were hired at the same time and work side by side on identical production machines. Both are conscientious workers and have the same production rates. The only real difference in their jobs is that if one of the machines breaks down, Craig has to fix it. As an ex–Machinist's Mate in the navy, he knows quite a bit about machinery. Fortunately, the machines are dependable and hardly ever break down.

While there is little overtime in the department, Craig gets most of the after-hours work that is assigned. This has always bothered Linda, but she's never said anything about it.

Today, however, Linda found out that Craig makes 80¢ an hour more than she does, and she's decided to complain to her supervisor.

Is there discrimination?

Decisions

Janice Nye has a case under the Equal Pay Act of 1963 since she performs substantially similar work in similar working conditions. The reasons the supervisor gave are irrelevant because they do not relate to job issues.

In *Bookkeeper,* the difference between the two jobs (independent judgment vs. close supervision) and the incumbent's difference in experience and knowledge justify different salaries.

In *Super Value,* the pay difference is discriminatory because the differences in job duties are minor.

Linda has a reasonable complaint. While Craig has an additional duty, it is infrequent. Since all other job factors are equal, pay and overtime should be too.

THE FUTURE: COMPARABLE WORTH

A related and even more difficult problem involves work that is not equal but "comparable." While the courts have not ruled definitely on the issue of "comparable" pay, the EEOC has pushed for a comprable-pay doctrine that would require employers to compare completely different job categories such as clerk and manual laborer. Clerical work usually does not pay as well as physical jobs; however, the disparity cannot be attacked using equal-pay arguments because the jobs are not "substantially equal."

At the same time, since clerical jobs are generally filled by female workers and manual-labor jobs by males, the pay differential is potentially discriminatory.

A comparable-worth doctrine would require employers to compare job categories. A "point system" would be devised to determine the level of skills required and the economic value of each job.

In a 1985 ruling in Alaska, the state's Human Rights Commission decreed that the comparable-worth doctrine required the state to pay public-health nurses (generally female) the same wages as physician's assistants (generally male).

If the EEOC succeeds in instituting a comparable-pay doctrine, the liability to employers will be great. For this reason, employers with categories that are heavily female or heavily male should take steps to minimize future damage by integrating the sexes at all pay levels. By eliminating the concentrations of women in traditionally female jobs and avoiding channeling women or men into sex-segregated job categories, an employer can reduce potential future liability.

12

Racial and Cultural Discrimination

Imagine the stereotypes that come to mind when you hear the word "hillbilly"—barefoot, pregnant, moonshine, feuds, poor, shacks. To have no images, you would need to have a "blank" mind that had never heard stories and jokes about hillbillies. Other words stir similar stereotypes: "Eskimo," "black," "Chinese," "white." Because these stereotypes can subconsciously bias employment decisions, the Civil Rights Act expressly outlaws discrimination on the basis of racial and cultural differences.

We don't like to think that we could be guilty of discrimination, yet most of us have unconscious stereotypes. Studies investigating hiring decisions show that supervisors tend to hire applicants who look most like the supervisor. This is easy to do. When faced with a choice involving an applicant who reminds you of yourself, you're likely to hire her. After all, you turned out to be a pretty good employee. As a logical extension, since most of us are most familiar with the members of our own cultural and social groups, we're more likely to hire from within the groups of people similar to rather than different from us.

Racism exists whether it is subtle or overt. One court found that an employer demonstrated "sophisticated and subtle racism" when passing over a black newscaster who had handled more than 1,200 broadcasts as weekend anchor for a promotion to a weekday slot. The network chose a white male with less experience. According to the court, the station attempted to disguise discrimination by "overdocumenting" the black's "errors" relative to the white's (*Lowery v. WMC-TV,* 1987).

A more obvious example of racial harassment cost Vons grocery store chain $12.2 million in 1987. This included a jury award of $39,833 for pain and suffering. The plaintiff, a black truck driver, filed suit because of racial slurs and loss of income. He claimed that the loss of income resulted when he was assigned short-distance, low-paying delivery routes in contrast to white truck drivers who were given more lucrative routes.

As a way of testing your knowledge, how do you respond to these cases?

1. A supervisor lets the personnel officer know that even though a janitor doesn't need to have a high school diploma, they are wasting his time if they send him applicants without high school diplomas.
   Discrimination? Yes__ No__ Don't know__
   Why?
2. No blacks are assigned to Mr. X's department because of his attitude.
   Discrimination? Yes__ No__ Don't know__
   Why?
3. Manager: "Look, I gave the job to him because he's black and the vice president has been bugging me for a long time because I haven't met my goals."
   Discrimination? Yes__ No__ Don't know__
   Why?
4. The technician pool had one Alaskan native left in it, and a pump-station manager had an opening. However, he refused to take the Alaskan native because fishing season was almost here.
   Discrimination? Yes__ No__ Don't know__
   Why?
5. The manager stopped training minority employees because each time she got one trained, that person left for a higher-paying job.
   Discrimination? Yes__ No__ Don't know__
   Why?

If you answered Yes in each case, you are right. The following guidelines provide the specifics you need to handle the more difficult cases.

CULTURAL AND RACIAL GUIDELINES

· You may not discriminate based on culture, race, or related characteristics such as

- height and weight requirements,
- the ability to speak fluent English,
- educational background,
- arrest record,

- record of financial problems,
- style of dress or hairdo,

unless these characteristics are directly job-related.

· Height, weight, and physical-fitness requirements discriminate against certain ethnic and racial groups (Alaskan natives, Hispanics, Orientals). Unless there is a relationship between the employee's height and job performance, height requirements should be eliminated or modified. In both *Davis v. County of Los Angeles* and *League of United Latin American City v. City of Santa Ana,* height requirements were struck down for firemen and policemen because the requirements disqualified substantial numbers of otherwise qualified Mexican Americans.

It is allowable to say that a person must be able to lift certain weights consistently to obtain a job requiring that ability but not to say that a person needs to be of a certain height and weight. Some small, seemingly delicate people are stronger in ability than large, husky individuals.

An example of where height is job-related is that of pilots of carrier operations, who must be at least five feet five inches tall to see over the instrument panel to operate the controls.

If you can demonstrate that a stringent physical requirement is necessary to co-worker or public safety, you will probably be allowed to use it. Physical-fitness requirements are often lawful for underwater demolition workers, iron workers, bridge builders, or jobs that require rapid reflexes, and speed, coordination, dexterity, endurance, or strength.

· Requiring fluent English discriminates against people in some cultural groups, and it isn't an ability needed for most jobs. It might be a job-related characteristic in certain public-speaking positions.

· Specific types of education or degrees can be required if they are job-related. However, many jobs unnecessarily require a high school diploma or college degree. Does a janitor need a diploma?

Education requirements can discriminate against some cultural and racial groups as well as older workers who are not as likely to have degrees. The college-degree requirement may be allowed for lower-level supervision positions, however (*Thompson v. Mississippi,* 1986).

· Many employers would not want to hire a person convicted of a crime, particularly for a security-related job. A prior conviction may be a legitimate reason to deny employment if the prior conviction is directly related to the job. For example, if a person was convicted of dishonesty and the new job involves handling customers' money, the employer may refuse to hire the individual. However, a conviction for reckless driving may not be a legitimate reason to deny a secretary a job.

Arrests, however, are different from convictions in that an arrest does not establish guilt. Members of certain minority groups have shown that they are more likely to be arrested without cause than are nonminority persons in similar circumstances. It is safer not to ask job applicants for arrest records.

At the same time, because of increasing numbers of lawsuits against employers for crimes their employees commit, a security check may be not only legitimate but advisable if the employee will have access to the public in vulnerable situations, as in hospitals or hotels.

· Similarly, a record of financial problems is more likely to be characteristic of some minority groups than it is of others. Unless the financial problem is job-related, it is information that should be ignored. There are a number of new restrictions against taking adverse personnel actions due to wage garnishment.

· Finally, unless style of dress or hair is job-related, as it might be in certain public-relations or cooking positions, it cannot be a factor in an employment decision because it might result in discrimination.

As an example of what is considered racial discrimination, a bus company fired a black driver for growing a beard, claiming that bus customers preferred clean-shaven drivers. The black employee had a skin condition, "pseudo folliculitis barbae," which is common among black males. Shaving aggravates this condition and causes inflammation. The employee won reinstatement and back pay.

· Avoid assumptions or stereotypes related to any of the following:

- physical strength,
- intelligence,
- criminality,
- dexterity,
- technical aptitude,
- aggressiveness,
- emotional stability—

that you may associate with a person's culture or race.

Assumptions about a protected group may not be used when making a decision about an individual.

Historical experience is not allowed as a basis for a decision when the historical experience is tied to an assumption related to a racial or cultural characteristic.

You may not use statistical evidence as the basis for making a decision about an individual member of the group.

· You may not use community standards or expectations as the basis for stereotyping jobs or groups. You may not segregate employees or create special assignments of customers due to protected-group status.

· Be careful of denying employment to a person based on a prior employer's reference if the prior employer shows discriminatory tendencies.

· The court cannot always assess whether discrimination is intended. The court instead looks for evidence of discrimination or nondiscrimination. If members of one ethnic group receive different treatment than persons of another group, the court may conclude that discrimination occurred unless there is a nonracial explanation available.

· In 1988, the U.S. Supreme Court ruled that employees or applicants can use statistical evidence to prove that an employer's subjective decisions violate discrimination laws.

· Tests, language requirements, and other measures that are used to determine whether someone gets a job or promotion and that may be culturally biased or negatively affect members of a specific group must be shown to be directly job-related.

For example, if an employer can show that high scorers on a test consistently perform better in a job than do low scorers, the test can be shown to be valid as a predictor of job ability. Such a test is job-related.

However, if the test questions and scores have no relation to a job, the test is not job-related and may not be used.

The burden of proof rests with the employer.

· There are very special and limited exceptions to the general rules against testing. You may test for emotional stability when hiring a police officer. You may test for stress and anxiety endurance when hiring an air traffic controller. You may test a typist for typing speed or a telephone salesperson for voice clarity. These tests are allowable because these characteristics are key to the successful performance of specific jobs. You might expect help in designing valid tests.

· Some employees may feel they are being discriminated against for *not* being a member of a racial or cultural group. In some instances, white employees have filed lawsuits and won. In *Commons v. Montgomery Ward,* a Kansas federal district court ruled that a white female supervisor who lost her position during a corporate reorganization was the victim of "reverse discrimination" when a similar position was created and given to a less experienced black employee.

· Court cases have shown that it is unfair to have quotas regarding how many minorities or women are hired. However, goals are allowable. Affirmative actions to eliminate the present effects of past barriers is legal.

Court rulings indicate that an employer must have evidence that its affirmative-action plan is based on conspicuous racial imbalance if it plans to make employment decisions based on affirmative action.

The rule: Employers cannot discriminate on the basis of "protected-group" membership.

· As a manager, you are not responsible for your employees' prejudices unless these prejudices result in behaviors that limit another race's or culture's employment opportunity. You are strictly liable for your own actions.

You must maintain a harassment-free work environment. Watch for racial or cultural slurs, jokes, insults, and criticism. If you know about employee harassment and take no action, you are liable.

CASES

Now that you've read the guidelines, please decide in the following cases: (1) Is there a case of discrimination? (2) Which guidelines apply?

Case 1: Nancy Baldwin

Nancy Baldwin has a number of "native" employees. Due to their cultural differences, she doesn't discipline them for some of the areas in which they are low performers. Her employees like her, and she's convinced that her respect for what she calls "native time" and other differences pays off in the long run. Unfortunately, she cannot promote employees who aren't alert to job standards such as punctuality.

Case 2: Jane Evans

Jane Evans, the EEO specialist, has been working very hard to get minority women hired in the accounting department. So far, that department's 25 employees include 23 white men, one white woman, and one minority man.

This morning she sent over three minority women who she believes were very qualified and career-oriented. Each met all the legal qualifications for the job.

This afternoon, she got a call from accounting's department manager. He was furious. None of the applicants had a high school diploma, and he has told her he wants to hire only someone with a diploma. Why, he wanted to know, is she wasting his time interviewing people he'll never hire?

Case 3: Joe Black

Joe Black is hired for a job and is doing good work. Three weeks after his hire, his supervisor discovers that Joe lied on his application. Joe claimed not to have a record of arrests, and he did. His supervisor does not want a dishonest employee, so he tells Joe he will be let go. Joe thinks what is past is past and claims discrimination.

Case 4: Michael Samelo

Michael Samelo has applied for a position as legal assistant with the legal department. He has two years of experience as a legal secretary, gained while he was in the navy, and four years as a part-time legal assistant for the Smith law firm.

Mr. Samelo holds an A.A. degree in justice from the University of Alaska. During the interview, Mr. Samelo is told that the job doesn't pay much. He indicates that he doesn't mind since he enjoys legal-assistant work.

Fearing reprisal from the minority community, Personnel readvertises for the position and hires a less experienced minority female.

Has Mr. Samelo been discriminated against? If so, how?

Decisions

Nancy Baldwin is guilty of discrimination. By withholding supervision, she has made it impossible to promote the employees she didn't discipline. Nancy will probably create a morale problem among her other employees, who have to be punctual. If Nancy disciplines any employee for lack of punctuality when other employees are free to be late, she'll probably face a charge of discrimination.

Jane Evans is not guilty of discrimination. The high school diploma is not job-related and is discriminatory to members of minority groups. If she had failed to send the accounting supervisor the three candidates who were qualified, she would have colluded with the manager's discrimination. He must interview them and the other legally qualified candidates and have a clear, job-related reason for the hire.

The supervisor will probably not be able to fire *Joe Black*. Although lying on a job application may be grounds for termination, it may be allowable to lie when faced with a discriminatory question. Joe may thus be protected.

Michael Samelo has been discriminated against, and the employer will be liable *unless* it can base its decision on a bona fide affirmative-action plan that was created to address a conspicuous racial imbalance. If it has a valid plan, however, Michael will lose, as affirmative action *is* legal.

13

Heard Any Good Polish/German Jokes? National Origin, Immigration

Many Americans have feelings about people of German (Mexican, Iranian, Arab) descent. Although the United States is a melting pot of many countries, we are often surprised when a job applicant looks or seems foreign. The Civil Rights Act of 1964 forbids discrimination on the basis of national origin.

At the same time, it is unlawful to hire an alien unauthorized to work in this country. Penalties for hiring an unauthorized alien or failing to maintain employment records for three years after an individual is hired (or one year after an individual is terminated, whichever is later) can amount to fines up to $2,000 for the first offense per illegal alien. The fines increase to $5,000 per illegal alien for the second offense and $10,000 for the third offense. Regular violators may face criminal penalties and six months in prison.

Given these basics, what would you decide in the following situations?

1. Although the manager of Christmas Electric knows it is illegal to hire aliens not authorized to work in the United States, he hasn't bothered to check new employees' documentation. He figures if he is asked to by the Department of Labor, he will comply.
   Discrimination/compliance problem? Yes__ No__ Don't know__
   Why?
2. Mexican Americans are always assigned to Rosa Guitterez's department to avoid language problems.
   Discrimination? Yes__ No__ Don't know__
   Why?
3. Eureka Telephone forbids Spanish-speaking employees from talking in their native tongue between calls.

Discrimination? Yes__ No__ Don't know__
Why?

4. Sales, Inc. denied a promotion to an employee with a heavy Italian accent because the job included telephone sales.
   Discrimination? Yes__ No__ Don't know__
   Why?
5. No Germans are assigned to Mr. X's department because of his attitude toward Germans.
   Discrimination? Yes__ No__ Don't know__
   Why?

If you answered Yes in cases 1 through 3 and 5 and Maybe in case 4, you are right. The following guidelines provide the specifics you need to handle these and more difficult cases.

NATIONAL ORIGIN DIFFERENCES GUIDELINES

· You may not discriminate based on national-origin characteristics such as

- height and weight requirements,
- the ability to speak fluent English,
- U.S. educational background,
- style of dress or hairdo,

unless these characteristics are directly job related.

Height and weight requirements often discriminate against individuals from Asian and Latin American countries. While you may require that a successful job applicant be able to perform certain physical duties that are job-related, you may not ask that a person be of a certain height and weight. Some small, seemingly delicate people are stronger than large, husky individuals. An example of height as a permissible job-related requirement is that of pilots of carrier operations, who must be at least five feet five inches tall to be able to see over the instrument panel to operate the controls.

· Requiring fluent English discriminates against people in some national-origin groups, and it isn't an ability needed for most jobs. It would be a job-related characteristic in certain public-speaking, public-relations, sales, or telemarketing positions. On the other hand, fluent English is not required in a food-processing or janitorial job. Language requirements must relate to job performance.

You may not forbid foreign-born employees from talking to one another in their native tongue unless it would endanger employee or public safety (*Guiters v. Municipal Court,* 1988). English-only rules may apply to emergency situations or when working around potentially dangerous substances or equipment.

· Specific types of education or degrees can be required when they are job-related. In some instances (such as medical licenses), you may even require that these degrees be from accredited U.S. educational institutions. However, many jobs unnecessarily require a high school diploma or college degree. Educational requirements could discriminate against immigrants.

· Finally, unless style of dress or hair (length, mustaches, beards, forelock) is job-related, as it might be in certain public-relations or cooking positions, it cannot be a factor in an employment decision because it might result in discrimination. For example, although you may ask that an employee dress "professionally," you cannot discriminate against saris, turbans, or the professional dress of other countries.

· The courts cannot always assess whether discrimination is intended. The courts instead look for evidence of discrimination or nondiscrimination. If individuals of one national origin receive different treatment than persons of another group, the court may conclude that discrimination occurred unless there is a nondiscriminatory explanation.

· Tests, language requirements, and other measures used to determine whether someone gets a job or promotion, which may be biased or negatively impact members of a specific group, must be shown to be directly job-related. For example, if an employer can show that high scorers on a test consistently perform better in a job than low scorers, the test may be valid as a predictor of job ability. Such a test is job-related. However, if the test questions and scores have no relation to a job, the test is not job-related and may not be used.

· You must maintain a work environment free from harassment based on national origin. For example, Polish jokes may be offensive to an employee of Polish origin.

While you are not responsible for what employees think, you are responsible for what they do. Watch for ethnic slurs, jokes, or insults.

· You may not segregate employees or segregate customer assignments on the basis of national origin unless a lingual capacity is directly job-related.

· Avoid prejudicial assumptions or stereotypes about individuals from different countries, such as

- Germans are warlike;
- Italians are frivolous;
- Irishmen drink a lot;
- Orientals make a lot of money by working cheaply;

· Indians steal;
· Englishmen are patronizing.

IMMIGRATION GUIDELINES

· It is unlawful to hire, recruit, or refer to employment for a fee an alien if you know, or should know, that the alien is not authorized to work in this country.

· You must verify every new employee's identity and right to work in this country.

· You may not continue to employ an individual hired after November 6, 1986, if you know that he is an illegal alien.

· All U.S. employers (individuals, corporations, joint ventures, agencies, businesses, and associations) must comply with these laws.

· "Employees" refers to anyone who receives compensation for services, unless those individuals are independent contractors or engaged in casual employment (sporadic, irregular, or incidental domestic services in a private home).

· Employers must complete an Employment Eligibility Verification form (Form I-9) on each employee hired, recruited, or referred for a fee after November 6, 1986. These forms and the related check of the employee's documents must happen within three business days of hire.

If an employer hires an employee for less than three days, the time deadline is moved up to the end of the first working day.

· You are not required to alert the INS when an applicant or individual cannot produce the necessary documentation. However, you cannot employ this person.

· Illegal aliens who have lived in the United States continuously since January 1, 1982, can apply for temporary resident status.

· Avoid using the ban on hiring illegal aliens as a reason to discriminate. In particular, you may not keep photocopies of eligibility documents for employees with "foreign-sounding" names or appearances but not for others. Also, you request nationality documents only *after* you've offered someone a job.

CASES

Now that you've read the guidelines, please decide in the following cases: (1) Is there a case of discrimination or compliance violation? (2) Which guidelines apply?

Case 1: The Korean Mechanics

The Maintenance Facility recently hired a number of Korean mechanics. Last Friday, Bill Smith, their supervisor, complained to the manager that he wanted the Koreans to stop speaking Korean at work. How could he supervise them if he didn't know what they were saying to each other? He was convinced by their smiles that some of their remarks were about him. He wanted them restricted to English.

The manager tried to calm Bill down. He asked Bill to give him reasons for his request that would be related to getting the work done. All Bill would say was that they were talking behind his back and that he wanted it stopped.

On Monday, when the manager talked to the mechanics, they said they preferred to speak in Korean among themselves. He told them to speak English during their time on the job, explaining that it would make things easier all around.

On Tuesday, the mechanics filed a discrimination suit.

Case 2: Jim Hendrix

Jim Hendrix is a Filipino engineering graduate. He has a heavy accent. While he has 10 years' experience in bridge construction, he was not hired under a recent contract to build 12 bridges because he tested poorly in knowledge of English engineering terms. The job was given to a recent U.S. engineering-school graduate. He filed suit. What will the verdict be?

Case 3: Joan Anders

While Joan is an excellent manager, she is fast-moving. As a result, she does the essentials. She does ask all new employees to fill out Form I-9. She doesn't ask to see their driver's licenses. Has Joan put her company at risk?

Decisions

The Korean mechanics have a good case for being allowed to speak Korean among themselves. If they were working on a dangerous project such as a drilling-rig operation, they would have to speak English. However, the requirement of speaking only English while on a job site in normal conditions is not job-related. If it were and if the supervisors needed to hear everything an employee said, it would be allowable to install "bugs" and eavesdrop on all our conversations.

Bill's problem in this situation (how he feels about his employees and their respect for him) is a different situation.

Jim Hendrix will probably win. He has the experience. The test was discriminatory. He could be given a "cheat sheet" transcribing English engineering terms into Filipino or be given two days to learn the terms.

However, most states have tough licensing requirements for engineers. Were Jim to be the supervising engineer, he would probably need to be licensed. In that case, the employer's test would be irrelevant. A more justifiable requirement would be: Does Jim have a license?

Joan Anders is potentially liable. She is fulfilling part 1 and not part 2 of the employer's obligation. As a result, she is liable for a penalty, warning, or fine.

14

Cases: I'm Sorry, but You Wear Glasses and Are Overweight: Handicaps and Accommodation

Imagine what it would be like if you had to be in perfect health to get a job. How many people do you know who wear glasses? Imagine what it would be like if none of them were eligible for managerial jobs because of their sight problem. How many people do you know who are five to ten pounds overweight? Imagine their being routinely denied job opportunities because of the extra five pounds. Both the need to wear glasses and the extra weight are minor physical handicaps. We live in a society where we are allowed to alter parts of us (glasses and hearing aids) or parts of job situations (ramps for wheelchair accessibility) to accommodate people who are capable of working despite some imperfections.

"Accommodate" means to restructure jobs or working conditions to open up employment opportunities for people with handicaps.

The central question of discrimination against and accommodation for people with handicaps is: Where do you draw the line? Most of us allow people to alter themselves through eyeglasses and hearing aids. Are people who need canes, crutches, or braces allowed in all jobs? Not if doing so endangers their safety, the public's safety, or the safety of other employees. Most of us have empathy for people with common problems that might affect us too: headaches, overweight, occasional backaches, arthritis. Can we and should we design jobs to accommodate people with epilepsy or more serious physical handicaps?

As a way of testing your judgment before you read the specific guidelines on handicaps and handicap accommodation, what decisions would you make in the following situations?

1. Jim was on an upward career path in the company until he suffered a nervous breakdown. Since then, he has been passed by for every promotion.

Discrimination? Yes__ No__ Don't know__
Why?

2. As part of company Y's safety program, all job applicants are given a physical examination after they pass the first screening. One supervisor routinely drops from consideration all those with a weak back.
Discrimination? Yes__ No__ Don't know__
Why?
3. A partially deaf employee is fired because she repeatedly gets confused when given verbal instructions.
Discrimination? Yes__ No__ Don't know__
Why?
4. No one with a handicap has ever been hired for a remote construction-camp job, though many have applied.
Discrimination? Yes__ No__ Don't know__
Why?
5. A blind applicant is not hired because she is not able to take a written test.
Discrimination? Yes__ No__ Don't know__
Why?
6. A woman with arthritis is not hired because she can do only some of the machine assembly jobs.
Discrimination? Yes__ No__ Don't know__
Why?

If you answered Yes in each case, you were right.

HANDICAPPED AND HANDICAP-ACCOMMODATION GUIDELINES

· You may not deny employment opportunities to handicapped persons if they can do the job.

· A handicapped person is one who has a handicap, a physical or mental impairment, that substantially limits one or more of a person's major life activities.

Life activities include areas such as communication, mobility, manual tasks, hearing, seeing, learning, and employment.

A person who experiences difficulty in securing, retaining, or advancing in employment qualifies as "substantially limited."

A person is handicapped if he has been classified as handicapped at one time or is regarded as having a handicap. For example, Thomas Eagleton, George McGovern's vice-presidential running mate in 1972, would fit this definition—he was "regarded" as having a handicap.

Similarly, a person who has a record of a handicap, such as a person who has suffered a nervous breakdown, a heart attack, or a bout with cancer is handicapped.

Generally, diseases such as hepatitis and tuberculosis are considered physical handicaps. So are physical or cosmetic disfigurement, a skin disease, or a lisp or stuttering. Epilepsy, asthma, migraine headaches, diabetes, arthritis, and obesity are sometimes considered handicaps.

A person who has suffered a nervous breakdown, a heart murmur, or a heart attack can be regarded as handicapped.

Short-term problems such as "whiplash" are normally not seen as handicaps.

Based on federal law and handicap-discrimination laws from a number of states, it is probable that mental disabilities such as post-traumatic stress syndrome (Vietnam Veterans Syndrome), schizophrenia, paranoia, manic-depression, and other mental disorders may be protected by the new amendments.

Blindness has been the issue in several lawsuits. In *Coleman v. Darden,* the court determined that the EEOC could reject a blind applicant because sufficient visual acuity was directly job-related. However, the court did *not* rule on the issue of accommodation.

Obesity is a questionable area. In New York, courts have ruled that the discrimination legislation protects obese individuals. A Missouri court of appeals, however, denied a claim brought by a woman refused a job because she had high blood pressure and weighed 205 pounds at five feet four inches. The court held that she was required first to seek help herself as both obesity and high blood pressure are treatable for many individuals.

Gambling is considered a handicap under federal laws. A court stated that when a federal agency dismissed an employee for losing $2,000 of government money through gambling that the action was illegal under the Rehabilitation Act.

You cannot refuse to hire an applicant because she suffers from a disease afflicting only one racial, ethnic, or religious group *unless* the *effects* of the disease make her unable to perform the job.

At this time, the status of alcoholism is uncertain. In 1978, Congress removed alcoholism and drug abuse from protection by the Vocational Rehabilitation Act of 1973 if the condition affects the employee's work ability or endangers safety. However, with a number of states including mental disabilities as handicaps, alcoholism may again be included as a mental disability.

As an exception to the alcohol exclusion, a man who drank a pint of gin daily and missed 14 months' work in three years won a job-discrimination suit against the National Marine Fisheries Service in 1988.

A U.S. district judge ruled that he was legally crippled by alcoholism and that his employers should have helped him get counseling. The judge based her ruling on a federal law requiring that federal agencies "make reasonable accommodations" for handicapped workers, including alcoholics and drug addicts. The man won $150,000 in back pay and the right to reapply for his old job.

The U.S. Supreme Court is currently scheduled to hear arguments that may legally define alcoholism as a disease.

In California, employers of 25 or more employees must accommodate any employee who wishes to enter voluntarily into an alcoholic rehabilitation program provided that undue hardship is not imposed on the employer. Texas, however, specifically excludes alcohol or drug addiction from handicap protection.

· AIDS raises special issues, because of fears of contagion. The U.S. Supreme Court ruled that a person with a contagious disease is "handicapped" and is thus protected by the Vocational Rehabilitation Act of 1973.

However, if reasonable medical judgment finds that an AIDS-infected employee poses a significant risk of contagion or the potential of harm to employees or customers, the employee may not be "otherwise qualified." Reasonable accommodations would still be necessary. According to the federal government, AIDS is not contagious in normal workplace settings.

The court left open the question of whether the protection extends to persons who are carriers of a disease such as AIDS but are not impaired.

Beware of verbally speculating if an employee has AIDS. You could open yourself to a defamation suit.

The Massachusetts Civil Liberties Union filed a lawsuit on behalf of a New England Telephone Company employee who said a supervisor forced the employee to admit being treated for AIDS and that when the information was released to co-workers, it became impossible for him to continue working there. The employee won (*Cronan v. Net Co.*).

A Florida district court ruled that a schoolteacher with AIDS was qualified under the Vocational Rehabilitation Act to teach school because medical evidence indicated the AIDS virus could not be transmitted through routine classroom contact (*Chalk v. District Court,* 1988). The school board had offered him an administrative position, which the plaintiff refused. The court held that preventing the teacher from teaching would cause a substantial emotional injury and that the plaintiff's harm outweighed the school's harm. According to the court, the risk of contagion was minimal and theoretical.

Similarly, while many fear tuberculosis is contagious, the U.S. Supreme Court ruled that an elementary schoolteacher with a record of tuberculosis who again tested positive for it was protected by handicap legislation (*School Board of Nassau County, Florida v. Arline,* 1987).

· You most easily fall into discrimination problems if you follow *assumptions* of what a handicapped person can or cannot do.

· When possible, employers must adapt work requirements or conditions to improve employment possibilites for handicapped people. Any kind of job adaptation, job restructuring, auxiliary aids, or equipment modification is classed as an "accommodation." Auxiliary aids may include Braille materials, audio recordings, telephone handset amplifiers, notetakers, and translators. For example, someone who is confined to a wheelchair may be hired as a receptionist because his handicap would not interfere with his job performance.

An employer may also build ramps or otherwise improve physical access to the jobsite. In most states, employers of handicapped employees are expected to make common areas such as meeting rooms, hallways, and eating facilities accessible. Also, under the architectural-barrier laws of many states, state buildings open to the public must be accessible to the handicapped.

Accommodations may involve retraining, reassignment, or the provision of interpreters. In some cases, accommodation means providing application forms orally or written in Braille.

Under the Vocational Rehabilitation Act of 1973, which applies to federal contractors and the recipients of federal funds, reasonable accommodation may include the following:

- Making facilities readily accessible to and usable by handicapped persons.
- Job restsructuring, part-time, or modified work schedules.
- Acquisition or modification of equipment or devices.
- Appropriate adjustment or modification of examinations.
- Provision of readers and interpreters.
- Retraining for a position for which employees have the basic qualifications and capabilities.
- Reassignment to a different position, including positions of different grades.

· Employers need to make adjustments and modifications only when the accommodation is reasonable. For example, if it costs an employer $25 to modify a piece of equipment so that a handicapped person can handle it, that will likely be a "reasonable" accommodation. A modification costing $25,000 is not so reasonable. A major company, however, might have to pay more than $25,000 to build a ramp or install an elevator to serve the needs of several handicapped employees or members of the public.

Because lawsuits are expensive, it may be cost-effective for an employer to expend several thousand dollars in accommodation rather than risk a handicap suit.

The employer does not have to provide a particular accommodation the *employee* wants so long as it provides "reasonable" accommodation.

· Employers do not need to make accommodations that would cause safety problems or undue hardships in work disruption, personnel problems, or excessive costs. You do not have to hire someone whose ability to perform the job requires unreasonable accommodation, such as severe work disruption or expense.

An employer is not required to hire or to continue to employ an individual with a physical or mental impairment who, despite accommodation efforts, is still not qualified to perform the duties of her position. Thus, if an individual cannot perform the duties of a position regardless of his disability and the employer's accommodation, then the employee may be discharged.

· Physical fitness requirements are recognized as reasonable factors as long as they are in fact necessary requirements for the job situation. Employers are more likely to have stringent physical requirements upheld when they can demonstrate that the requirements protect the safety of others. Physical requirements are probably appropriate for jobs such as iron workers, bridge builders, underwater demolition, or for jobs requiring rapid reflexes or high degrees of speed, coordination, dexterity, endurance, and strength.

· When an employer uses a physical fitness standard, it may be advisable to use a formal medical examination as documentation.

· An employee who is able to perform now, but not if employment continues, is treated separately. Issues to consider are 1) the potential future deterioration, 2) the employee's or applicant's present ability to work, and 3) co-worker safety.

In Oregon, a court ruled that an employer could terminate an employee because the employee's condition would increase the risk of incapacitation if he continued to perform the job. Similarly, a New York employer was allowed to refuse to hire an applicant because of the probability that the employee's dermatitis would be worsened by exposure to work.

· An employer is allowed to ask questions to ascertain a person's job ability if these questions are asked of all applicants.

A neutral question might be "Do you have any disability, medical condition, or health problem that would prevent you from fully performing the duties associated with the advertised job?"

· If physical abilities are job-related, an employer may advise successful job candidates that employment is contingent upon completion of a preemployment physical.

· Watch for employment tests that negatively affect older workers as a category. Why? Younger applicants are assumed to be more "testwise," so you may have a problem under age discrimination.

· Employers must ensure an employee's confidentiality concerning her handicaps. If you have a question concerning whether someone else needs to know about the handicap, ask yourself whether there is a need to know. If an employer is later sued for defamation of character, an employer's defense of "privilege" will be upheld only if the confidential information concerning the employee was communicated within the need-to-know management group.

· The employee has a responsibility also: He must let you, the supervisor, know that he has a handicap or disability that will affect work performance.

· Generally, allowable terminations will be those in which an employee is unable to work because of a chronic illness or a disability with an indefinite and long duration, and a doubtful potential for recovery or rehabilitation. Because of the importance of these decisions, medical advice is required.

Five factors affect such decisions:

- the nature of the disability or illness;
- the likelihood the employee will return to work or return to a satisfactory level of performance;
- the employee's length of service;
- the position's impact on the unit or department's effectiveness;
- how employees who had similar jobs and also had extensive absenteeism due to medical reasons were handled.

An employer's decision will impact the employee directly involved and the morale of other employees, who may view the company as "kicking a person when he is down."

· Is left-handedness a handicap? In Chicago, a jury awarded a grocery-store checker $136,700 when she quit after being required to check out groceries with her right hand.

CASES

In the cases below, please decide (1) Is there discrimination? (2) Which guidelines apply?

Case 1: Bob Jackson

Bob Jackson, who is deaf but can lip-read, has applied for the receptionist position on the first floor of Dynco. About 10 percent of his job would be to answer phone calls. The rest of his job would be public contact. He is turned down.

Case 2: Dynco

Over the past four years, Dynco's personnel manager has hired several handicapped people: a person confined to a wheelchair, a person with only one functional arm, and a mentally retarded person. The manager has always found them a job at which they could succeed, even though the jobs were essentially "dead-end" jobs.

Case 3: John Elliot

John Elliot was hired as a management trainee five years ago. Sixteen months after he was hired, he had a nervous breakdown. Since then, he has repeatedly been passed over for promotion. He believes he is being discriminated against.

Is this discrimination?

Case 4: Mary Landers

Mary Landers was a blind applicant for a legal-research analyst position. When turned down, she filed suit, contending that she was experienced in legal analysis and would require only someone to read to her.

Was she discriminated against?

Decisions

Bob Jackson can and probably should be hired. The employer can accommodate his handicap by having incoming calls routed to another clerical worker who will take over that 10 percent of Bob's job. Bob's extra time can be spent doing other duties.

Dynco's case resembles affirmative action more than it does discrimination. In each case, the manager has found the applicant a job at which success is possible. The manager can extend his action by finding jobs with more potential; however, the manager is not guilty of discrimination.

John Elliot appears to be discriminated against. A nervous breakdown is not permanent; however, his employer appears to see it as a lasting handicap.

Mary Landers lost her suit. Having sufficient sight to read was seen as a valid job requirement. The court stated that it was unreasonable to expect the employer to hire a second employee as a reader.

15

What Do You Mean You Don't Work After the Sun Sets on Friday? Religious Accommodation

If an employee comes to you in October and says, "I need two days off in January to celebrate a religious holiday," must you give him the days off? What if he's a deacon or a leader in his religious group? What if you've never heard of the religious group? Must you give him time off? With pay? What if another employee says, "I know we've got a rush order to get out, but I've just joined a religious group, and I need the next two days off to celebrate a holiday"?

The Civil Rights Act of 1964 outlaws discrimination against any religious group. You can't refuse to hire a person because he's Catholic, Mormon, Jehovah's Witness, Hindu, or a member of religion Z. The act also requires that employers not set up employment barriers against members of any religious group. Most American companies allow employees Christian holidays or pay them at overtime rates if the employees are needed at work on a holiday. Employers must also accommodate other religious groups by allowing employees time off to observe their holidays.

The central question of accommodation is one of balance:

1. How much notice must an employee give?
2. How much time off must the employer allow?
3. How strongly must the employee be connected with the group?

Considering all the shades of gray in this area, test your knowledge and assumptions in the following situations.

1. The company's religious holidays include Easter and Christmas but not Yom Kippur.
   Discrimination? Yes__ No__ Don't know__
   Why?

2. The applicant for a crucial position was told before her hire that she needed to be "on call" seven days a week. She makes a practice of telling people who ask her for help (even emergencies) on Sunday to put it off until Monday. She is fired.
   Discrimination? Yes__ No__ Don't know__
   Why?
3. A supervisor says, "I'm not against any religious group, but standard policy here is that you have to work a weekend now and again."
   Discrimination? Yes__ No__ Don't know__
   Why?
4. A person is fired from a conservative company because he is an atheist. The company says that because he has no religion, there is no religious discrimination.
   Discrimination? Yes__ No__ Don't know__
   Why?
5. The founder of the company starts every staff meeting with a short prayer. Staff members who must attend the meetings but who have differing religious views are not required to participate in the prayer.
   Discrimination? Yes__ No__ Don't know__
   Why?

In situation 1, if you answered No, you're right. No company has to make every religious holiday a work holiday. However, if employees request those days off, the company must accommodate.

Although situation 2 is a somewhat gray area, if the company has followed standard disciplinary procedures, it can probably fire the applicant. Her position is crucial, and she knew at the time of hire that it was an "on-call" seven-days-a-week job. However, if the calls can be transferred to another employee, accommodation may be possible and thus required.

Situation 3 involves discrimination. Despite standard policy, the employer must accommodate religious needs. Business convenience is not a reason for failing to accommodate.

Situation 4 involves discrimination. Atheism is protected; to discriminate against atheists would allow religious bias to enter the workplace.

Similarly, situation 5 allows religious bias to enter the workplace. An atheist must be allowed to skip the introductory prayer.

RELIGIOUS-ACCOMMODATION GUIDELINES

- An employer must not discriminate on the basis of religion by letting religious bias or belief negatively affect employment decisions.

· "Religion" includes any religious belief or observance, regardless of how little known the religion is. Beliefs are protected even if they seem offensive or bizarre to others.

Religious observations include a churchmember's duties.

Employers cannot interfere with an employee's beliefs or lack of beliefs. A religious supervisor is not allowed to create an atmosphere in which a certain religion is "preferred."

· An employer must maintain a working atmosphere free from religious bias.

· An employer must make a reasonable effort to accommodate the religious beliefs of all employees.

· Due to religious convictions, some employees are unable to work on Saturdays, Sundays, and certain religious holidays. Accommodation would mean restructuring the working schedule to allow for this.

· An employer may be unable to make an accommodation for the religious activities of some employees because of undue hardship in work disruption, personnel problems, or excessive costs. In these cases, accommodation is unreasonable, and an employer need not accommodate.

An example of undue hardship is an employee's asking to take a religious holiday during a peak worktime, with almost no notice.

The employer has the burden of proof in proving undue hardship.

· When the courts determine whether an accommodation is "reasonable," they look closely at all issues involved. For example, an employer was not able to apply a policy of "a whole weekend's overtime or none at all" to an employee who couldn't work one of those days. The court ruled there was no significant business reason for the policy.

In another example, a court ruled that an employer should have tried to find or train a substitute for an employee who wanted to transfer to another department because the other department's hours would allow him to meet certain religious obligations. Another court ordered an employer to reinstate a Saturday-Sabbath observer. The company claimed that it was undue hardship to ask other workers in a rotation schedule to fill in for the employee. However, the employee offered to work extra Sunday shifts, and the court said the problem was one of business inconvenience, not business necessity.

Dress is another area of accommodation. A court ruled that a member of a religious sect required to wear a close-fitting headcovering at all times need not observe the dress code for nurses at her hospital.

Union dues are another area of accommodation. An employee with religious objections to unions can make charitable contributions in lieu of paying union dues (*Machinists v. Boeing,* 1987).

Another court upheld an employer who fired a worker as extra help for the Christmas rush season when she refused Saturday work for religious reasons. The court accepted the employer's defense that it was too difficult to find a one-day substitute for a two to seven month job.

Another court upheld a company's refusal to hire an engineer who couldn't work crucial weekend hours. The job called for 24-hours-a-day 7-days-a-week availability.

· While employers must reasonably accommodate if possible, they need not make the specific accommodation the employee requests.

In *Ansonia Board of Education v. Philbrook,* a teacher sued the school administration that refused his request for paid sick or personal leave for religious holy days. He (and other employees) were allowed to use a limited amount of sick leave for other personal business. The administration allowed him to take unpaid leave on holy days. The U.S. Supreme Court ruled that the employer's accommodation was reasonable. According to the Court, "We find no basis in either the statute or its legislative history for requiring an employer to choose any particular reasonable accommodation. By its very terms the statute directs that any reasonable accommodation by the employer is sufficient to meet its accommodation obligation." However, in this specific case, the Court questioned the employer's policy of allowing paid leave for all reasons except religious ones.

· Employees have responsibilities also:

- to notify the employer of their religious needs, giving adequate time;
- to establish the sincerity of their beliefs (though this is not an area in which the employer should challenge the employee);
- to cooperate with the employer.

· Religious institutions are exempt from some aspects of these guidelines.

CASES

With these guidelines in mind, please decide in the following cases: (1) Is this discrimination? (2) Which guidelines apply? (3) Case 2: Describe both the employer's and the employee's line of reasoning and decide who will win.

Case 1: The Booksellers

The Booksellers hired seven Hasidic Jews for accountant positions in May. During the hiring process, Personnel learned that the new accountants could not work on Saturday or after sundown on Friday because of their religious beliefs.

This was accepted by the employer, and other workers consented to take additional Saturday shifts as long as they did not have to work extra overtime during the week.

As winter advanced and the days got shorter, the supervisor noticed the Hasidic Jewish accountants leaving earlier and earlier on Friday afternoons.

The company made a decision to terminate the Jewish accountants, based on business necessity. What would the court say?

Case 2: The Dress

When Image Design, a Los Angeles public-relations firm hired Mary Jorgenson, they hired her based on her references and her résumé. Since she had worked in New York prior to her hire, she was not interviewed in person. However, a lengthy phone interview with Jim White, the owner of Image Design, established that Ms. Jorgenson had the verbal skills and expertise he sought. During the interview, Mary asked Jim how she would be judged. He said two things were important to him: the business and profits she brought in and the appearance she presented to the public and clients.

Jim was also impressed with Mary when she appeared for work. Since he was rarely in the office on Friday, it wasn't until the second month after Mary's hire that he noticed she dressed in a bizarre, rather gypsylike dress on Friday. When he asked her about it, she explained that she always dressed like that on Fridays because of her religious customs. In checking with her, he discovered that she was really convinced of the value of those customs. Though her Friday dress continued to bother Jim, he decided not to push the matter, as Mary wore business suits Mondays through Thursdays.

Unfortunately, a client mentioned Mary's dress to Jim one day on a golf course and laughed. Arnold James, a third member of the golfing party, who represented an account Jim wanted, was there and asked the client about Mary's dress. Arnold's reaction showed that he thought it was weird. Jim was horrified, and the next day he brought Mary into his office. He asked her to wear a business suit on Fridays. She said she couldn't because of her religion. He told her it was grounds for termination. She filed suit.

Who do you think will win? What will be the line of reasoning for each?

Case 3: Matching Headdress

As manager of the public-relations department, you're proud of the appearance of your employees. When the new public-relations assistant arrives wearing a long dress with a matching headdress, you're upset. When you speak to her about her appearance, she explains that she dresses according to her religious customs. You tell her that's fine, but not in your department. You let her know you'll try to arrange a transfer for her.

Is this lawful? Who will prevail?

Case 4: Short Notice

A long-time employee asks for a leave of absence to attend a special religious celebration. The request comes on short notice, and a replacement cannot be found without the burden of paying overtime.

What does the law require of you?

Case 5: Saturdays

An employee tells you that because of the teachings of a religion that he's just joined, he can no longer work on Saturdays. He asks to be transferred to a shift where Saturday work is not required. However, an employee who has a lot more seniority would also like such a transfer and has a superior claim to it.

Whose rights come first?

Case 6: Johnson

In *Johnson v. U.S. Postal Service,* a post office had only five employees, one of whom converted to the World Wide Church of God. Because all personnel were crucial and Johnson was only third in seniority, the manager could not grant him every Sabbath off. He did try to give him as many as possible and offered to recommend him for a transfer to another branch.

Case 7: Blue Bell

In *EEOC v. Blue Bell,* seven members of the Jehovah's Witnesses demanded a leave of absence for a religious celebration. The demand was made two days prior to the expected time of departure. The employer said that the job involved special skills, making it impossible to procure substitutes on such short notice. He refused to let more than three go.

Would the court find this reasonable accommodation?

The Findings

The Booksellers will *probably* have to accommodate. During the hiring period, the new accountants notified the employer that they could not work on Saturday or after sundown on Friday because of religious beliefs. This problem is a seasonal one since the other workers agreed to cover the workload on Saturdays. The only problem is the extra overtime during the week.

The Booksellers has two possible ways to accommodate:

1. It can hire a part-time employee to cover the extra overtime during the week.
2. It can see if the other employees will cover the extra overtime during the week in return for having some daytime hours off, during which the Jewish accountants cover for them.

This case is not clear-cut. If The Booksellers cannot reasonably accommodate, either because of excessive work disruption or problems with the other employees, it may be able to discharge the accountants. The Booksellers has the burden of proof.

The plaintiffs, however, may have a breach of contract. In their initial interview, they arranged for no work after sundown on Friday.

In a similar case, the court allowed an employer to fire an employee hired as extra help for the rush season. Although she refused Saturday work because of her religious beliefs, the company would have faced undue hardship in hiring a replacement for one day per week. In another case, the company's decision not to hire an engineer who could not work after sundown Friday or on Saturday was upheld because the job required him to be available on a seven-day-a-week basis.

Image Design will *probably* need to accommodate. Jim White's reasoning will be that Mary's appearance causes the public-relations firm an undue hardship in potential loss of revenue. Further, he can argue that he let Mary know during the hiring process that her appearance was one of the two areas on which he judged employees.

Mary will argue that her dress is appropriate and professional, although different from the traditional. She will ask to be judged on her dress without bias. She will argue that there will be no loss of revenue or that the loss will be minor compared to the revenue she'll generate.

Although the case is not clear-cut, Mary will most likely win because there are several accommodations the company can make. One reasonable accommodation might be to let Mary work four 10-hour days and take Fridays off.

Another accommodation would be to let Mary work on Fridays but to have no client contact on that day. If the company can *prove* that it would suffer undue hardship, either in making these accommodations or in keeping Mary on as she currently is, it may win. The company, though, has the burden of proof.

In a comparable case, the courts ruled that a company could *not* enforce dress codes on a Black Muslim employee whose religion required her to wear ankle-length dresses.

In *Matching Headdress,* you have a possible defense, business necessity, to a religious-discimination suit. Because she works in a public-relations department, you have a concern about her appearance.

The strategy of a transfer, if the employee accepts it voluntarily and without duress, may work.

If the employee contests the transfer, however, the courts may decide your issue is "business convenience," not "business necessity." Because this employee is not the manager, her "different" appearance becomes less important.

In *Short Notice,* the law requires you to accommodate *if you can.* Due to the shortness of the notice and the difficulty of finding a replacement, you'll probably be allowed to turn the request down.

In *Saturdays,* you are asked to balance between accommodation and seniority. A number of issues enter into this. For example, if an employer has a union contract, it may argue that "bumping" the employee with seniority would be undue hardship. In *TWA v. Hardison* (1977), the U.S. Supreme Court said that the seniority system served all employees and that accommodating Hardison's religious needs would "deny the shift and job preference of some employees as well as deprive them of their contractual rights." If that employee with seniority has been waiting a long time, you could argue that personnel problems would be the result of accommodation.

In *Johnson,* the employer tried two forms of accommodation: a transfer and the attempt to give Johnson as many Saturdays off as possible. While these were not the requested accommodation, they were reasonable.

In *Blue Bell,* the employer made reasonable accommodation by letting three of the seven go. The employees would have had a strong argument had they given more than two days' notice.

16

It's Such a Little Thing: Routine Decisions and Stereotyping

IT'S TOO SIMPLE NOT TO TRIP YOU

One of the likeliest times for a manager or supervisor to get caught in illegal discrimination is when making routine decisions. Most of us act as we've been conditioned to act without thinking. To show you how strongly you've been conditioned, please cross your arms, one over the other. Notice which hand is on top, your right or your left. Now, uncross your arms and cross them the other way so that the other hand is on top. If you're like most of us, it took you longer to cross your arms the second way because for 20, 30, 40, or 50 years, you've been crossing your arms consistently one way.

We're equally consistent in many of our routine decisions (the decisions we make without considering their implications), and that's how we get into trouble. Imagine, for example, that you have good rapport with one of your employees and use him as your sounding board. When it comes time to promote one of your employees, that employee is the one you chose—not because he's your friend but simply because he knows the most about the operation. That might be a fine reason to promote someone, except that you set up this employee to be the only one who had a chance to get that inside information.

You may have been conditioned to "protect" women routinely. Suppose you always give the women on your shift the easier jobs. Could you be found guilty of discrimination? You bet. The men may complain, and so may the women. Perhaps they need to learn the harder jobs to have an equal chance to get co-worker respect, new skills, or promotions.

Consideration is not illegal. However, it is illegal to treat two people differently solely because of their sex. It's our assumptions about what a person can or cannot do because of her sex or age that get us into trouble. Assumptions and stereotypes are an expensive habit.

With these general ideas in mind, review each of the following cases, and decide whether it involves illegal discrimination.

1. "Say, Jane, could you take the minutes while you, Jim, and I hash this out? Women have better handwriting."
   Discrimination? Yes__ No__ Don't know__
   Why?
2. All the men in the department belong to Dom Piers, an exclusive men's club. Mary Eden gets frustrated because she often misses out on the latest news by not being able to play racketball. When the manager left on his vacation, he put Jeff Dustin in as acting manager because he was "up on things." Mary had seniority.
   Discrimination? Yes__ No__ Don't know__
   Why?
3. "I was thinking about seeing if Peggy was interested in the job. I know she's new, but I knew her father, and he was great."
   Discrimination? Yes__ No__ Don't know__
4. Supervisor: "There aren't any women who can lift a hundred and fifty pounds."
   Discrimination? Yes__ No__ Don't know__
   Why?
5. Supervisor: "The minority women have a chip on their shoulder."
   Discrimination? Yes__ No__ Don't know__
   Why?
6. Supervisor: "I'd rather you didn't. That's awfully hard work for an older man."
   Discrimination? Yes__ No__ Don't know__
7. The manager stopped training minority employees because each time she got one trained, she left for a higher-paying job.
   Discrimination? Yes__ No__ Don't know__
   Why?

If you decided that discrimination was involved in each of these cases, you're right. Since routine decisions and stereotypes trap so many of us in unconscious discrimination, please read the following guidelines carefully.

STEREOTYPING AND ROUTINE DECISIONS GUIDELINES

· You cannot deny opportunities to individuals who are minorities, women, and other protected classes because of your assumptions about what they can or cannot do. These assumptions include ones related to

· physical strength,
· aggressiveness,
· physical characteristics,
· intelligence,
· dexterity,
· technical ability,
· emotional stability.

You cannot assume that women have more emotional stability, that men are stronger, or that "you can't teach an old dog new tricks."

· Routine decisions that have a discriminatory impact, regardless of their intent, can lead to problems. A routine decision is a relatively minor decision that you make without considering the implications that may be seen as giving preferential treatment.

Avoid informal word-of-mouth communications that would leave some employee regularly uninformed about needed information. Avoid word-of-mouth recruiting.

· In making decisions affecting shift assignment, discipline, training, counseling, referrals, recommendations, job assignments, and overtime, watch for decisions that favor individuals or that "protect" individuals. Favoritism and protection may result in denied opportunities. Unconscious discrimination is as costly as conscious discrimination.

· Nepotism and other policies favoring relatives result in denied opportunity for members of protected categories not currently employed. As a result, these policies should be omitted.

· The "old-boy network" is another example of a practice that could result in a lawsuit. The practice denies opportunities.

· When making an employment decision, consider the merits of the individual case rather than your own experience with "women employees" or "minority foremen." At the same time that you recognize the individual on the basis of his abilities, weigh each decision for consistency.

· Avoid making employment decisions that give preference to individuals you socialize or have a personal relationship with.

· If any decision has the long-range effect of denying employment opportunities to a protected group, it may be seen as discriminatory, regardless of good intentions.

CASES

As a means of testing your understanding, in each of the following cases decide (1) Is there discrimination? (2) Which guidelines are involved?

Case 1: Sandy Lomas

Sandy Lomas is the personnel officer–recruitment specialist for the Bishop Company. Joe Rand, the supervisor for the contracts department, asks her to find him a replacement for a contracts engineer.

Sandy interviews seven applicants. The most qualified person is a woman. Since she knows that the supervisor does not work well with women employees and would give a woman employee a difficult time, she recommends two male applicants for the job.

Given all the information you have and can assume, was this a wise decision?

Case 2: Joe Murphy

Julie is a young employee who works for Joe Murphy. Joe is a good supervisor and treats all his employees well. Julie doesn't want to charge Joe with discrimination; however, she has an economic problem. She's hurting for money and could really use some overtime. Joe distributes the overtime unevenly, tending to give most of it to the older workers and the "family men." When Julie asked Joe about this, he said, "Look, Julie, an opportunity for overtime is a benefit. I'll give it where I know it's needed. Tell me that you've got a money problem, and I'll see that you get a share too." Julie doesn't want to tell Joe about her credit problems for fear that that would bias him against her.

Case 3: Jack Webber

Jack Webber is a raquetball addict. When he hired Mary and Chuck as his assistants last year, he was pleased for two reasons: They both did excellent work, and he found that Chuck was a racquetball player. He and Chuck play every weekend, usually with customers of the company.

Meanwhile, Mary has become pretty frustrated. She's been told she's doing excellent work, but during recent months, Chuck always seems to know more about what's going on in the department than she does. This puts her in an awkward position when new projects are discussed and assigned.

Last week, a promotional opportunity occurred, and Webber put Chuck up for the job. His reason: Mary and Chuck have equal skills, but Chuck is more "on top of things" in the department and gets along better with the customers. When the promotion was announced this morning, Mary asked for a meeting with Webber.

What issues will be discussed? What's your conclusion as to the possible discrimination?

Decisions

Sandy Lomas made a discriminatory routine decision. She colluded with Joe Rand's prejudice by denying women applicants a chance to compete for a job. Regardless of her knowledge of Joe, she should have referred the best-qualified applicants to him. She might have been lucky and sent him the one applicant who would have changed his prejudice.

Joe Murphy, regardless of his motives, is discriminating on the basis of his assumptions about which groups of employees need the money the most and his relationships with the employees. No one doubts that Joe is a good supervisor. His intentions are good.

However, based on Joe's routine decision, an employee who wants overtime needs to have a relationship with Joe so that Joe will know about her money needs. This will favor those who have a more personal relationship with Joe and those who don't mind discussing their money needs.

Joe's routine decision results in discrimination. Overtime is an employment benefit that can be accepted or turned down by an employee but that should not be withheld.

Jack Webber could be found guilty of discrimination. Although he promoted Chuck because Chuck was more "on top of things," Jack created the situation in which Chuck had access to additional information. This created unintentional discrimination.

Regardless of whether Mary files suit, her morale has been lowered by being outside information channels. Since she apparently does excellent work, Mary's frustration costs the company.

17

Asking for What You Want: Defining Job Requirements

CATCH-22

The catch-22's of discrimination are the traps that occur when managers define job requirements. You define job requirements when making hiring, promotion, performance evaluation, discipline, and discharge decisions. If you state job requirements professionally, you'll be able to avoid potential legal problems when hiring, promoting, or conducting employee appraisals.

In hiring or promotion situations, if you believe successful job applicants must have a certain level of abilities to perform a job successfully, you must state those abilities as minimum job requirements. Otherwise, you'll have no reason to turn down applicants who lack those abilities. If you do turn down an applicant who doesn't meet an unstated requirement and he is a member of a "protected class," he may file and win a discrimination suit. The job requirements you state must be nondiscriminatory.

According to the federal Equal Employment Opportunity Commission, more discrimination charges are filed because of the wording of job requirements or who is selected (and isn't) for the job than are filed in any other area of employment practice. Because of this, every manager who interviews job candidates must be aware that an apparently innocent but poorly worded requirement can leave her company open to a costly discrimination charge. As is true with traffic violations, ignorance is no defense.

In performance appraisal and disciplinary situations, managers often use failure to meet performance standards as a reason for low evaluation in discipline. Again, the wording and quality of the performance standard are crucial to preventing and winning lawsuits.

OUCH

The OUCH test is your tool. If your job requirements and performance standards pass the OUCH test, you've stated them in nondiscriminatory terms. The test

*O*bjective,
*U*niformly applied,
*C*onsistent in effect,
*H*ave job-relatedness.

Figure 17.1 summarizes OUCH (p. 112).

In Chapter 28, you'll learn that in some cases, an employer may ask for a requirement that doesn't pass the OUCH test if there is a legitimate defense. However, learning the OUCH-test guidelines is a manager's best safeguard.

Objective

Each requirement or standard an employer sets in terms of skills, educational background, or experience should be phrased in terms that are *factual, observable,* or *measurable.* For example, "passed the commercial pilot's exam" is objective in that an applicant can show that she has passed the exam (or hasn't), and any two people can reach the same opinion when doing a brief check of an applicant's résumé in this area. The requirement that any applicant have a "warm and friendly attitude" fails the O of the Ouch test. What's warm and friendly to one person may be obnoxiously sugary to one person or distant to another. How do you tell, for sure, a "warm and friendly attitude" when you see one?

A performance standard such as "handles assignments responsibly" is subjective. If you promote one employee rather than another because the first is more "responsible," the second may charge you with discriminatory decision making and sue. If you state your expectations in terms of "completing assignments by deadlines" or "meeting production quotas with budget," you protect your right to evaluate or promote employees without dispute.

A disciplinary expectation such as "improve attitude" is highly subjective and thus leaves a manager vulnerable to a suit from a disgruntled employee. If you ask, however, that an employee demonstrate improvement by reducing the number of customer complaints he receives by 50 percent, you're setting an objective standard.

FIGURE 17.1 The OUCH Test for Job Requirements and Standards

Each requirement and job standard must pass the O U C H test:
*O*bjective,
*U*niformly applied,
*C*onsistent in effect,
*H*ave job-relatedness.

Objective	Required skills, educational background, criteria, experience, or performance measurement must be put in terms that are factual, observable, or measurable. Example "passed the commercial pilot's exam" vs. "warm and friendly attitude" or "types 60/3 wpm"
Uniformly applied	This means that you ask the same questions of each applicant and that you apply the same standards to all employees in equivalent positions.
Consistent in effect	Each requirement, criteria, or standard: screens out about the same number of women as male applicants; screens out about the same number of minority as nonminority applicants; screens out about the same number of protected class as nonprotected class applicants. Example "are you willing to work overtime?" vs. "do you have 2 years of military experience?"
Have job-relatedness	Each requirement must be *necessary* for people entering or continuing in job if they are to do a good job.

Team spirit will hang you. Most supervisors are able to write objective job requirements and performance standards for three-quarters of the abilities they require of an applicant. Other qualities, such as "having a positive attitude" or being "able to be a member of a team," are difficult to put into objective terms. These subjective requirements, while critical, lead to lawsuits.

So that you can ask for these characteristics without winding up in court, translate "positive attitude," "team spirit," and other subjective measures into factual, observable, or measurable terms. For example, "positive attitude" translates into specifics such as "a history of being at work on time without using much sick leave," "being able to state three reasons why they want to do this type of work rather than another," and other specifics. I can ask an applicant, "Do you prefer to work alone or as a member of a team?" and get a yes or no response directly related to "team spirit."

Intentions do not count. In 1988, the U.S. Supreme Court ruled with 8–0 unanimity that bias in subjective judgments such as "ambition," "loyalty," "tact," "common sense," and "originality" can lead to illegal discrimination. Their decision stated that the Civil Rights Act of 1964 applies to subjective marginal practices that work to the detriment of women and minorities. Thus, even if your intentions are positive, if your subjectivity shuts "protected categories" out of positions, denies them promotions, or works to their detriment in performance-evaluation or disciplinary situations, you'll lose in court.

Translating your gut. Many of us tend to size up applicants quickly before we have much specific information. Sometimes our "gut sense" helps us to hire terrific employees. Sometimes, we think we've hired a quality employee, and it turns out that we got fooled. The translation process of taking our "gut-sense" requirements and putting them into objective terms not only keeps supervisors on the right side of the discrimination law but also gives more concrete information on which to base hiring decisions.

Uniformly Applied

This guideline means that each question you ask of one applicant is the type of question you could ask of any applicant. It means that any promotional criteria or performance standard would apply to any employee in a similar position. This prevents you from biases you might unconsciously hold related to sex, age, race, and other protected areas. For example, if you accidentally discovered that an applicant is the mother of five small children, you might be tempted to ask, "Are you sure you can get to work at eight

A.M.?" or "Do you think you'll use a lot of sick leave when your kids are sick?" You're not likely to ask these same questions of a 50-year-old male applicant. Questions such as these indicate a discriminatory bias against the mothers of young children.

As a supervisor, you have real and important concerns related to attendance. You can ask, "Is there anything that would prevent you from being at work on time each morning?" without discrimination. This question addresses the same concerns yet is a question you would ask of any applicant, and thus it's uniformly applicable.

Consistent in Effect

A job requirement or question that you ask an applicant or a standard that you apply to an employee is consistent in effect if it screens out the same proportion of nonprotected applicants as protected applicants. This guideline gives you a chance to prevent unintentional discrimination.

To be "consistent in effect," each question or requirement must screen out approximately the same number of male as female candidates, the same number of white as black applicants, the same number of young and middle-aged as older workers, and so forth. As an example of the intent of this guideline, consider a question you might innocently and casually ask a woman applicant: "Do you have young children at home?" If you have a concern that a mother with young children won't be willing to work overtime and overtime is legitimately a requirement for someone in the position, you can ask a more neutral quesion: "Are you willing to work overtime?" This is consistent in effect because it screens out equal numbers of applicants. It screens out everyone but those willing to work overtime and those willing to lie. It doesn't focus more on women than on men.

If one of your requirments does screen out a category of people and yet deals with an important ability, try stating the question in a less discriminatory way. For example, suppose you have a requirement of 2 years of military experience because you think there are positive qualities such as leadership that individuals gain from military experience. The military-experience requirement discriminates against women. Instead, you can ask for these positive qualities less discriminatorily by asking, "What do you have in your background that *demonstrates* leadership ability?" Then you will not be screening out women.

Have Job-Relatedness

Each requirement or question you ask of an applicant must have job-relatedness. A requirement is job-related if it is necessary for someone entering the job to have to be able to do a good job. For example, you may ask applicants specific questions related to their job skills, work experiences, training, education, and licenses. To assess their degree of responsibility or their ability to work under the job's conditions, you may ask for information related to their past job responsibilities, attendance record, and the degree of direct supervision they've had. You may check out their willingness to travel and their acceptance of your organization's work hours and schedule. You may ask questions related to an applicant's job-related physical impairments and health problems if these are related to the physical skills needed for a job.

It is important to remember that if you state that a particular skill is a minimum requirement and later hire someone without that skill over a minority person with that skill, you will have discriminated. Similarly, performance standards and promotion criteria must be objective, job-related, and applicable to any employee in a similar position in your organization.

CASES

With these guidelines in mind, please take a look at the following questions as a means of testing your understanding.

1. Which of the following types of information that a job interviewer might note about an applicant are objective?
   a. excessive hair length
   b. good attitude
   c. sex
   d. marital status
   e. a good "team" person
   f. good public-relations background
   g. six years of clerical experience
2. Which of the following requirements could be uniformly applied?
   a. All applicants must have a high school diploma.
   b. All applicants and employees must be willing to work overtime.
   c. All applicants and employees must be at least 5 feet 7 inches tall (for security guards).
   d. All female employees must wear dresses.
   e. All male employees must have short hair.
   f. All applicants must have two years of accounting experience.
3. Which of the following requirements are consistent in effect?
   a. All applicants and promotional candidates must have a history of military experience.
   b. All applicants and promotional candidates must have a high school diploma.

   c. All applicants and promotional candidates must weigh at least 120 pounds.
   d. All applicants must be willing to handle irate customers.
   e. All applicants must have one year of work experience and/or education in a job-related field.
4. Which of the following requirements are probably job-related?
   a. Typing skills for a typist.
   b. High school diploma for a shift supervisor.
   c. Mechanical ability for a typewriter salesperson.
   d. Experience with generators, pumps, turbines, and engines for an operator in a gas plant.
5. Which of the following pass the OUCH test?
   a. Management trainees must be under 45 years old.
   b. Truck drivers must be at least 5 feet 6 inches tall.
   c. Shift supervisors must be willing to work overtime.
   d. A cook must have a positive attitude.
   e. Employees of remote pump stations must be willing to work a "week-on, week-off" schedule.

Decisions

Number 1: c and d are objective. Except for a person who is undergoing a sex-change operation, a person's sex is objective information. It may be hard to tell at first glance if someone is a man or a woman, but it can be determined. Similarly, although there are many innovative marital and nonmarital relationships these days, a person's marital status can be legally defined.

"Excessive" hair length is not objective. To a bald person, any hair might be excessive. "Good attitude," good "team" person, and "good" background are also subjective. Six years of clerical experience is time-defined and thus objective.

Number 2: a, b, c, and f can be uniformly applied; c, however, will fail a later part of the OUCH test as it discriminates against some Orientals, Latin Americans, Alaskan natives, and Spanish-surnamed individuals. Choice d asks a question of female applicants that wouldn't be asked of male applicants. Men can wear pants; women cannot. Similarly, male employees must be willing to have short hair, while women may have long hair.

Number 3: Only d and e are consistent in effect. Choice a screens out more women than men, at least among the current working population. Choice b screens out members of minority groups and some older Americans. Although asking for a high school diploma is not consistent in effect, an employer may ask for the specific degrees that a person needs to perform a job successfully. Choice c screens out more women than men and screens out disproportionate numbers of Alaskan natives, Orientals, and Americans of Spanish descent. Choices d and e are consistent in effect, in that they will screen out relatively equal numbers of "protected" and "non-protected" individuals.

Number 4: Only a and d are job-related. A person can be an excellent shift supervisor without having a high school diploma. An excellent salesperson can sell typewriters with no mechanical ability. Though mechanical ability may be an asset, it's not a necessary requirement.

However, typists and gas plant operators need the skills listed in a and d.

Number 5: c and e pass the entire OUCH test. Both are job-related, objective, can be uniformly applied, and are consistent in effect. Both a and b are requirements that aren't job-related and aren't consistent in effect. Choice d is not objective.

18

Protecting Your Right to Hire Whom You Want: Practical Ins and Outs of Interviewing Questions

Hiring decisions may be the most important decisions you face. Good employees can make or break a manager's reputation. With the advent of discrimination laws and the increasing numbers of employees and applicants who file and win complaints and lawsuits, a manager's skill in conducting hiring interviews is even more crucial. Poorly worded questions can lead to legal action.

Good interviews are both legally and organizationally important. Some managers interview so subjectively that they decide whom to hire based on *impressions* of job applicants. Objective and thorough interviews give a manager a realistic *assessment* of what each applicant has done for past employers, can do for a new employer, and is *likely* to do if hired. After an effective interview, the manager knows each applicant's skills, strengths, and job-related abilities.

RECRUITMENT

Effective nondiscriminatory interviewing begins with recruitment. You can't hire a mix of qualified applicants representing several age, sex, and racial groups if none apply. Unfortunately, some managers are caught in this trap—no minorities or women or older applicants apply. Thus, they are left with an unbalanced work force and are more open to charges of discrimination.

If you're a manager in a large organization, you might consider sending a recruiter to reach into organizations representing protected categories as a supplement to your newspaper classified ads. In fact, using a broadcast or print medium that reaches only a predominantly white or a predominantly black audience is discriminatory if your community is racially mixed. Also if you recruit *only* in institutions that reflect the same imbalance you have in your work force (i.e., recruit from an all-male institution when your work force is all male), you violate the Civil Rights Act.

Beware of relying on word-of-mouth recruiting. If you have a work force that's heavily one race or one sex, word-of-mouth recruiting brings you large numbers of similar applicants. The federal Equal Employment Opportunity Commission has held that word-of-mouth recruiting that reaches only a specific group when there is an existing imbalance in the work force is illegal (*U.S. v. Georgia Power*).

MINIMUM JOB QUALIFICATIONS AND JOB DESCRIPTIONS

Your next step in effective interviewing is ensuring that you know what an applicant must be able to do if hired. Your two tools are

1. a listing of minimum job requirements;
2. a job or position description.

Minimum Job Qualifications

Minimum job requirements

1. help you clarify your thinking concerning what job skills or knowledge is needed in the position you'll be filling;
2. give you a basis for wording your classified ads;
3. give you a tool for objectively turning down unqualified applicants.

All of the minimum qualifications should pass the OUCH test: objective, capable of being uniformly applied, consistent in effect, and job-related. A sample listing of five of the requirements for one corporation's executive director position is below.

Sample Minimum Qualifications

1. Three or more years of senior management experience (requirement relates to the complexity of staff and project issues handled by the executive director; "senior" means supervising at least two levels of subordinates, having budgetary control, and having final program authority in at least two areas).
2. Management background that reflects an understanding of more than one industry/area of expertise so that the executive director will be able to oversee personnel in different positions (or other experience or background giving this same ability).
3. Skills and/or experience in working with Alaskan native people or people of several races and/or cultures.

4. Experience or background in either construction, fiscal management, or project management.
5. Experience (as shown by specific examples) that demonstrates the ability to sort through complicated regulations and paperwork.

Job Description

Job descriptions are useful for orienting new employees once hired and serving as a basis for conducting hiring interviews. For example, if you're hiring an executive secretary, you'll want to make sure the successful applicant is skilled in screening telephone callers, and this skill will be listed on your job description. As a manager, you can use the job description for evaluating your employee's performance.

Table 18.1 gives a sample job description for a Receptionist/Secretary.

TABLE 18.1 Receptionist/Secretary Job Description

Principal Function(s):

Greets and assists customers as the initial point of contact (in person or by phone) and sees that customers receive the appropriate referral to other staff. Provides routine clerical assistance to other employees and managers.

Responsibilities:

Answers/screens telephone calls; takes appropriate messages when necessary.
Greets customers and directs them to appropriate staff member.
Sorts and delivers mail to appropriate staff.
Files loan documents; other filing as requested.
Maintains confidential files of items such as salaries, expenses, personnel records, and routine correspondence.
Types forms, standard letters, and memos.
Types confidential correspondence, other material from handwritten copy, primary or semifinished source material, dictating-machine recordings, or shorthand notes.
Provides other clerical assistance when requested.
Assumes additional responsibilities as requested.

If you were interviewing a finalist for the receptionist position you might ask questions based on the first responsibility, "answers/ screens telephone calls," as follows:

"Have you ever screened telephone calls?"
"What does 'screening' telephone calls mean?"
"If the customer is angry, but there are no employees available to take the call, how would you handle the situation?"

By asking specific questions based on the job description, you'll be able to make a realistic assessment of each interviewee's job-related experience and skills.

While good job descriptions are useful, poor job descriptions will get you into, not out of, trouble. What's wrong with the following job description?

Tool Crib Man

Major Responsibilities:	Care and inventory of testing equipment, machine tools, drill bits, special machine attachments, and related equipment.
Qualifications Required:	Machine-shop experience, good health, ability to work accurately with numbers.

If you noticed the sexually biased job title and the broadly stated health requirement, you're on target. Also, job descriptions like this above are too brief to be really helpful.

PREPARE A LIST OF STANDARD QUESTIONS

Your screening and hiring interviews will move more smoothly and be more effective if you first prepare a list of 7 to 15 standard questions or question areas that you'll ask each applicant or finalist. This list of questions will also later demonstrate your essential fairness if you do get challenged with an equal-employment-opportunity complaint.

Many managers make copies of the question list and use each copy as a basis for taking notes on those interviewed. If you are later called into court, this practice will provide you with ready documentation for defending why a job applicant was not selected, provided your decision was based on his lack of experience or lack of a success in one or more question areas. Your standard questions must pass the OUCH test (see Chapter 17).

The standard question list also gives you a basis for later comparing all finalist interviewees. Naturally, you'll use the standard questions as a base and will ask other questions as well to delve into particular job-related experiences.

Sample questions follow.

Sample Questions

1. Could you give me some examples of the most difficult management situations you've had to handle?
2. Could you give me some examples of the most difficult personnel situations you've had to handle or resolve?
3. What leads you to apply for this position?
4. Could you give me information concerning your ability to oversee personnel and projects in these areas?
   a. construction
   b. fiscal
   c. engineering
   d. maintenance
5. This position calls for skills as an administrator. Could you give me some background on your skills and abilities in this area?
6. In what situations have you used negotiation skills?
7. This position requires the ability to handle regulations and paperwork. What education and/or experience do you have that indicates your ability in that area?
8. What experience do you have in working with Alaskan natives? Village governments? What other experiences do you have that relate to this area?

CONDUCTING THE INTERVIEW

If you have hired someone you thought would be terrific who turned out to be awful, you know that there is skill to creating an interview climate.

In an effective interview, the applicant does most of the talking, and the applicant gives complete and accurate information. Because few applicants talk freely before they've relaxed, a good interviewer first relaxes an applicant.

The most effective way of relaxing job applicants and at the same time avoiding violations of equal-employment-opportunity laws by getting into personal areas is to ask the applicant job-related questions that are easily answered. Your first step is thus asking easy, almost throwaway questions to get the applicant talking. Ask your more important questions one-third to halfway through the interview when the applicant is talking more easily.

The questions must be job-related so that you avoid potentially discriminatory areas and accurately assess the applicant's job-related skills. If you don't ask enough questions or enough of the right questions, you'll get an *impression* of what the person is like, not a realistic *assessment*.

Important questions include ones concerning the applicant's past two to three jobs, job responsibilities, and past relations with supervisors.

The job-related questions you ask should be reasonably detailed, so that you know what the person has actually experienced or demonstrated. Using the position's job description as your guide, you should ask questions concerning each aspect of the position that the applicant is applying for. The quality of your questions is crucial; the best questions get the best answers.

You want to watch for someone who can't respond to your questions, seems glib, or bad-mouths a past employer. Remember, you've got to work with the person you hire.

Types of Questions

Three types of questions work well in hiring interviews:

1. open-ended questions;
2. clarifying questions;
3. narrowing questions.

Open-ended questions normally start with "what," "how," "tell me about," or "tell me more" and are questions that encourage an applicant to answer fully. Closed-ended questions call for a yes, no, or short answer. Using open-ended questions gives you more information.

Clarifying questions allow you to recheck information and to let an applicant know you're listening. They also allow you to lead from one question area to another. A sample of a clarifying question: "So you've had seven years of experience as a supervisor. In your last position, what numbers and types of employees did you supervise?"

Narrowing or either/or questions help in interview control and in clarifying answers. A sample narrowing question: "Did you have full or partial responsibility in preparing the budget?"

Because climate is important in interviews, it helps to avoid questions that start with "why" or "did." Both words subtly increase an interviewee's defensiveness and thus give you less information. As an example, read these two questions aloud; the major difference is that one begins with "why" and one with "what":

"Why did you leave your last job?"
"What led you to leave your last job?"

Finally, you'll want to avoid asking leading questions that give away the answer. An example of a leading question: "Would customers state that you leave a positive impression?" Few applicants would say no to that question because the phrasing leads to a yes.

Testing

Employment tests help some managers decide among a number of applicants. An employment test is valid if it

1. assesses characteristics and skills that are directly related to good job performance;
2. assesses the skills that will actually be used in performing the job; and
3. later proves by test results that those who do best on the test perform best on the job and that those who do least well on the test do most poorly on the job.

Employment tests that negatively and disproportionately screen out minority or women applicants may be illegal.

Asking for References

Asking questions of former employers is one of a manager's best tools for assessing how well the applicant has performed in the past.

However, avoid the trap of rejecting a job applicant when the only reason is a negative job reference from a former employer. If the former employer's opinions grew from prejudices, you'll inadvertently have discriminated. A number of federal Equal Employment Opportunity Commission decisions have shown that employers should give job applicants an opportunity to rebut negative reports (EEOC Decisions #72-0974, #72-2103).

Documentation and Records

Discrimination charges are often more difficult for an employer to disprove than they are for a rejected applicant to prove. Without records, you're on your own.

Although the federal Equal Employment Opportunity Commission and the similar state and municipal commissions and courts approach each claim on its individual merits, it's the employer's job to show that the criteria used in the hiring process were rational. Records allow you to prove your objectivity without spending an excessive time in court.

Good records include the list of standard questions the interviewer asks of each applicant who possesses the initial screening and the minimum job qualifications. Your objective set of minimum job requirements or screening criteria and standard questions on which you based the interviews show an effort to treat each applicant fairly and consistently.

If you keep notes about each applicant on a sheet listing the standard questions, you'll be able to explain, with documentation, why an applicant was not hired. For example, if you're looking to hire a secretary who types at least 70 words per minute and the rejected applicant types only 50 words per minute, you rejected her based on objective criteria that you applied to all applicants.

Before you complete your records, train yourself to do one last review of any notes you've made to ensure that no discriminatory remarks were recorded.

Depending on your state, you might want to keep your records for 5 years. For an exact answer concerning how long to keep your records, contact your state's department of human rights.

Do Intentions Count?

Occasionally, managers who face legal action find that they have inadvertently discriminated. As part of their defense, they state that no discrimination was intended.

Discrimination cases, however, are based on the evidence presented. No one can read a mind. If your employment practices have the *effect* of discriminating, they are illegal. The U.S. Supreme Court stated in a precedent-setting case, *Griggs v. Duke Power Company,* that any action or policy is unlawful if it is discriminatory *in effect* unless there is substantial business justification for the policy. In fact, even a practice that appears neutral can be discriminatory if its *effect* leads to discrimination.

Because discriminating unconsciously is as easy as discriminating consciously, an effective interviewer is aware of his biases and avoids their influence.

PROMOTION

Promoting one employee and not another can get you in almost as much trouble as hiring one applicant and not another. Several guidelines:

- Make sure that all your subordinates are kept informed concerning available promotional opportunities; this will protect you from charges of routine discrimination.
- Learn about the promotion potential of all employees, including women and minorities.
- Eliminate practices that could restrict promotion opportunities for minority or female subordinates—such as giving complex assignments only to men when that experience is a requirement for advancing to higher-level jobs.

- Eliminate any stereotyped ideas (such as thinking that women aren't interested in long-range career paths).
- Base your promotional selections on objective, job-related factors.
- Use only job-related standards for promotions.
- Base your promotion selections on objective and not vague or subjective evaluation of the candidates.

CASES

Case 1: Herman Walker

Herman Walker applies for a job. While interviewing Herman, you can't help noticing that he has one blind eye. You ask him if he has any specific health condition that would prevent him from doing all portions of the assembly-line job. He answers no.

When you finish all the applicants, Herman and two other men are similarly qualified; however, Herman scores the highest on the aptitude test. Despite this, you hire one of the two others. If Herman sues, what are your chances of a problem?

Case 2: Mary Landers

Mary Landers applies for a job. You are careful not to ask any discriminatory questions. She volunteers information concerning her recent divorce. When she learns that the secretarial position went to a male, she asks why.

When you tell Mary that the male candidate had more office skills and experience than she, she accuses you of discriminating against her because she's a divorced woman with three kids.

You tell Mary that you considered only how each applicant measured up to or exceeded the job's requirements. You mention that you asked each applicant the same standard questions.

Mary leaves, obviously unhappy, and files a claim.

Case 3: Which of These Questions Could You Ask?

1. How do you feel about having to work with a woman supervisor?
2. Many of your co-workers will be black. Does that create any problems for you?
3. That's an interesting name. What nationality is it?

4. Would you be willing to work for a supervisor who is younger than you are?

Case 4: Which of These Questions Could You Ask?

1. "This job frequently requires overtime, including Saturdays. Would that be a problem for you?
2. Of an applicant who says he is 18 but looks younger: "We cannot hire people under the legal age. You must bring your birth certificate before we can hire you."
3. "Do you have any handicaps?"
4. "We need a photograph. If you are hired, will you bring one for your personnel file?"
5. "This job requires you to be on your feet a lot. Do you have any physical condition that we should know about in considering your application?"

Decisions

Herman Walker could potentially sue and win unless you come up with a specific and objective reason for selecting the applicant you chose. If Herman's disability would not affect his ability to do the job and he is the most qualified, he should be the one hired.

Mary Landers has a complaint, but no case. If you had let the information she volunteered influence your decision, even if it was not information you asked for, you would have been out of line. However, you didn't. The records you kept, which include the applicant's answers to the standard questions and the fact that another applicant had better qualifications, demonstrate your fairness.

Case 3: All questions are illegal. Questions 1, 2, and 4 appear to show consideration for the applicant and an effort to prevent future problems. Their effect, however, is to discriminate or to imply discrimination. For example, 1 suggests that a woman would be more likely to get the job; 2, a black; and 4, a younger person. Question 3 suggests that the interviewer would then be specifically aware of national origin.

Case 4: Questions 1, 2, 4, and 5 are allowable. Question 1 asks for information that is job-related, objective, consistent in effect, capable of being uniformly applied, and related to no special category other than someone who would work overtime. Question 2 relates to an employer's need not to violate the working-age laws without discriminating against lawful younger applicants. Question 4 is a procedural one, which does not impact the interview. Question 5 is an example of a lawful way to check for the same type of information.

Question 3 is too broad. Asking this type of question might give you non-job-related information about handicaps.

AREAS TO AVOID

Based on what you've read in Chapter 17 and other chapters, you know that there are question areas that would lead to illegal discrimination. Table 18.2 provides you with a reference guide to the most common areas to avoid (pp. 129, 130, 131). The right side of the chart shows what you *can* ask.

In general, you'll want to avoid questions related directly to categories protected by the Civil Rights Act of 1964:

- sex,
- race,
- age,
- culture,
- national origin.

You'll want to avoid questions related to those areas, such as the applicant's

- home ownership,
- lineage or ancestry,
- family or marital status,
- living arrangements,
- birthplace,
- mother tongue,
- pregnancy or number of children,
- overdue bills,
- height or weight (unless *directly* job-related).

While you cannot ask about a person's marital status or number of children, you can ask whether the applicant can meet specific work schedules and attendance commitments. You can ask females about anticipated absences as long as you ask all applicants, including males, the same questions.

Educational standards have been the subject of frequent litigation. In *Griggs v. Duke Power Company,* the Supreme Court determined that a high school diploma is an unnecessary and potentially discriminatory requirement for certain jobs. Its reasoning was that at that time in North Carolina (where Duke Power Company was located), only 12 percent of the black males had a high school diploma as opposed to 34 percent of white males.

TABLE 18.2 Avoiding Traps: Interview-Question Dos and Don'ts

YOU CAN'T ASK OR REQUIRE	YOU CAN ASK OR REQUIRE
AGE	
"What's your age?" May I have a copy of your birth certificate? Questions such as "When did you graduate from high school (or college) or other questions that might be asked by someone trying to assess age. "Would you mind working for a younger person?"	"Do you meet minimum age requirements? Require that an applicant provide you with proof of age after hire. Ask a minor for proof of age in the form of a work permit.
SEX	
"What sex are you?" Unless sex is a bona fide occupational qualification. "What would you do if people made sexist remarks to you?" "Do you get along well with other women?" About an applicant's discharge status unless it is the result of a military conviction.	If sex is a bona fide occupational qualification, such as a wet nurse or sperm donor, you may ask, "What sex are you?" You can ask about an applicant's experience and education in military service or other educational settings as they relate to a particular job.
FAMILY-MARITAL STATUS; PREGNANCY	
Questions related to spouse, child-care arrangements or problems, unwed motherhood, contraceptive practices, pregnancy, spouse's preferences concerning job conditions. For example: "Do you have any young children?" "Do you really need to work?" "How does your husband feel about your coming back to work?" "Will your husband mind if you have to travel on business trips?"	Whether the applicant can meet specified work schedules or has activities, commitments, or responsibilities that may prevent him from meeting work-attendance requirements. "Is there any reason why you couldn't be out of town for a few days occasionally?" (Remember to ask *all* applicants the same questions.) Whether an applicant can meet the job's work schedule. For example:

TABLE 18.2 (cont.)

"Do you expect to be transferred because of your husband's job?" Any questions about marital status or pregnancy. Questions about national origin, ancestry, prior marital status, lineage, descent, or mother tongue.	"This job frequently requires overtime, including Saturdays. Would that be a problem for you?" "Is there any reason why you could not be consistently at work at 7:30 A.M.?" Whether the applicant has commitments, responsibilities, or activities that would hinder her from meeting attendance requirements. (If you ask this question of some applicants, ask it of all applicants.) Whether the applicant has ever worked under a different name. Whether the applicant is legally eligible to work in the United States.
RACE, NATIONAL ORIGIN, CULTURE	
"What would you do if people made racist remarks to you?" "Have you ever been arrested?" "That's an unusual name. What nationality are you?" Questions about the applicant's charge accounts or credit rating, unless they relate to performing a particular job. For a degree, unless you can show that this specific degree is the only way to measure a candidate's ability to do a specific job. "How do you feel about having to work with members of a different race?" "Your supervisor will be white. Does that create any problems for you?" "Where were you born?" You can't ask applicants questions about their national origin. You can't ask them who they live with or whether they own or rent their home. You can't ask for a photograph before hiring.	You may ask about an actual conviction that *reasonably relates* to performing a particular job. You may ask about degrees, courses, licenses, or equivalent experience that relates to a particular job. You can ask people to submit proof of their U.S. citizenship after they are employed. It's okay to ask applicants if there is any additional information related to a name change that will be necessary for you to check on their past jobs and education. Watch out for asking any questions that seem to search out information about national origin or ancestry.

TABLE 18.2 (cont.)

You can't ask questions about membership or affiliation in other organizations to determine the race, color, religion, sex, national origin, or age of an applicant. You can't ask questions about complexion, color of skin, height, or weight where it is not related to legitimate job requirements.	
HANDICAP OR DISABILITY	
"Do you have any disability or handicaps?" or any other *general* question that would gain information about disabilities, handicaps, or health conditions that do not relate to a particular job. You cannot ask questions about a disability that doesn't relate to the job.	"Do you have any specific health condition that would prevent you from doing all portions of this job?" "Do you have any sensory, mental, or physical disabilities or handicaps that may affect work performance?" Require that the applicant have the ability to perform all job-related tasks. You may ask if there are types of jobs for which the applicant should not be considered because of a handicap, disability, or health condition.
RELIGION	
"What's your religious affiliation?"	You may ask questions about whether an applicant can meet work schedules. For example: "This job requires weekend work on a rotating schedule. Would that be a problem for you?"

Also, the company had employees who lacked high school diplomas currently performing their jobs satisfactorily.

Similarly, a court struck down a municipality's requirement that fire fighters have high school diplomas (*Dozier v. Chupka*) because of the negative impact on blacks and the lack of demonstrated business necessity. However, in *Castro v. Beecher,* another municipality was able to demonstrate a sufficient business necessity that police officers have high school diplomas, and the requirement was upheld.

The courts also upheld a college-degree requirement in *Spurlock v. United Airlines* because of the public-safety factor. College degrees may be job-related when

- successful job performance requires knowledge of technical or professional subjects;
- the job requires a high level of judgment; and
- the consequences of employing an unqualified person are serious and involve public health or safety.

Airlines, school systems, and hospitals have been able to require that pilots, teachers, and medical technicians have college degrees. A manufacturer, however, was not allowed to use a college degree as a requirement for salespersons since the requirement negatively affected minority applicants.

While you cannot ask about an applicant's birthplace, you can ask newly hired employees to submit proof of their U.S. citizenship.

You can ask applicants if there is any additional information related to a name change that will be necessary for you to check on their past jobs and education. Watch out for asking any questions that seem to search out information about national origin or ancestry.

Generally, you can't ask a person about her arrest record. You can ask her about actual convictions when those are job-related. Similarly, you can't ask questions about credit ratings.

While there are areas to avoid, there are hundreds of thousands of questions one *can* ask. Table 18.3 gives you some samples.

You can ask questions concerning:

- previous work experience,
- reasons for termination of past employment,
- job training and job duties, and
- job-related views toward previous jobs and responsibilites.

TABLE 18.3 Interview Questions You Can Ask

To open communications, ask job-related questions that require candidates to draw on their experience and know-how. For example:

"Explain your job duties in your present or past job."

"If you had your druthers, what will you be doing five years from now?"

"What were two of your greatest accomplishments in previous jobs?"

"What skills do you have that are relevant to this position?"

TABLE 18.3 (cont.)

"From what you know about this job, what would you need to learn and develop in addition to the strengths you already have?"

"What makes you feel that this is the kind of job for you?"

"What is your image of the job? What interests you about it?"

"What do you feel are the major requirements for being successful on this job?"

"Pick one of your bosses whom you particularly like. How would she describe you?"

"What kinds of people do you find it most difficult to work with?"

"What do you judge to be your major assets and resources?"

"What do you want from this job that you are not getting from your present one?"

"In your past job, which duties did you like best? How come?"

"In your past job, which duties did you like least? How come?"

"What are your reasons for wanting to leave your present employer?"

"What led you to leave your past employer?"

19

It's Human Nature: When Employees Discriminate

Old prejudices die hard. If we wait until the last prejudice has died before we take action, we may wait forever. It's not enough for companies to hire women or minority employees if they then deny those employees a chance to work. No employee should have to learn that while she is equal, others with similar qualifications and job titles are more equal. Employers have an obligation not to use other employees' prejudices as a reason for denying some employees equal employment opportunity.

With this general principle in mind, what is your decision in each of the following situations?

1. Although the bathrooms aren't marked, it's generally understood that the first-floor bathroom is for white employees, the second-floor bathroom for Hispanic and Puerto Rican employees.
   Discrimination? Yes__ No__ Don't know__
   Why?
2. Because the policemen's wives complained, policewomen are scheduled to ride with other policewomen, not policemen.
   Discrimination? Yes__ No__ Don't know__
   Why?
3. If possible, all the Alaskan natives and American Indians are put in Bertha's department to give them an American Indian supervisor.
   Discrimination? Yes__ No__ Don't know__
   Why?
4. Every year, the company sponsors a special Oriental picnic. Non-Orientals aren't invited.
   Discrimination? Yes__ No__ Don't know__
   Why?

5. A state organization employs several mentally retarded persons. Because of employee complaints, they are told not to eat lunch in the company cafeteria.
   Discrimination? Yes__ No__ Don't know__
   Why?
6. One construction shift is all black, and one is all white because the blacks want it that way.
   Discrimination? Yes__ No__ Don't know__
   Why?
7. Ms. Lowe, a supervisor, was transferred to another assignment because the men working for her didn't want to work for a woman.
   Discrimination? Yes__ No__ Don't know__
   Why?
8. Because of racial tension, all Japanese were transferred to the day shift.
   Discrimination? Yes__ No__ Don't know__
   Why?

If you thought that each of the above situations involved discrimination, you were right.

EMPLOYEE-DISCRIMINATION GUIDELINES

· Discrimination based on employee preference is a subtle form of discrimination. An employer is not responsible for what employees think but is responsible for what employees do. It is unlawful to deny anyone an employment opportunity because of another employee's bias or preference.

· Employers may not make decisions that deny other employees opportunities because of spouses' complaints, social repugnance, language or cultural barriers, activism, or stereotypes.

· Watch out for job assignments that are made to accommodate employee prejudices. Job assignments must be made on the basis of job-related requirements.

· Watch out for preferentially hiring employees' relatives or those referred to the company by an employee if the effect of this practice will continue past discrimination by selectively informing only members of one race, sex, or group about a job opportunity.

· Watch out for segregated facilities such as bathrooms. Even if the sign doesn't say Whites Only, a company should watch out for an "unwritten rule."

· An employer has a responsibility to maintain an equal employment opportunity for every employee, despite the reaction of any employee to another's outside activities. For example, one employee may not want to work alongside an employee who wears a Black Power T-shirt. The reaction to the T-shirt should not form the basis for an employment decision.

· If a company sponsors a social or recreational activity, it can't be segregated on the basis of protected-class membership.

· Employers must be careful not to take sides when intervening in racial or ethnic conflicts.

CASES

In the following cases, is discrimination involved? Which guidelines apply?

Case 1: Bill Pomeroy

Jim Smith turned red when he saw Bill Pomeroy wearing a Castro button on his jacket. Jim told Bill to take the button off. When Bill refused, Jim socked him. Nancy Davis caught the tail end of the skirmish and suspended both employees for violence. Bill protested, saying that he was not violent. Nancy said, "Sorry, but you both were involved."

Case 2: Janson Enterprises

Janson Enterprises employs 300 clerical workers who work in 10 typing pools of 30 employees each. Recently, Janson's top management instituted the quality-circle concept in which representative employees meet in groups to discuss problems related to their jobs. These groups then make recommendations to the management.

One of the groups recommended that the typing pool be structured so that workers who smoked cigarettes were segregated in some pools and workers who didn't smoke were assigned to other pools. They also suggested that black and white employees be assigned to different pools or at least be seated in groups. Management decided to go along with both recommendations.

Case 3: Mr. Blue

When Mr. Blue's department hired two new employees, one of them was a woman. Because she was the first Indian employee, Mr. Blue introduced her to the other employees and stated that he wanted her to be a full member of the team.

During later weeks, he became aware that the other employees teased her, called her "Token," and sometimes used an insulting tone of voice when talking with her. He stayed out of it because he thought it best for the employees to work things out for themselves.

Could the Indian employee charge discrimination? Did the supervisor act properly?

Decisions

Bill Pomeroy has a case for discrimination. Although he did no more than wear a button and get hit, he was suspended. His employment opportunities were denied because of the reaction of another employee. Bill's suspension would have been justified only if he had said something inflammatory and thus provoked the violence.

Janson Enterprises. The guidelines that apply to the black-white segregation in this case are very clear. It is discrimination to group employees in typing pools on the basis of race, even when the suggestion comes from the employees involved. That it was the employees who initiated the prejudiced suggestion does not change the fact that discrimination is illegal.

Mr. Blue should have done more. Supervisors have a responsibility to provide an equal-employment-opportunity environment. Although he made a positive initial effort, he should have handled the employees' harassment with verbal counseling and disciplinary action if necessary.

20

"It's Just the Way Things Are": Customer Discrimination

"But the passengers want females as stewardesses – it's part of what they fly planes for!" "Management will just never listen to a female consultant." Many employers defend discrimination in hiring by saying that their customers want only men or only women, only whites or only blacks. Whether their customers really have those biases is a fact according to some people, an opinion according to others. What is certainly true, however, is that there are only a few jobs, such as sperm donor or wet nurse, that are sexually or racially exclusive.

Is illegal discrimination involved in the following situations?

1. "Sorry, a female cannot play the godfather!"
   Discrimination? Yes__ No__ Don't know__
   Why?
2. "We just can't hire minorities as door-to-door salespeople for that district. No one will let them in their houses."
   Discrimination? Yes__ No__ Don't know__
   Why?
3. "Our clients are young people. They buy makeup and hard rock records. An older employee will do better elsewhere. Kids talk to young salespeople."
   Discrimination? Yes__ No__ Don't know__
   Why?
4. "A woman executive simply can't do the entertaining necessary to make the contracts. If she tried, she'd get harassed. I'd rather not put a woman through that. We'll hire the man."
   Discrimination? Yes__ No__ Don't know__
5. Due to public pressure, the only women the police employed were clerks and dispatchers. When forced to integrate, the police accepted

two female rookies but created a special rape squad for one and assigned the other to Dispatch.
Discrimination? Yes__ No__ Don't know__
Why?

6. Because two customers wouldn't let minority repairmen in their homes during the day, the appliance company reassigned minorities to other service areas.
Discrimination? Yes__ No__ Don't know__
Why?
7. While Acme Security Rent-A-Guard Division has male and female security guards, it listens to customers' requests. If a company requests male guards, that's what Acme sends them.
Discrimination? Yes__ No__ Don't know__
Why?

Situation 1 does *not* involve illegal discrimination. Situations 2–7 do.

CUSTOMER-DISCRIMINATION GUIDELINES

· You are not responsible for the prejudices or biases of customers. However, you cannot deny employment opportunities because of these biases. If you respond to a customer's bias with discriminatory action, *you* are discriminating.

You may not base an employment decision on fear of a customer's harassment of an employee, a spouse's complaint, tradition, physical appearance, a preference for one sex, the obligation to entertain customers, community standards, or customer preferences.

· Avoid making an employment decision based on customer harassment of employees. (On the other hand, employee harassment of customers is not covered by discrimination laws.)

· In a few instances, only one group will be able to do a specific job. For example, male actors are needed to play some male roles; a woman who is able to nurse can be an effective wet nurse; only a man can be a sperm donor.

CASES

On the basis of these guidelines, consider the following cases: (1) Is there discrimination? (2) Which guidelines apply?

Case 1: Joe diManno

Joe diManno owns an exclusive men's clothing store. He hires only men salespeople because he feels that some customers would feel uncomfortable talking to a woman salesperson about some clothing items, particularly underwear.

Joe feels that his policy can be justified as a legitimate business necessity. He has talked with several customers who back him, stating that they need to discuss their clothing needs with the salespeople and that the men can relate best to their needs.

Case 2: Worldwide Enterprises

Worldwide Enterprises, which sells many products to Arab countries, has a policy of placing its Jewish employees in non-client-contact positions in the Middle East. In some cases, this means that Jewish employees have to wait for promotion vacancies in other parts of the world when client-contact positions open in the Middle East.

Company management feels that being Jewish is a real liability in Arab countries. They point to the fact that they do allow Jewish people who don't look Jewish and who don't have Jewish names to work in the Arab countries. They say that this fact shows that it's the customers and not the company that cause the problem.

Case 3: John Donnert

John Donnert works in a high-stress customer-relations job. At the end of a very difficult week, he noticed one of the customers glancing at his Afro and face. When the customer made a remark to another person, John heard a sarcastic tone and the word "Afro." That was enough. He exploded and told the customer off.

The customer walked out. John was fired. Is there discrimination?

Case 4: George Kanas

George Kanas is sales manager for Trouble, Inc. He has an opening for a salesman to service Trouble's industrial customers and a candidate who is qualified and wants the job. But the candidate is black, and George is worried that if he gives him the job, sales will be lost ("those industrial guys can be real 'unpleasant'"). If he doesn't give him the job, he fears the EEO consequences. After stalling as long as possible, George has promised the black an answer this afternoon.

What guidelines should he consider? If he doesn't hire the black, would there be discrimination?

Decisions

Joe is talking about business convenience, not business necessity. Also, it's his opinion that customers will prefer salesmen. The majority of his customers may actually prefer saleswomen.

In a case involving a firm doing business in the Middle East, a court allowed a company like *Worldwide Enterprises* to discriminate based on a defense of business necessity. In another case, a federal court ruled that a company did not violate the law when it refused to hire a woman for an international marketing position. The position involved selling to business executives in South America and Southeast Asia. According to the court (*Fernandez v. Wynn Oil Co.,* Cent. Calif., 20 FEP Cases 1162), the perceived sexual bias would have been a real obstacle to business success.

Both of these cases should be seen as examples rather than precedents. A company needs strong evidence to prove business necessity.

John Donnert's case can be interpreted in many ways. John might think firing was too severe a punishment. The company might respond that courtesy to customers is part of John's job.

What we don't know from the brief case description is John's past performance record. If John's record is poor and if other employees have been similarly disciplined for breaches in customer relations, the firing may be deserved. If John's record has been good, however, his explosion probably warranted a written reprimand and not a termination. In any case, his explosion was out of line. Although the customer provoked him, he responded more aggressively than necessary.

George Kanas should choose the most qualified applicant. If the black man is chosen and is excellent, sales may increase. If George gives the job to someone else, he is discriminating.

21

Disciplining and Firing

To many managers, discipline is a necessary evil. They discipline to correct work-performance problems and to send a message to all employees that good performance is expected. They discipline to maintain productivity and a well-functioning organization. Discipline is both an issue of potential conflicts among managers, supervisors, and employees, and an issue with potential legal consequences.

FIRINGS CAN BACKFIRE

Can you imagine having to supervise an employee you've fired? This situation can happen to managers who don't operate legally when disciplining employees, particularly if one or more of those employees files a grievance, lawsuit, or discrimination charge. A manager's protection lies in acting fairly and legally.

Employees fight terminations or discipline when they believe they have been unfairly treated. Employees may retaliate by spreading negative stories about the manager or company, or they may seek legal recourse.

If the courts find that a manager has unfairly fired or disciplined an employee by singling out that employee, given one employee harsher discipline than would be received by another employee in similar circumstances, violated the organization's personnel policies, or "harassed" an employee by closely monitoring and documenting one employee's poor performance while letting other employees' performance slippages go unnoticed, the courts may reinstate the employee. Further, the courts may issue a protective injunction protecting the employee from further harassment.

If you believe that managers need the right to discipline employees fully for not living up to performance standards and job requirements, it is important that you protect these rights by understanding exactly where discipline crosses over into inequity or harassment.

DISCIPLINARY GUIDELINES

Discipline: The bottom line is it's your job. The best way to handle it painlessly is to prevent problems. If you cannot prevent a problem, handle it early before it grows. These guidelines may make your life easier.

· Don't discipline nondisciplinary problems. If the system is such that an employee cannot possibly meet a deadline, that's not a discipline problem. You need to attack the system, not the employee. If the employee does not perform to your expectations because you did not make them clear, it's a communications problem. If an employee lacks critical skills, it's a training problem. An employee who clearly understands the job and the job's performance goals often needs no discipline.

Some problems are clearly discipline problems. For example, if an employee attempts to sabotage you or the operation, you need to deal with it. If an employee could perform well but does not because he'd rather not, discipline is critical.

· Deal with performance sabotage early on. Most problems grow while managers hope they'll go away. Not only does one employee get used to coming in late, but other employees notice the way the tardy employee gets away with it. Low performance can affect whole groups. If lateness is an issue for you, by the third time an employee is late, say, "I noticed you were twenty minutes late. Being on time is really important here."

Depending on your organization, one or more of the following may warrant disciplinary action:

- failure to comply with important policies or procedures;
- deliberate destruction of company property;
- failure to follow instructions;
- reporting to work or working under the influence of illegal drugs;
- excess absenteeism, short workdays, inefficient use of time;
- undermining company policies or programs;
- poor work performance;
- disclosure of confidential information to customers or competitors;
- personal work on company time;
- personal work conduct dangerous to others;

- insubordination;
- gambling or unprovoked violence on company property;
- theft;
- falsifying company records;
- sleeping during working hours.

· Keep disciplinary issues work-related. If you don't, you start dealing in issues that are outside your scope. An employee's drinking away from work is not normally your problem. If, however, the employee comes into work hung over, intoxicated, or late every Monday, her lowered work performance is within your range. If your personnel policies include information stating that intoxication is a disciplinary offense, intoxication is clearly a violation of work performance.

· Keep disciplinary issues objective, tangible, and specific. If you can't explain it, don't try. If something in your employee's attitude vaguely troubles you, wait until you can define it in specifics. Saying "I don't like your attitude" is asking for trouble. You may hear that he doesn't like yours. Worse, he may challenge you by asking what you don't like about it. Now you're in trouble; how are you going to explain it? You can say, "I want you to be at work by eight. I want you to work productively until five. By 'productively,' I mean achieving the results we laid out two months ago."

· Keep records of each employee's job performance, so that if you must discipline an employee, you'll be able to back up your decision with documentation. Keep all performance standards job-related, using objective criteria such as

- accuracy,
- sales volume,
- customer complaints,
- quantity and quality of production,
- operating within a budget,
- safety,
- meeting deadlines.

· Base your discipline on objective standards applied consistently to all similarly situated employees. Avoid discipline based on subjective or vague issues such as "attitude" or "personality" unless you define the issue objectively, specifically, and tangibly. You must keep all disciplinary issues and performance standards objective and job-related.

· Keep a record of the disciplinary actions you take so that you can show you treat all employees fairly and equitably. Termination records must document the reason for the firing.

· Be able to support your observations in disciplinary reports with facts by referring to

- production records,
- disciplinary reports,
- attendance records, and
- other examples of work quality.

· Remember that disciplinary actions may include

- verbal counseling,
- written reprimands,
- loss of privileges,
- suspension,
- demotion,
- discharge, and
- adverse performance appraisal comments.

· Focus on what you want rather than what you don't want. No one likes criticism. Employees respond better when you say, "My expectation is that you will not make personal phone calls on worktime" than when you say, "You've been making too many personal phone calls." After all, if your goal is results in the future, why focus on the past?

· Show why and how good performance matters. Sometimes you'll expect an employee to change, and she won't. Why? Because she doesn't think it matters. Perhaps the employee returns a half hour late each day from lunch. She may have decided it's a small issue. However, if that employee makes $13.00 per hour, that half hour costs a minimum of $32.50 per week, or $1625.00 per year. Don't hesitate to explain the bottom line.

· Be straight. Avoid pussyfooting. Discipline scares some supervisors to the extent that they sugarcoat what they're saying. If you bury negative feedback with indirect language, you may confuse your employee. Most employees want to know where they stand and can handle direct, constructive talk.

· Remember to discuss the positive as well as the negative. If you want highly productive employees, spend at least twice as much time on noticing what's right as on what's wrong. You'll notice a decrease in discipline problems and an increase in morale and productivity.

· Be consistent. If one employee is allowed to come in late, you can't crack down on another. If you set high standards for your employees, you'll need to follow them as well.

· Promise only what you can deliver. Know your personnel policies and what the courts say about fair practice. It's best to be able to carry out a firing action before you offer to do so.

· If a company must lay off employees, the employer must be able to show that the layoffs were necessary and that the criteria used in selecting employees for layoff were rational.

· Be aware that ex-employees may bring suit protesting termination on a number of grounds, including the following:

- abusive or wrongful discharge,
- bad-faith denial of the existence of a contract,
- defamation by libel or slander,
- economic injury or duress,
- fraud,
- implied covenant of good faith and fair dealing,
- violation of public policy (whistleblowing),
- intentional and negligent infliction of emotional distress (outrage),
- interference with contract or breach of contract,
- loss of consortium,
- malicious termination of contract,
- privacy invasion, and
- trespass.

"JUST CAUSE" AND STANDARD DISCIPLINARY PRACTICE

Most personnel policies state that a supervisor can fire an employee for "cause" if the supervisor has followed standard procedures. "Cause" may include an employee's incompetence, poor work performance, violation of company rules, or excessive absenteeism. Standard progressive disciplinary procedures in most companies are first to explain job standards to an employee, and then to counsel an employee orally if standards are not met. If improvement doesn't result, a supervisor or manager gives an employee a written warning or reprimand, outlining the improvement expected and a time frame or deadline. It is wise to include a warning that further lack of improvement may result in further disciplinary action, up to and including termination. If, after a reasonable period of time, the employee does not improve, management may then be in a position to terminate the employee.

In recent years, courts and arbitrators have begun to scrutinize and second-guess closely firing decisions made by employers. Montana's legislature passed the first statute protecting private-sector employees from termination without "good cause." Numerous courts have held that if an employer fires an employee without following guidelines set out in an organization's personnel handbook, the employee can sue for breach of contract. For instance, in *Weiner v. McGraw-Hill* (N.Y. 1982), McGraw's handbook had stated that the company would dismiss employees "for just and sufficient cause only." When the company then discharged an employee, the employee's legal claim was based on McGraw's personnel policies.

The bottom line is that an organization needs to protect itself from successful employee lawsuits by assuring that each firing decision will have to satisfy a just-cause standard. Just cause says that you as manager have valid, nondiscriminatory, and good-faith business reasons to discipline or fire a particular employee. If a disciplinary or termination action fails to measure up to the just-cause standards, you may be in trouble. The following paragraphs outline just cause more specifically.

Forewarning or "Notice"

The first standard is forewarning or foreknowledge. Did the supervisor give the employee advance notice that continued poor performance might result in being fired? If not, the first step is communication, not discipline. The supervisor might say, "This job requires that you be at work each morning at eight. Being late repeatedly is a disciplinary offense." Written job standards in job descriptions and personnel manuals are often considered forewarning and thus provide an added level of protection. The employer should be able to document that the employee has seen these standards. Often, employers accomplish this by having employees sign a statement that they have read the personnel policies. The "notice" requirement is also a reason for documenting, through an acknowledged or signed written reprimand, that the supervisor has told an employee his poor performance could result in a firing.

Work-related

A supervisor can discipline an employee for issues that relate to the employee's work performance but not for issues that do not affect work (such as being drunk at home on Friday evening or dating certain individuals, unless circumstances exist in which these situations *directly* and harmfully affect the employer).

Investigation

Supervisors should reasonably investigate the facts before discharging an employee. If the supervisor has not directly observed a problem, the supervisor must conduct a fair and objective investigation. An employee is presumed innocent unless proven guilty. Any firing should be based on substantial evidence—enough documentation that another reasonable person looking at the information would also decide to fire the employee. The more severe the prospective discipline, the stronger and more substantial evidence required.

Evenhanded

The final standard is fairness. One employee should not be disciplined for late arrival at work if other employees' late arrivals are ignored. If one employee is fired for an offense that another employee received only verbal counseling for, the termination action may not be defensible in the absence of other extenuating circumstances.

Also, the harshness of the discipline must fit the offense. While this standard is often used to dispute a termination, it's as problematic to underdiscipline as to overdiscipline. If an employee does obviously shoddy work over a long period of time, it may be time to move from oral counseling to a written reprimand to, possibly, termination for cause. On the other hand, no employee should be fired for a first offense unless it's particularly serious, such as theft, unprovoked violence, or a serious and reckless violation of safety rules that endangers other lives.

A just-cause standard requires satisfaction of certain questions prior to disciplinary action:

- Have I communicated what I expect to the employee?
- Are the same performance standards applied to all similarly situated employees? Are there other employees with a similar record who were treated differently?
- Has the employee been given adequate training and counseling on how to improve his performance? Has this been documented?
- Has the employee been warned of the action that will be taken if performance fails to improve? Has the employee been given adequate time and opportunity to improve? Has this been documented?

Management has the right to expect punctuality, productivity, a reasonably professional appearance, notification when an employee expects to be late or absent, honesty, nonuse of alcohol or illegal drugs on the job, attention to supervision, proper use of company equipment, obedience to safety regulations, quality workmanship, confidentiality of records, and obedience to company rules.

Using just cause and other disciplinary guidelines means that when you do take disciplinary action, even if those actions will be contested, you'll be on solid ground.

WRITTEN REPRIMANDS

Often, as a manager, your role in assuring organizational productivity will require that you do things you would rather not. Chief among these occasions will be the writing of a negative memorandum to an employee who is sure she has no problems. Then you not only feel like the "Grinch that stole Christmas," you run the risk of alienating that employee and thus further reducing work productivity.

The easy route would be not to write the memo. And truly, if honest performance appraisals are done, you will never have to write a memo for 9 out of 10 employees. Sometimes, however, written disciplinary memos are necessary as a last resort.

Memos become necessary when oral counseling fails. You've discussed the problem with the employee, and he has listened, but the problems have continued. Worse, you may have someone who genuinely believes he has no deficiencies. Instead, the belief is that you as the manager expect too much or see the situation incorrectly. In this situation, ongoing verbal discussions often tend to prolong the problems with no improvement. The employee ultimately governs his performance, and if the employee believes the manager is off-base, little improvement will occur.

Memos are necessary when the problem is damaging the work productivity of other employees, including yourself. Despite the fact that discipline is difficult, your real choice is between not offending one employee who has lower than expected productivity and indirectly sabotaging the productivity of others. Even if the problem is "only" with the office receptionist, it is a major problem. That person is the front line between your organization and its customers. That person affects other employees and can greatly influence office morale. If your secretarial or support staff person is working more slowly than you would expect, that can slow down an entire office's production and frustrate everyone. If one of your professionals has a problem, it will affect the image of your organization and directly reduce the results you are expected to achieve.

You need to write the memo because you owe it to the employee with the problem. If this employee does not improve, you will never promote him. This employee will be the last to be given challenging responsibilities.

You need to write the memo because you owe it to your other employees. If you choose inaction over taking steps to resolve the problem because you do not want to cause a conflict, you indirectly penalize the other employees who must adjust to reduced performance. Worse, you may find that your better employees simply leave, since high performers tend to be attracted to other high performers.

It is necessary that you write the memo because it is your job. If you do not do it, no one else will. And you have let everyone down: your customers, the employee, your other employees, and yourself.

Finally, this memo, signed by the employee, is your documentation that you confronted the employee with a problem and gave him a reasonable deadline to make expected improvement, prior to termination.

FIRING WITHOUT BACKFIRING

All of a manager's skills are needed when terminating an employee. If you fire an employee, you protect yourself and your company by

- making the firing decision after fully considering all relevant options;
- assuring yourself that the firing decision is fair, consistent with treatment of others, and supported by documentation;
- preparing for the firing interview carefully;
- notifying your supervisor and personnel officer;
- realizing you may need to deal with an employee's anger, depression, shock;
- realizing that the employ may deny the situation, attempt to bargain;
- realizing you'll need to be specific about your reasons.

Your preparation should include advance decision making concerning

- the employee's last date of work (today or 5 or 10 days later);
- amount of severance pay;
- outplacement or other services;
- statements and references;
- compensation issues related to salary and accrued leave;
- pension issues;
- contractual issues.

Your meeting will go more smoothly if you or your personnel officer has prepared all of this information for the employee.

You may want to have a witness to the interview, or you may choose to meet with the employee privately. Prepare yourself to keep control of the interview and of your own emotions. Avoid any inflammatory remarks.

Finally, you'll want to collect the employee's keys, company credit or identification cards, and equipment.

CASES

Case 1: Jay Hanson

When Jay Hanson took over the manager's job, he briefly reviewed the personnel files. All of the employees had been given "excellent" ratings by the previous manager.

Within a few weeks, however, he found that one employee consistently turned out sloppy work. He gave this employee a verbal warning and when things did not improve in two weeks, gave her another warning.

When things didn't improve after another week, he told the employee that if her work didn't improve, she'd be terminated. The employee responded, "Your problem is you can't motivate employees. You can't fire me—I've been here a long time and have always had 'excellent' ratings."

Jay called the former manager, who said that the employee had given him trouble too but that he had given her an "excellent" rating because he was trying to motivate her.

What do you recommend that Jay do?

Case 2: Chuck McKearney

Chuck McKearney has been a problem employee for six years. He has had repeated problems with excessive absences, but never enough to be fired. Yesterday he got into a fight with a coworker. When the supervisor investigated, he found that Chuck was at fault and fired him.

Chuck charges discrimination, stating that other workers have not been fired for fighting. Chuck is black.

Does Chuck have grounds for a discrimination suit? Did the supervisor act properly?

Case 3: Joe Murphy

Stan Sales, manager of Bendell Auto, sent Mike Shephard home for coming to work intoxicated. The next day, Stan left word for Mike to speak with him when he arrived.

Moments after their meeting began, Mike threw a stapler at Stan and, grabbing Stan by the shirt, began shaking him back and forth. Stan, a

55-year-old man with a known heart condition, fell to the floor with a stroke.

Joe Murphy, Bendell's owner, investigated. Sue Thomas, Stan's secretary, said that Mike began shouting a minute after he entered Stan's office. Joe fired Mike.

Mike protested, saying Sue "had it in for him" since he had never responded to her sexual advances. Joe found this allegation inconsistent with what he knows about Sue's normal behavior.

If Mike sues, what do you think the court might decide?

Decisions

Jay Hanson should first consult the personnel policies to find out what the company's disciplinary standards and procedures are. Then he should ask the employee in for a problem-resolving discussion in which he asks for the employee's viewpoint and gives the employee his assessment.

Next, Jay should consult with his manager or personnel officer and begin constructive and progressive discipline. This should include documentation of poor performance followed by a written reprimand that gives a reasonable timetable for improvement. If the employee improves, Jay should reinforce the improvement; if not, a termination action may be the best choice. Because of the groundwork laid, this decision will be defensible.

Jay has the supervisory right to terminate a poor performer. At the same time, since disciplinary action may result in a grievance or lawsuit, Jay should carefully review his actions to ensure that his actions are fair and consistent, and that he has given the problem employee sufficient chance to correct her behavior.

Jay's mistake is that he moved too fast in threatening termination.

Chuck McKearney's case lacks enough information for a decision. He may have grounds to prevail in a discrimination suit, however, if fighting is not mentioned in the personnel policies as a dischargeable offense and other employees have fought without being terminated.

Managers should beware of firing an employee for one offense (fighting) when part of the reason for the termination is a series of other offenses (absences). The value of unrelated offenses is primarily to dispel the employee's claim of a good record. Two or more unrelated problems provide a less substantial basis for a disciplinary action than do two related problems.

The supervisor acted properly by investigating Chuck and *may* have acted properly by terminating him. An independent body such as a court would look at these issues:

- Was Chuck given forewarning or notice that fighting would result in termination?
- How have other employees been disciplined for fighting or similar events?
- Was the investigation objective and fair?
- What were Chuck's work record and length of employment?
- Was discharging the employee appropriate or overly harsh?

Joe Murphy investigated what he understood was an apparent act of assault. Sue's statement indicated that Mike was at least partially at fault. Mike's actions injured the supervisor's (Stan's) health. Given the circumstances, termination may have been a valid and defensible alternative.

22

Documentation: Paper Trails Made Easy

You're pretty unique if you like paperwork, which means that when it comes to documenting an employee's performance, you'd rather not do it. The problem is that your paper trail is what makes it easier to discipline, appraise, or fire an employee. If a grievance or discrimination complaint is filed against you and you have no documentation, it's your word against the employee's. This is especially difficult where the employer bears the burden of proving the justification for personnel action. With a paper trail, you can show the reasoning that led you to discipline, fire, or fail to promote an employee.

Your documentation of each employee's positive and negative work performance can win or lose a future lawsuit. The rules are simple.

As it happens. Document as it happens. If you try to write a year's worth of notes on an employee's performance over a weekend, it is obvious. It is also a waste of a good weekend. Date each note, so that it's believable that you made your notes promptly.

Balance. If you've got 12 employees and you're writing performance notes on one, it will appear to an outsider that you're out to get that employee. You should be keeping performance notes on all employees, so that you have a memory jogger for performance reviews, promotions, raises, and disciplinary actions. It is in *your* best interest to write and file these memos.

Job-related. Keep your notes focused on work performance, and use only objective criteria. You can keep notes related to sales volume, accuracy, customer complaints, productivity, quantity and quality of work, safety, meeting deadlines, operating within a budget, and other specific areas. Avoid comments about what is subjective or outside the job: such as comments about initiative, attitude, or personal life. These areas leave you vulnerable to the attack that you're personally biased.

Support. Make sure that you can support your observations with facts such as attendance, disciplinary or production records and samples of work quality. If you get challenged, you'll have an easier time. You'll also be less likely to get challenged. If you allude to frequent customer complaints, attach a complaint letter or your phone notes on a called-in complaint.

Factual. Keep your documentation factual and accurate. If it's your opinion, feel free to think it. Just do not write it down. Saying that someone did a "poor job" or a "good job," "wasted time," was "too ambitious," or "did not delegate properly," are all judgments. Any personality description is sure to be an opinion. Instead, you want to record the specific facts that would lead anyone else to make the judgments.

Avoid emotion. If you're angry when you write your file notes, your frustration will come through in statements such as "this employee obviously should never have been hired," and "this is the worst employee I've ever supervised." As a supervisor, you're supposed to handle yourself professionally and not react in anger. If this case does go to trial, it may take you hours to explain those two statements. It's important to write about an employee with respect, despite his misperformance. Factual and respectful criticism can still tell the story.

Avoid conclusions. A frequent documentation mistake is writing conclusions and characterizations rather than sticking to the facts.

Documentation is best when it is an obviously unbiased accounting. Writing that "the employee's arrival time varied from 10 to 45 minutes late during the week of March 4th" is specific and factual. Writing "This employee can't be counted on to get to work on time" is a conclusion. Almost any statement using the words "attitude" or "initiative" are conclusions.

Conclusions are particularly dangerous in that they prejudice neutral outsiders, such as judges or juries, against the supervisor.

Remember that others will read it. Your documentation is not the "last word." It will be read by the employee and may be read by a grievance officer, the employee's attorney, a judge, or a jury. Insulting statements prejudice neutral outsiders against you. For example, in 1987, Frederick Stauber won a suit stating that his National Guard co-workers threatened to make negative reports against him and sabotaged his work. He said his supervisor slandered him by writing negative performance comments. For reasons including the documentation, the jury ordered the supervisor to pay Stauber $61,000 for punitive and other damages. Two co-workers were ordered to pay $20,000 and $25,000.

Review. Regularly review your documentation to ensure that your notes are accurate and that you are documenting facts, not opinion.

It's yours. You can document only what you see or hear. If someone else overhears something, have him write the performance note. Otherwise, it is only hearsay.

Enough. You want to have enough of a paper trail so that another reasonable person, reading the documentation, would understand why you took the disciplinary action you did. This means that if you plan to fire someone, the documentation should show you've made ample attempts to help the worker improve.

Stay short. Another mistake is writing paragraphs rather than sentences. In long paragraphs, it's likely that the supervisor will be tempted to replace factual observations such as "there were repeated typographical errors on outgoing letters" with subjective descriptions. The longer the descriptions, the more it seems that the supervisor is out to get the employee.

As a manager, you have every right to require productivity, honesty, punctuality, attention to supervision, and quality workmanship. If you've got an employee who is not performing, you have every right to take action. Your paper trail protects your rights.

CASES

Many of the most important guidelines can be boiled down to A and B.

A = accurate:

- objective facts
- actual performances as they occur (not memory)
- job-related behavior
- direct observations, not hearsay

B = behavioral:

- specific behavior
- not evaluative statements
- not personality descriptions

Using the A/B code, please grade these file notes. Give an item an A if it meets all the criteria for accuracy, a B if it meets all the criteria for behavioral, and an NA if A and B are not applicable.

Documentation of a secretary's performance:

1. The secretary made only two errors on a major proposal (October 12, 1989).
2. The secretary was able to compile a revised mailing list while maintaining usual production in other areas (October 12, 1989).
3. The standard of 98% of all correspondence with no errors was met last month (October 31, 1989).
4. I've heard that secretary wastes time when making copies (November 5, 1989).
5. During the year the secretary was too ambitious for her own good (November 11, 1989).

Documentation of a technical employee:

6. Employee prepared technical report on her own with little assistance. Report summarized all variables (December 3, 1989).
7. Employee met following objective: to create cost reduction procedure for project XYZ that is usable by purchasing contract administration and field construction people. This was done two months after starting the project (December 20, 1989).
8. Employee's "know-it-all" attitude interferes with her work (December 28, 1989).

For a trainer:

9. Seven of eight "students" have reported that trainer is abusive in class, cuts students off, does not answer questions, and humiliates students for being wrong (January 5, 1990).

For an accountant:

10. Accountant didn't cross-check "11" report figures with "9" report. This resulted in incorrect data being given to the project engineer (January 12, 1990).

For a supervisor:

11. Supervisor doesn't delegate or discipline properly. This resulted in low productivity and two grievances (January 30, 1990).

Decisions

Numbers 1, 2, and 3 are both A and B.
Number 4 is hearsay and thus not A and is evaluative and thus not B.
Number 5 is subjective and evaluative and thus neither A nor B.
Numbers 6 and 7 are A and B.
Number 8 is subjective and evaluative and is thus neither A nor B.
Numbers 9 and 10 meet both A and B criteria.
Number 11 is both subjective and evaluative, so meets neither A nor B.

23

Harassment and Retaliation: When Enough Is Too Much

Imagine that one of your employees who's always been a problem files a discrimination complaint against you. Or imagine that you're involved in a tricky legal situation and that an employee leaks a story to a newspaper, accusing your company of violating a safety law. Or imagine that an applicant mentions during an employment interview that she successfully sued her last employer for race discrimination.

Any of these situations might cause you to take protective action. In the first situation, you might begin to monitor closely the employee so that you can document poor work performance. In the second, you might immediately discipline the employee with a written reprimand, suspension, or termination. In the third, you might cut the interview short.

Any of these actions could get you into trouble: the accusation: harassment and/or retaliation.

Harassment includes singling out an employee by monitoring and documenting her performance and actions more carefully than you would ordinarily. Obviously, you'll monitor an employee with a disciplinary problem more carefully than an employee without a problem. However, if you're noticing and documenting all the employee's behaviors while your files on other employees, even those with discipline problems, are thin, you may be guilty of harassment.

Managers are also guilty of harassment when they don't maintain a neutral work atmosphere in which employees can be free of harassment related to their sex, age, race, or religion. You are responsible in this situation for the actions of the other employees that you supervise.

Finally, supervisors should be careful that they don't set up harassment situations by telling other employees that a particular minority or woman was hired simply because of the equal-employment-opportunity guidelines and not because of her qualifications. Think back to the instances in which you've heard a supervisor say, "I only hired her because she was black, a woman, handicapped...." The supervisor intentionally or inadvertently invites employees to give the new employee a hard time.

Retaliation refers to the protective actions you take when an employee files a discrimination complaint, mentions a past discrimination complaint, or protests against a safety or other public-policy violation.

In harassment and retaliation cases, if the courts find for the employee, they not only award monetary compensation but may also issue a protective injunction protecting the employee from further harassment by a specific manager. Since all managers need the right fully to manage and discipline employees, it is important that they protect their rights by understanding exactly where discipline and protective action cross over into harassment and retaliation.

Do any of the following cases involve harassment or retaliation?

1. Even though the new minority manager didn't mention the company she represented, after she spoke about discrimination as the guest on a radio "hotline," she found herself excluded from several managers' meetings.
   Discrimination? Yes__ No__ Don't know
   Why?
2. When the supervisor found out the applicant was a civil-rights activist, he cut the interview short by not asking the last six questions.
   Discrimination? Yes__ No__ Don't know__
   Why?
3. When a minority person overheard a co-worker insult a minority leader who had just died, he hit the co-worker. He was suspended for violence.
   Discrimination? Yes__ No__ Don't know__
   Why?
4. Racially insulting graffiti etched into the restroom walls wasn't covered by a light coat of paint for several months.
   Discrimination? Yes__ No__ Don't know__
   Why?
5. After Anne made a number of remarks to her supervisor about his use of the phrase "the girls," he stopped. He also resolved to be careful of how he acted around her. In keeping such a close eye on her, he began to notice a number of problems with her performance. After six weeks, he called her in to discuss her file since some of the problems suggested grounds for termination.
   Discrimination? Yes__ No__ Don't know__
   Why?

6. Mary, a white clerk, has been late for work on occasion, but she always calls in and has a good reason. Jane, a black clerk, calls in when she is late, but her reasons just don't seem to be as good as Mary's. The manager writes a letter to Jane asking her to improve her attendance.
   Discrimination? Yes__ No__ Don't know__
   Why?
7. Supervisor to Polish employee: "Look, why don't you just stop complaining about Polish jokes?"
   Discrimination? Yes__ No__ Don't know__
   Why?
8. John Technician has a *Playboy* calendar hanging in the control room of the pump station. One of the female technicians asked John, then the supervisor, to remove it. The calendar is still hanging in the control room.
   Discrimination? Yes__ No__ Don't know__
   Why?
9. A warmhearted supervisor regularly says things like "We've tried to help you people." "He's a credit to his race." "It's for your own good." "I really like you people."
   Discrimination? Yes__ No__ Don't know__
   Why?
10. Supervisor to employee: "Look, I think you'd better drop this civil-rights bag. You're just asking for trouble."
    Discrimination? Yes__ No__ Don't know__
    Why?
11. Two days after a black filed a claim of race discrimination, he became the first person fired for violation of a long-standing safety rule.
    Discrimination? Yes__ No__ Don't know__
    Why?
12. Supervisor to employees: ". . . and if you men get bored with the paperwork, ask one of the girls to take care of it."
    Discrimination? Yes__ No__ Don't know__
    Why?
13. The one exception to the stuffy environment in the executive office is that the secretaries are usually called by their first names.
    Discrimination? Yes__ No__ Don't know__
    Why?

Harassment or retaliation was involved in cases 1, 2 and 4 through 13, and possibly was involved in case 3. The following guidelines explain why.

HARASSMENT AND RETALIATION GUIDELINES

· You are not responsible for what employees *think*. You are responsible for what they *do* if their actions result in diminished opportunities for women, minorities, or the handicapped. You are responsible for making every reasonable effort to control discrimination.

You must maintain a *neutral* working environment free of harassment in the form of bias, abuse, insult, or intimidation. If you allow harassment, it is assumed that you have given your okay to it. Things to watch for include slurs, jokes, insults, criticism, demeaning remarks or tones of voice; racially, sexually, or other derogatory literature; and forms of address that might be insulting (*Anderson v. Methodist Evangelical Hospital,* 1972; *Murray v. American Standard,* 1972).

The general principle is that one person's joke may be another person's harassment. If you occasionally tease a woman about being a woman and she laughs with you, that's humor. If you talk about the "Limey" or the "woman" repeatedly and the person involved feels insulted or "set apart" by this, that's harassment. No employee should have to be teased constantly for being a Mormon, a Jehovah's Witness, or a "Britisher."

In the sample situations, both the racially insulting graffiti and the Polish jokes created a harassing environment.

A supervisor is responsible for maintaining a neutral work environment. In sample situation 3, the minority person was provoked. Disciplining this person for violence may be appropriate if the co-worker is also disciplined.

· Once an employer knows that harassment or a racially combative atmosphere exists, the employer must take immediate reasonable steps to remedy the situation (*Shell v. Suffolk County,* 1986).

· An employer has an obligation to make subcontractors or third parties aware of company policies regarding harassment. If the supervisor learns that a subcontractor is repeatedly harassing one of the employer's (not the subcontractor's) employees, the employer must take steps to correct the situation.

· Discipline must be shown to be fairly applied to all employees. For example, one worker cannot be disciplined for repeated late arrivals at work if another is not.

· These guidelines are difficult to follow. A supervisor tends to feel emotionally involved when an employee files a protest against a company action or a discrimination charge. Despite the difficulty of the situation, a supervisor must adhere to the ideal of evenhanded treatment.

Any excessive discipline or monitoring may become harassment or retaliation.

Consider employees who file a charge or protest as members of a "protected class." Even if their work habits are atrocious and their complaint is bogus, any discipline will be subject to extra scrutiny and likely be considered illegal reprisal. While it's not necessary suddenly to avoid disciplining employees who have filed a charge, you must treat them as you would any other employee. If they are discipline problems, treat them as you would any other discipline problem, following standard procedures.

In sample situation 5, the manager violated this guideline and began to keep an unusually close watch on one employee.

· Retaliation claims may arise where discipline follows an employee's

- public statements;
- prior employment activities;
- complaints or lawsuits filed;
- protests or demonstrations;
- outside activities; or
- interracial relationships.

· The courts may find retaliation on the basis of

- departures from customary practices;
- the timing of discipline actions (just after the employee took part in an equal-employment-opportunity-related event or protest);
- heavy monitoring or surveillance of one worker (more than another employee in like circumstances).

· Normal protection under antiretaliation principles may not extend where the employee's actions are in bad faith or illegal.

· Finally, a supervisor must avoid setting up potential harassment situations. A supervisor who says "We only hired her because she's a woman" or "because she's black" creates advance resentment for a new employee.

CASES

In the cases that follow, decide in each case: (1) Is there harassment or retaliation? (2) If so, which guidelines apply?

Case 1: Kit Jasper

When Kit Jasper was hired as the public-relations assistant four months ago, she understood that her job was to improve the company's image in any way possible. Her job description was very explicit about supporting company policies and protecting the company image in public.

Since hiring her, the department manager has learned that Kit is an ardent feminist.

Last night he blew up. On the six o'clock news he saw Kit taking part in a discrimination protest against one of the company's subcontractors.

He calls her into the office and tells her to cut it out. She responds by saying that the demonstration was on her own time and that discrimination is illegal, even if done by a company subcontractor.

He fires Kit for not living up to the conditions of her job. She files a discrimination suit.

What is her line of reasoning?

Who will win?

Case 2: Support Group

Soon after the female support staff began organizing a women's support network on their coffee breaks, the supervisors noticed that the staff coffee breaks were sometimes as long as 30 minutes. A rule was issued that coffee breaks were to be taken in departmental areas only and would last 15 minutes. While this had been outlined in the employee handbook, it had never been enforced. Is discrimination involved in this case?

Case 3: John Anderson

After the department manager hired John Anderson, he told his assistant to "keep a close watch on John. We had to hire him, even though we found out he has been arrested. I just want to make sure we don't have a problem." Is discrimination involved in this situation?

Case 4: Bob Best

Bob Best has been a problem employee for six years. He has had repeated problems with excessive absences, but never enough to fire him. Yesterday he got into a fight with a co-worker. When the supervisor investigated, he found that Bob was at fault and fired him.

Bob charges discrimination, stating that other workers have not been fired for fighting. Does he have grounds for a discrimination suit?

Decisions

Kit Jasper's case involves three issues. First, the company will probably contend that Kit's actions were harmful to the company because they insulted or harmed a subcontractor. Kit may counter that her actions improved the company's image by demonstrating the company's stance against discrimination.

Second, the company will probably insist that Kit Jasper has a responsibility to the company, even on her time off. Kit may counter with the argument that her off time is her own. The eventual decision in this case will partially depend on Kit's position in the company. The president of a company is so closely identified with a company that in some ways a president is always "on company time." Kit is only an assistant.

There is also a balance in whether Kit involved the company or not. In many companies, employees can do what they want on their off time as long as they don't involve the company. Employees can take part in bar fights as long as they don't say "This is on behalf of the X Company" as they slug the other patrons. They can wear sheets or strange clothing as members of any group as long as they don't embroider their company's name on the sheet.

Finally, the case involves retaliation. On this issue, Kit will probably win. The employer cannot fire her on the basis of her participation in a discrimination protest.

Support Group case is a very gray one; the employer stepped over the line between acceptable discipline and into retaliation only slightly. It is completely acceptable for the employer to insist that coffee breaks last only 15 minutes, particularly because that had already been outlined in the employee handbook. However, when the employer stated that coffee breaks were to be taken in departmental areas only, that appears to be retaliation or insurance against women organizing on a companywide basis. If the employer had left this off the memo, the memo would have been okay.

In *John Anderson*'s case, the manager discriminates by singling the employee out. Arrest records are generally not information that an employer can seek or use against an employee. Information about arrests can be discriminatory against certain groups unless it is clearly job-related. Convictions are more likely to be job-related than arrests.

As a result of the manager's actions, at least one other employee will watch, distrust, and possibly talk about another employee. This violates the need for a neutral work environment in which each employee is judged solely on his merits and performance.

Whether or not *Bob Best* has grounds for a discrimination charge depends on whether fighting is listed in the company's personnel policies as grounds for immediate termination and whether other employees who have fought have also been terminated. Despite his excessive absences, Bob has grounds for a suit if he is fired on grounds that don't apply to other workers. However, if the policies state that the infractions of different violations are cumulative, there may be justification for his being fired.

24

Why Reverse Discrimination Usually Isn't

What rights do men and nonminorities have? If a white man is passed over for a job or promotion that goes instead to a woman or minority, does he have rights?

1. Recently, a supervisor hired a qualified American Indian employee in preference to a more qualified white male applicant.
   Discrimination? Yes__ No__ Don't know__
   Why?
2. Bil Bilko compained to his supervisor's supervisor that his supervisor, Priscilla Willing, had sexually harassed him. The senior supervisor laughed at Bill and said, "Come now, you should be able to handle that!"
   Discrimination? Yes__ No__ Don't know__
   Why?

If you answered No in the first case, you're probably right. If you answered Yes in the second, you're right.

REVERSE-DISCRIMINATION GUIDELINES

· Discrimination guidelines protect all individuals—men and women, minorities and nonminorities, young and old.

In situation 2, Bill had as much right to be protected from sexual harassment as a woman. It's illegal to discriminate on the basis of sex or race, regardless of which sex or race complains.

· Technically, there is no such thing as reverse discrimination.

Although discrimination is illegal, affirmative-action efforts to eliminate the present effects of past barriers may be legal. This is why situation 1's answer is a No.

As part of voluntary affirmative-action efforts, a company may create a special intern or trainee program that is open only to women or minorities.

For example, in *United Steelworkers of America v. Weber* (1979), a company's voluntary agreement with a union to *prefer* minorities in a training program was found to be legal. This program did not bar whites, had a time limit, and was used by an industry in which a clear practice of past discrimination existed.

A company's affirmative-action efforts must be designed to address specific problems. Once these problems are resolved, protected persons can no longer be given preferential treatment.

For example, in *Wygant v. Jackson Board of Education* (1986), the Supreme Court found the school district's union contract to be illegal. This contract stated that the percentage of minority teachers would not be reduced if there were layoffs. The Court's decision was based on the absence of a pattern of past discrimination.

A company may use affirmative action in its hiring practices and not in its promotional policies or may use affirmative action in both areas.

· Organizations can carry affirmative action too far. For example in *Commons v. Montgomery Ward,* a federal district court (Kansas) found that the company had practiced "reverse discrimination" against a white woman supervisor.

During a corporate reorganization, the company eliminated her position and then created a similar position that was filled by an inexperienced black employee.

The court stated that if a company intends to use its affirmative-action plan to justify its employment decisions, it must produce evidence that the plan corrects "conspicuous racial imbalance." Without that justification, the company was practicing discrimination, not affirmative action.

A similar ruling was issued in *Lucas v. Dole* (1987) when the FAA selected an underqualified black for promotion based on an interview process using five broad and subjective questions.

· It is to a supervisor's advantage never to say that an employee was hired because he is a member of a protected class (women, minorities, handicapped, veterans). Supervisors who do so create a backlash against the new employee and are thus creating a discriminatory climate.

CASE

Please test your knowledge in the following case by deciding: (1) Is there discrimination? (2) Which guidelines apply?

Case: Glucose

At a recent training session on equal employment opportunity and affirmative action, Glucose's director of employee relations, Jim Dugan, told supervisors that the company had an affirmative-action program. Fred, one of the supervisors, asked Jim, "What is the quota for minority supervisors?"

"We don't have a quota," Jim answered. "We do have a goal of ten percent minorities in supervisory positions."

The supervisor then asked, "What's the difference between a goal and a quota?"

Jim answered, "A quota is a number we must reach; a goal is a voluntary figure we try to reach."

Yesterday, Fred asked a senior manager why he was passed over for a supervisory position. The manager said, "You both had good qualifications. It was a toss-up. We chose him so that we could meet our affirmative-action goal."

Fred protested, "That's discrimination! I'm more qualified!"

Was there discrimination?

Decision

In this case, the management were legally within their rights. Affirmative action goes beyond equal employment opportunity to correct past discrimination. By giving a qualified minority person a chance, they were acting affirmatively.

Affirmative action to rectify past discrimination is legal. It is legal to give some kinds of preferential treatment to previously disadvantaged groups. In this case, the minority applicant was well qualified and was in fact roughly equal in qualifications to the nonminority candidate.

The senior manager should not have created a hostile situation by telling Fred that the other applicant's minority status was the only reason for the final decision. A manager best maintains morale by spending time developing honest reasons *not* related to minority status.

25

Collusion: The Nice-Guy Syndrome

Who is in trouble when a manager handles a situation "diplomatically," knowing another's biases? Suppose a personnel officer knows that a supervisor will not manage women or minority employees well. Will the personnel officer act in the company's best interests by sending the supervisor qualified minority and female applicants, or should the officer protect both the supervisor and the applicants from a difficult situation?

If you've ever worked with a manager or a supervisor who has prejudices but is otherwise in a position of authority, you may have been tempted to "collude."

GUIDELINES

If you collude with another person by protecting her from situations in which she would work with people of another sex, race, age, or category, or if you act to protect the minority, female, or older or younger employees *by denying them an opportunity,* you have discriminated.

Your actions are illegal, *regardless* of your intentions.

CASE

AIB Service, Inc.

According to Janice Jordon, personnel officer for AIB Service, Inc., she was caught between a rock and a hard place. Her story:

"A supervisor in our company has asked me to find him a replacement for one of the vacancies in his department. As the personnel officer, I want to be able to please him. I've interviewed twelve applicants.

"The most qualified applicants are two women. However, I know this supervisor doesn't work well with women and refuses to hire a woman employee. If he was forced to hire a woman employee, he'd just give her a hard time. So I sent him the three best qualified male applicants.

"Was I wrong? Part of my job has to include keeping the organization functioning smoothly. If a woman had been hired, it would have been no service to her."

Did Janice act wisely? Who is most at fault?

Decision

Janice is in trouble. The employer is liable for her discrimination, and the supervisor she "covered for" may not be. She colluded with his prejudice and denied the two most qualified applicants a chance even to compete for the job.

Beyond the legal issue, there is another real business issue in this case. One of these qualified women applicants may have turned the supervisor around. And that would have meant increased opportunities for other women employees in the future. Also, since a male who is allowed to keep biases toward women employees may show them at some point to women customers, Janice's actions were not in her organization's best interests.

26

Employment at Will

HOW NOT TO GET BURNED WHEN YOU FIRE AN EMPLOYEE

It used to be that a manager could fire an employee after deciding to do so. No special reason was needed. Most employer-employee relationships were considered by law to be "at will." "At will" means that employees can resign when they decide to and that employers can terminate employees, even without notice.

Now, however, increasing numbers of ex-employees are suing their former employers for firing them unjustly or without adequate notice. Theodore St. Antoine, professor of labor law at the University of Michigan Law School has determined that nearly 10 percent of the 2 million non-union and non-civil-service employees fired each year sue their employers.

The courts in many states (among them, Alaska, California, Massachusetts, and New Hampshire) are ruling that employers have an implied duty of acting fairly and in good faith. These court decisions, related to "unjust dismissal" and "abusive" or "wrongful discharge," are based on theories of contract and tort law and "public policy."

Court decisions have in almost every state drastically modified the employment-at-will principle. For example, in Arizona, an appeals court allowed a credit analyst to sue American Express for firing him; a Connecticut court allowed an employee to sue Aetna Life and Casualty for wrongful discharge; the New Jersey Supreme Court allowed a midlevel manager to sue Hoffman-LaRoche. The Alaska Supreme Court held that an employee hired for a definite term (in this case, "until retirement") would not be discharged except for cause (*Eales v. Tanana Medical Surgical Group,* 1983). Alaska courts also recognize the covenant of good faith and fair dealing (*Mitford v. de Lasala,* 1983).

In some cases, courts have ruled in the ex-employee's favor, despite the absence of written contracts. For example, California federal judge J. S. Letts stated, "The unilateral involuntary termination of employment is inherently unfair." Courts in Alaska and other states have rewritten the traditional common-law rule that employers may fire for any reason.

The costs of losing, or even winning yet suffering through a lawsuit, warrant good management. Legal actions by employees protesting at-will terminations have convinced many employers to fire employees only with reasonable notice and for just cause.

Employers who lose wrongful-termination cases may owe former employees back pay, front pay, attorney fees, punitive and emotional-distress damages, and even reinstatement. In the period 1978–1983 employees won 48 of 74 jury verdicts in California; in other states 64 percent of all trial verdicts favor the employees. Six of the California plaintiffs received more than $1 million each. The average jury award is currently $602,000.

A variety of factors (such as the employee's length of employment, standard industry practices, and the employer's verbal statements) related to continued employment protect the employee. In essence, employees have a bargain with their employers. Once the bargain is made, employers must have good reason to change the relationship. Employers must act in good faith with the process and the reasons for termination.

GUIDELINES

· Treat employees fairly and in good faith. Make sure that all terminations follow constructive and progressive disciplinary procedures. These procedures may include

- Precede terminations with written reprimands.
- Precede written reprimands with verbal counseling.
- Precede verbal counseling with explaining performance standards.
- Use objective standards to eliminate arbitrariness from disciplinary decisions.
- Terminate only for "good cause" and after adequate investigation.
- Discipline consistently.

· Keep records of all unsatisfactory work conduct and performance. Document all employee discipline with clear and dated notes.

· Read your company's personnel policies and employee handbook. Make sure your personnel actions comply. Realize that any policies that are unfair or that are not followed may be used against you if you are sued. In effect, you will have breached your "contract" with the employee.

· Make sure you have no language in any employee documents (handbooks, contracts, personnel policies) that assures employees of continued employment or that employees are terminated *only* for just cause. If your handbooks specify grounds for termination, make sure they don't say that those specific issues are the *only* grounds.

Eliminate any language that suggests employees are "permanent" after a trial or probationary period. Economic conditions change, and no employer can grant unconditional permanence. You might replace "permanent employee" with "regular employee" and "probationary period" with "orientation period."

For example, in *Yartzoff v. Democrat-Herald Publishing* (1978), the Oregon court determined that employee handbook provisions regarding a "normal probationary period" might indicate that an employee could be terminated only for just cause after the probationary period.

· Realize that any of the following may create an implied contract:

- letters offering employment;
- business custom;
- oral statements;
- employment-offer letters;
- employment application forms;
- employee handbooks;
- personnel manual;
- an organization's rules, policies, or practices;
- positive performance appraisals;
- long-term employment;
- noncompetition agreements;
- words that might appear to be a basis for an expectation of lifetime employment.

In *Thompson v. St. Regis* (1984), the Washington Supreme Court echoed the sentiment of courts across the country when it ruled that an employment relationship is terminable by the employer only for cause if there is an implied agreement to that effect.

· Realize that statements in employee handbooks or personnel policy manuals may be sources of unwitting commitment and may limit your ability to terminate an employee.

For example, a New York court of appeals found breach of contract when the employer fired an employee for "lack of application" without following procedures set out in its handbook (*Weiner v. McGraw-Hill,* 1982). The handbook stated that "termination would be for 'just cause.'" The employee sued, and won, on breach of contract.

When Equitable Life Assurance Society fired four employees for "gross insubordination," the employees won more than $500,000 (1981). Equitable's handbook said that "no employee [would] be discharged without previous warning and a period in which to bring performance up to a satisfactory level. . . ."

In *Toussaint v. Blue Cross and Blue Shield of Michigan* (1980), the court decided that personnel-manual or employee-handbook policies stating discharge be only for cause can become part of an employment contract.

When a credit analyst sued American Express for firing him, he used the company's employee manual that stated, "We have enthusiastically accepted our responsibility to provide you with good working conditions, good wages, good benefits, fair treatment and the personal respect that is rightfully yours. . . ." The Arizona Appeals Court stated that such "representations made by an employer in a personnel or policies manual may become part of an employment contract and may modify the employer's right to terminate an otherwise at-will employee."

· Include a statement in any employee handbook that the handbook does not constitute a binding agreement or contract. This provides some protection. However, the decision of state courts are split on whether such disclaimers insulate employers from liability.

· Realize that promotions, raises, advancement, job longevity, and the absence of negative performance evaluations or disciplinary action may establish a contract for continued employment, assuming continued acceptable performance, and thus any firing needs to be justified.

Employment of long duration may give rise to a doctrine known as the implied covenant of good faith and fair dealing. For example, in *Pughs v. See's Candies* (1981), the California court decided that the employer-employee relationship—32 years of service, with routine raises and promotions—implied a commitment by the employer of good faith and fair dealing that eliminated the employer's right to terminate at will and without formal warning and notice.

· Never promise job security. Verbal and written statements concerning job security in job applications, employment and orientation interviews, and personnel handbooks can be assumed to be binding.

For example, a statement in the employer's policy handbook that the company required "good cause" for discharge and that the employees would have a job as long as they did the job well gave the employee a legitimate expectation of job security.

· You may want to have your employee handbook reviewed by counsel to eliminate provisions constituting, or giving the appearance of, binding employment commitments.

· Consider developing an employment contract that spells out the general or broad reasons for which an employee may be terminated.

· Eliminate unintended or misleading language in "letters of hire," employee handbooks, or personnel policies that suggest employees are "permanent" after a trial or probationary employee.

Similarly, avoid telling employees they will be terminated only for good or just cause. The courts may find this statement to be a binding commitment.

· Tell job applicants that employment is "at will" in your organization. The employment application may indicate that the employment is at will. Then ask newly hired employees to sign a written acknowledgment that the employment is "at will."

In *Novosel v. Sears Roebuck* (1980), the court found that the employee had no legitimate expectation of just cause due to signing an employment application stating that employment could be terminated by the employer with or without cause or notice and at any time.

As another example, in *Walker v. Modern Realty of Missouri* (1982), a letter of agreement stating that employment would "last as long as mutually satisfactory to both parties" created a relationship that the employer could terminate at will.

Realize that your written assurances or oral promises concerning continued employment may negate the validity of your employment-at-will statement (*Schipani v. Ford Motor Co.*).

· Have an attorney who is skilled in labor law review your employment contracts, personnel policies, and employee handbooks.

· Realize that oral promises or verbal assurances may bind you. When Avis transferred a manager from its San Francisco to its New York operation, it assured the manager that if the new position didn't work out, he could have his old job back. He was also told that he would not be fired unless he "screwed up badly" and that he "would never get hurt." He then signed an "employment-at-will" waiver.

He was fired and he sued. The federal appeals court said that the company's oral promise was binding and enforceable, and not a "casual pep talk." The manager won $300,000 in lost wages and benefits.

· If you are a public-sector manager, realize that court precedents indicate that public-sector employees have "a property interest" in their jobs and are entitled to notice and an opportunity to be heard before termination, notwithstanding contractual provisions for contesting the discharge after the fact (Cleveland Board of Education v. Loudermill, 105 S.Ct. 1487, 1985).

There is generally no application of an employment-at-will concept in the public sector, save for the very highest positions that serve at the pleasure of an executive.

In many situations involving arbitrated grievances, this property-right principle has been extended by arbitrators to include instances in which management, for whatever reason, has chosen to suspend employees without pay, pending the outcome of an investigation. Even if the investigation subsequently supports the termination of an employee, the temporary removal from employment (i.e., suspension) prior to investigation is now considered to be a deprivation of a property right and requires procedural due process. In fact, *any* adverse action taken against an employee, including a letter of warning, must now be preceded by notice of the alleged wrongdoing and an opportunity to respond.

Given this extension of *Loudermill,* supervisors now have three choices with regard to interim suspensions prior to full invesitgative proceedings. They must (1) notify the employee of the charges and provide an opportunity to respond prior to the unpaid suspension, (2) suspend with pay, or (3) provide alternate employment in some fashion, pending the outcome of the investigation.

In almost all cases where it is essential to remove an employee from a particular set of duties or worksite while an investigation is under way, managers may reassign the employee or conduct a preliminary hearing to determine if there is sufficient cause for a suspension without pay. In some cases, managers may suspend without pay.

· Realize that these issues are all potentially "gray" and that factors specific to an individual situation may alter any legal decision.

EMPLOYMENT-AT-WILL DISCLAIMERS

It may be defensible to use an employment-at-will disclaimer or waiver. While a number of court decisions have held these disclaimers to be valid—that is, a discharge without cause is then not a breach of contract (*Batchelor v. Sears Roebuck,* 1983; *Crain v. Burroughs Corp.,* 1983)—other courts have not upheld disclaimers.

Because of the potential of litigation in the employment-at-will area, you may want to have an employment-at-will disclaimer reviewed by an attorney.

A disclaimer adds a level of protection. It is not a guaranteed safeguard.

A statement may read like the following:

Version 1

In consideration of my employment, I agree to conform to the rules, policies, and regulations of ______________________________ organization.

I agree that my employment and compensation can be terminated with or without cause, with or without notice, and at any time, at the option of either myself or the organization.

______________________________________ ___________________

Employee signature Date

Version 2

The management of X Company hope that your employment with X Company is rewarding and satisfying.

We believe that the Company offers exceptional employment opportunities and that our compensation and benefits package is one of the best in the industry.

It is important that all employees understand the terms and conditions of their employment status with X Company. X Company is not able to guarantee or promise employment for any specified length of time.

At some time, it may be in the best interests of X Company to terminate employees on an individual basis or on the basis of a reduction of the work force. The Company reserves the right to make these decisions at its sole discretion.

Employees must realize that their employment may be terminated at any time at the option of X Company.

________________________ ______________

Employee signature Date

Version 3

I certify that I have read, understood and will abide by all the rules, regulations, directives and policies contained in the Company Personnel Policies Handbook, a copy of which has been provided to me.

I also understand that the statements of policy contained in the Personnel Policies are not a contract nor are they to be interpreted as a covenant of employment and may be changed without notice.

The purpose of this handbook is to provide me with essential information needed for me to function effectively as a member of the organizational team.

In order to preserve the greatest freedom of association, I understand the length of my employment is not guaranteed. Just as I will be free to voluntarily terminate my employment with or without cause, the company will be free to terminate my employment at any time with two weeks notice, with or without cause.

No Company representative has the authority to enter into any agreement contrary to this disclaimer.

________________________ ______________

Employee signature Date

Version 4

This handbook is intended as a guide concerning organization policies and benefits.

These guidelines are not a contract.

The organization reserves the right to make changes in these guidelines as it deems appropriate, with or without notice.

It should be understood that employment is terminable at the will *of either* the employee or the organization at any time.

No representative of the organization other than the Chief Executive Officer has any authority to make any contrary agreement.

Your signature certifies that you have read the handbook and that you accept the provisions stated above.

________________________ ______________

Employee signature Date

A Statement of Understanding should then be signed and dated by the employee. You might consider having the waiver separate from the employment application to highlight its importance.

Another alternative is to state, in the employee policy handbook, that the employer is an "employment-at-will" organization. If so, you'll want employees to sign a statement stating that they have read and understand each of the policies.

For example, the statement may read: "I have read and understand the policies contained in the employee handbook."

REVIEWING EMPLOYEE HANDBOOK

In reviewing your personnel and employee handbooks, you may find statements that unwittingly commit you and your company. You may want to rewrite these handbooks and remove all references to job security or permanence, or to just or good cause as a requirement for termination.

You may want to include waivers and disclaimers such as

- "This manual is subject to change at the employer's discretion."
- "The employer retains absolute discretion concerning the decision to discharge an employee."
- "Any employment agreements or understandings must be reduced to writing and executed by an authorized officer of the company. No oral agreements or understandings are binding."
- "If a supervisor's statements are not consistent with this manual, the statements in the manual will govern."
- "None of the policies contained in this manual are intended to entitle any person to remain employed indefinitely by the employer."
- "Only specific persons [names] may give authoritative interpretations of this manual. Other management personnel have been instructed not to interpret the manual to employees."
- "As an employee of the X Company, you have the right to end your employment at any time. The X Company retains the same right to end your employment, regardless of any other documents or oral or written statements issued by X Company or its representatives."
- "Employment is *at will* and terminable *at will* by the employer or employee, with or without cause. Any oral statements or promises to the contrary are not binding. The employer is not responsible for such statements that are not confirmed *in writing* and by the President or the Personnel Department."

· The statements contained in this booklet are not to be considered binding and may be revised from time to time by the management."
· "Because of the need to change policies to accommodate organizational and economic changes, the following rules are subject to change without prior notice. This manual does not constitute a contract."

Finally, consider having each employee sign this statement, acknowledging that he has read the handbook.

> I acknowledge receipt of the Employee Handbook and agree to comply with it and the rules and policies of the Company.
>
> I understand that the Handbook and all other written or oral material provided to me are intended for informational purposes only.
>
> I understand that the policies and benefits in the Handbook, or communicated to me in any fashion, are subject to change by management at any time and without notice.

CASES

Case 1: Saul Jones

Saul worked for Bell, Inc. for one year and one day, and was terminated. He sued, contending that he had not been given a performance review or any written indication that his performance was unsatisfactory. He did admit that he and his immediate supervisor had a "personality conflict."

When company officials looked for the employment-at-will waiver that Saul had signed, they could not find it. They believe it was removed from the file. Saul states that he never signed one. The company is able to document that it has a signed employment-at-will waiver for every employee hired before and after Saul.

There are no written personnel policies or employee handbook.

What would happen if this case goes to court?

Case 2: Lynn Landon

When hired by Management, Inc., Lynn Landon signed a statement that in consideration of Management's training program, she would remain at Management for one year.

One month after completing Management's six-month training program, Lynn resigned. Management was an employment-at-will employer. Two weeks later, she joined Professional Management, Inc. Management's president and personnel manager discussed whether or not to pursue legal action against Lynn. This is the second employee trained by Management who has been hired by Professional Management.

Case 3: Joe Cody

When Thomas, Inc. hired Joe Cody, they sought him out. He was employed by Smith, Inc. and told the Thomas personnel manager that he valued job security. The Thomas personnel manager told him that Thomas was a good company and that Joe's job would be secure, provided he did a good job.

Six months later, Joe was asked to sign an employment-at-will disclaimer. He refused, saying that he would not have taken the job if he knew he would be terminable at will.

Thomas then fired Joe as part of a staff reduction. Joe sued, alleging breach of contract.

Decisions

Saul's case is complex, a good example of one that might go to a jury.

Saul's supervisor should have followed standard procedures and given Saul written warning of potential termination. Even though Bell is an employment-at-will company, supervisors protect themselves and their companies from the costs of legal action by operating in a visibly fair manner.

It's a matter of dispute whether Saul signed an employment-at-will disclaimer. Given that all employees hired before or after Saul signed one, it appears that Saul did also and that the copy is simply missing. However, Saul may be able to contend that his supervisor bypassed the disclaimer in his case.

Given the strength of the arguments that both sides will be able to present, this case is too close to call. However, the bottom line is that even if Saul loses, the legal costs to Bell will be high. Companies do best when they set up systems that avoid problems.

Lynn's case shows the other side of employment at will. Employees may quit without notice and may join competing firms.

If an employer wants the right to terminate employees at will without cause or notice, it generally must grant employees similar rights. Given that Management is an at-will employer, it probably has no hope of any legal action, despite Lynn's written promise. Such promises are often more morally than legally binding.

In the future, Management may want to protect itself with a noncompetition agreement or proprietary-materials policy. Equally, it may want to learn what Professional Management offers that lures away Management employees.

Joe may win his case. In a similar case, a federal appeals court stated that a company had breached its oral employment contract when the interviewer promised job security and then terminated an employee who had performed well. The court stated that the "contract" was formed during the interview.

In a comparable case (*Ebling v. Masco Corp.,* 1980), an employee promised job security if he was "doing the job" sued when discharged two years later. He won an award of $300,000.

Finally, in *Glover v. Sager* (Alaska, 1983), drivers were told they'd keep their jobs "as long as they kept their noses clean." They filed suit when terminated and won.

27

Employee Rights

Can you read notes in a file kept in an employee's desk? Can you insist that an employee explain your viewpoint as you want it explained to a government investigator? Can an employer monitor employee work habits by videotape? Does an employee have the right to see what's in her personnel file? Can an employer ask applicants to take a polygraph test for security reasons? How public and derogatory can employees be when protesting company working conditions before the company has the right to fire or discipline them? What rights do employees have to be notified in advance concerning a potential layoff?

Increasing numbers of employees are suing, and winning, when they believe their rights have been violated. Not all suits are won by employees. Employers have rights too. There is a sometimes shifting balance between employee and employer rights.

Employee rights include rights

- to privacy;
- to off-the-job associations;
- to information that concerns them;
- to free expression;
- to protest and seek investigation of unsafe working conditions;
- to protest discrimination;
- to self-organize and form unions;
- to fair treatment;
- to file worker's-compensation claims;
- to pursue wage-and-hour claims.

GUIDELINES

· *Privacy:* The right to privacy includes both the right to be free from the publicizing of one's private affairs with which other parties have no legitimate concern and the wrongful intrusion into a person's private activities so as to cause mental suffering, shame, or humiliation. The roots of the right to privacy lie in the first, third, fourth, fifth, and ninth constitutional amendments.

According to the Bureau of National Affairs, the number of privacy-related lawsuits in which employees prevailed increased 20-fold between 1984 and 1987. The average award for suits brought in the last 2 years was $316,000.

While the only federal privacy law, the Privacy Act of 1974, applies only to federal agencies and not to private employers, many states are developing privacy legislation. In states with no legislation, employers best protect themselves when they follow guidelines based on court rulings.

The courts balance the employer's right to know with the employee's right to privacy.

Successful suits include the 1983 Ninth U.S. Circuit Court of Appeals ruling that California officials invaded the privacy of a police-department job applicant by asking her questions about her sexual history on a polygraph examination. The court held that her sexual activities were off-limits to her potential employer and were protected by the Constitution.

In an unusual case, a nurse refused to "moon" her fellow employees while singing "Moon River." When her employer fired the nurse for her refusal, she sued. The Arizona Supreme Court approved her right to sue for wrongful discharge, as a matter of public policy.

In 1984, an employee who was discharged after he took a polygraph test concerning alleged drug use sued his employer for invasion of privacy. He received almost $400,000 in potential lost wages and benefits.

In 1987, the U.S. Supreme Court ruled that a psychiatrist working in a California state hospital had a reasonable expectation of privacy at his workplace. His employer seized personal items from his desk and file cabinets while investigating charges of sexual harassment against him. The psychiatrist's successful suit contended that the employer's search violated his Fourth Amendment rights of protection from unreasonable search and seizure.

Similarly, a Texas employee won $108,000 from an employer that opened her padlocked locker to look for stolen property when it had no justifiable suspicion that she was the thief (*K-Mart Corporation Store #7441 v. Trotti,* 1984).

Your guideline related to searching employee desks? Do not search unless you can prove a pressing business need. The employee has the right to be free from unnecessary, overbroad, or unregulated employer investigations (*Showengerdt v. General Dynamics,* 1987).

If you conduct a search unreasonably, you may be sued for assault, battery, false arrest, false imprisonment, trespassing, intentional infliction of emotional distress, defamation, or invasion of privacy.

According to Frederick Krebs, director of the U.S. Chamber of Commerce's Employee Relations Policy Center, the courts realize that an employer has a "need to monitor, to know, but want him to behave fairly." For example, courts have upheld drug-testing programs for airplane pilots and railroad engineers but have dismissed random, compulsory tests for salesclerks and other clerical personnel as too intrusive.

Another likely offense is publicizing information that is true but private. Most state courts recognize that employers should disseminate information about employees only to a need-to-know group within management (*Schneider v. Pay 'N Save,* Alaska, 1986). As another example, a California court ruled in favor of an ex-employee discharged by an employer. The employer prepared a termination memo listing the reasons for the termination and then posted the memo in a public area.

Similarly, an employer may have liability if it provides information negligently. In one case, a husband called a company and asked about his wife's attendance at a night-shift job. He committed suicide after being told she had missed several nights. In this case, the employer prevailed on the grounds that it provided the information on a need-to-know basis.

In another case, a Massachusetts employee won $50,000 when his employer told other employees he had been discharged for drug use. Information kept in an employee personnel file can also get you into trouble. While you have the right to keep records, these records should not be exaggerated, malicious, or available to those with no need to know.

Some states, including California, Connecticut, Maine, Michigan, Oregon, and Pennsylvania, have stringent laws limiting disclosure of employee records to third parties. Ten states and the Federal Privacy Act of 1974 set limits on the data that the government can disclose to employers about individuals.

There are exceptions to an employer's right to disclose. When two employees left their firm to start a business, the former employer notified clients that the employees had been fired. The court ruled that despite the misinformation, there was no invasion of privacy. According to the court, the employees' departure was no secret. Only the circumstances were at issue.

For employers, commonsense guidelines are apparent from court rulings:

- Avoid collecting secretive information gained by unfair methods.
- Collect only information about individuals that is relevant to specific job-related purposes.
- Make confidential or sensitive information known on a limited and need-to-know basis only.
- Be careful about statements to prospective future employers, in employee personnel files, and in conversations.
- As employers, realize that your rights end where the rights of an innocent employee begin.

· *Job references:* Control who gives job references on behalf of your organization. Carefully control what is said about past employees. You may be sued for slander or defamation.

According to Jury Verdict Research, Inc., one-third of all defamation and slander cases are filed by discharged employees, who win in 77 percent of the cases. The median verdict is $81,750 (1987).

For example, Larry Buck won $1.9 million from a Texas jury after his former employer told an inquirer that Buck was disliked, ruthless, and a failure.

In 1985, Gail Davis, former executive assistant to Diana Ross, sued the singer for circulating a letter naming Davis and six other former employees: "If I let an employee go, it's because either their work or their personal habits are not acceptable to me. I do not recommend these people."

Davis asked for a retraction and did not get it. Maintaining that she had resigned voluntarily and was a good worker, she sued Ross for $12 million in compensatory and punitive damages. Ross's defense was that the letter was a matter of "subjective opinion" and did not state outright that Davis was unfit. After the Second Circuit said that the case should go to a jury, the suit was settled.

In *Geyer v. Steinbronn,* the employee won $105,000 in damages, contending slander, defamation, and invasion of privacy for a reference deliberately designed to hurt him.

Truth *is* a defense against a defamation charge. But what is "truth"? Truth is a question for a jury, and you'll save money by avoiding a needless lawsuit.

Your safest route: Simply give the dates the employee worked for you, or ask the prospective employer to get a written release from your former employee, authorizing you to make statements about her. If you do release information, make sure it goes only to someone with a legitimate need to know.

· *Polygraphs:* A new federal law effective in 1988 bans polygraph tests used by private employers, whether in job interviews or to question randomly selected employees about items missing, damaged, or stolen.

Federal, state, and local governments and firms doing sensitive work under contract to the Defense Department, FBI, and CIA are not covered. Pharmaceutical firms and companies that employ security guards are exceptions.

Employers may not fire, discipline, or discriminate against employees who refuse to take a polygraph.

In certain circumstances, employers may be able to give strictly regulated lie-detector tests, provided there is *evidence* of a theft or wrongdoing that caused economic loss or injury. Prior to the test, the employer must give the employee a written statement describing the loss or wrongdoing and the reasons why the company believes the employee is involved.

Polygraph testing violates the employee's right to privacy if questions of a personal nature are asked. If the tests are given only to members of a protected group, civil-rights laws may be violated. Other grounds for liability include assault, battery, negligent or intentional infliction of emotional distress, and outrageous conduct. Not only the company may be sued; in some cases, supervisors have been sued individually as well.

More than 27 states[1] have statutes preventing employers from using polygraph exams for job applicants or as a condition of employment.

Four women discharged by Rite-Aid (Maryland, 1984) for refusing to take a lie-detector test won more than $1 million each in punitive and compensatory damages.

In another case, the court, viewing freedom from polygraph exams as a matter of public policy, found for an employee who refused to take a lie-detector test (*Perks v. Firestone Tire and Rubber Co.,* 1979).

Polygraphs are not the only tests that may be illegal or unwarranted. It is generally held that employers must have good and sufficient cause to insist that employees undergo psychiatric examinations.

· *Off-the-job associations:* Except in special instances, employers have no right to curtail an employee's off-the-job associations.

If an employee's actions outside of work hours don't concern work, ignore them. For example, if one of your employees parties heavily, that is not your concern. If his work performance during working hours is poor as a result, however, that concerns you. Critique the work performance; leave the partying out of it.

[1]These states include (as of the date of writing) Alaska, Arkansas, California, Connecticut, Delaware, the District of Columbia, Hawaii, Idaho, Iowa, Maine, Maryland, Massachusetts, Michigan, Minnesota, Montana, Nebraska, Nevada, New Jersey, New York, Oregon, Pennsylvania, Rhode Island, Tennessee, Utah, Vermont, Virginia, Washington, West Virginia, and Wisconsin.

If the employee's off-duty actions do not harm the employer or cause the employee to perform work unsatisfactorily, the actions are outside the manager's rights to manage. If you believe you can show harm, remember that you will have the burden of proof. An example of harm would be where the employee is legitimately "on call," as with a doctor.

Avoid criticizing, commenting on, or interfering with an employee's private life.

If you have a concern that an employee may leak secrets to a competitor, talk to an attorney or your personnel officer. You can protect confidential and proprietary interests through other methods, such as policies agreed to by all employees.

If you set up guidelines concerning an employee's outside actions, check these guidelines with an attorney first. You'll want to make sure your policies are both legal and enforceable.

If you decide you want to talk to an employee about a sensitive private issue, plan your conversation carefully. You may want to seek advice first.

An employer may restrict employees from moonlighting if it negatively affects the employer's business.

As an example of how strictly the courts view these issues, Air California fired an employee for streaking in front of the Los Angeles terminal after he went off duty. The company's reason was that the employee's off-duty conduct injured the company's image. An arbitrator overturned the firing, saying that because the employee wasn't wearing his uniform, the firing was out of bounds.

However, when Ohio National Life Insurance Company fired an employee for associating with a woman not his wife, whom he presented as his wife at a convention, the firing was upheld (1985). The courts did not view the firing as a public-policy violation.

· *Access to information:* Laws in 19[2] states and the District of Columbia grant public-sector and often private-sector employees access to their personnel files.

Twenty-five states have "right-to-know" laws, requiring companies to divulge information concerning hazardous substances used in the workplace.

A new federal law and laws in three states require that employers provide notice of plant shutdowns and severance pay for affected workers.

[2]These states include (as of the date of writing) California, Connecticut, Delaware, District of Columbia, Illinois, Maine, Massachusetts, Michigan, New Hampshire, New Jersey, Oregon, Pennsylvania, Rhode Island, South Carolina, South Dakota, Tennessee, Utah, Vermont, Washington, and Wisconsin.

· *Free Expression:* Except in special instances, employees have the right to speak freely.

Courts in 24[3] states have specific laws protecting employees who report legal violations by their employer or refuse to violate a public policy such as an environmental law. A number of states have specific statutes for refusing to commit perjury or for blowing the whistle on unsafe or defective products or procedures.

Employee rights are balanced by employer rights. For example, an employment relationship may require accuracy and good faith in employee statements in matters of public concern, an unusual degree of confidentiality, or discretion and avoidance of bad-faith public criticism.

In *Pickering v. Board of Education* (1972), the U.S. Supreme Court devised a "balancing" test to measure an employee's right to free speech versus the employer's rights. In this case, a schoolteacher was fired because he wrote a letter to the editor criticizing the board of education for using funds for athletic programs rather than education. He did not attack any individual and did not upset normal school operations. The Court stated that "free and open debate is vital to informed decision-making by the electorate. Teachers should not be compelled to relinquish First Amendment rights they would otherwise enjoy."

The Virginia Supreme Court (1985) allowed two employees to sue for wrongful discharge after they were fired for opposing a merger forced by management. The court found that the terminations violated public policy.

In another case, an Arizona employee told a customer that his employer had stolen items salvaged from a wreck. When the employer fired him, the court stated that the employee could sue for wrongful discharge as a matter of public policy (1985).

When the International Brotherhood of Teamsters fired their business agent for refusing to give false testimony to a legislative committee, the court allowed him to sue for wrongful discharge as a matter of public policy (1959). Similarly, the court found for an at-will employee who was fired for refusing to participate in an illegal price-fixing scheme (*Tameny v. Atlantic Richfield,* 1980).

In yet another case, the court found that a nurse who was fired after she wrote an article on the right of terminally ill patients to die had a right to sue on the basis of freedom of speech.

[3]These states include (as of the time of writing) Arizona, Colorado, Connecticut, Delaware, Florida, Hawaii, Illinois, Indiana, Iowa, Kansas, Kentucky, Louisiana, Maine, Michigan, Minnesota, New Hampshire, New Jersey, New York, Ohio, Pennsylvania, Rhode Island, South Carolina, Texas, and Utah.

Employees don't win every suit. An Alaskan assistant attorney general protested his 1982 firing, stating the state's attorney general violated his right to free speech. The assistant was fired for writing a memo protesting a suspension. He said that because the suspension was a "threat," he would not "do or think anything different" as a result of it. His employer said that since "discipline clearly will not work," the assistant would be fired. The Alaska Supreme Court said that while it would uphold an employee's right to free speech, this case related only to a "personal dispute" with a supervisor.

· *Unsafe working conditions:* Employees have the right to protest unsafe working conditions without fearing reprisals. Specific federal laws include the Toxic Substances Control Act, the Resource Environmental Conservation Act, and the Occupational Safety and Health Act.

OSHA recently levied some of the largest fines in U.S. history. It fined a defense contractor $615,000 for accident-reporting violations and fined a car manufacturer more than $1.5 million for safety violations.

An employee has the right to refuse to do a job when "a reasonable person would conclude that there is a real danger of death or serious injury and there is in sufficient time, due to the urgency of this situation, to eliminate the danger through resort to statutory enforcement channels."

For example, when a foundry employee was fired after pointing out a smoke problem caused by burning scrap metal, he was fired. The OSHA ruling granted him $14,857 in back pay and compensatory damages, and cleared his personnel record (1987).

Employee fears must be reasonable, however. In 1986, the court upheld the right of MarkAir to fire a pilot who refused to deliver cargo to Aguacate, a Contra base in eastern Honduras. The court stated that the pilot's fears were unreasonable and totally unfounded since they were grounded in speculation and hearsay, not fact.

A number of states have additional regulations to protect the health and safety of employees. These include regulations related to sanitary facilities, ventilation, heating, and seating.

· *Protesting discrimination.* Employees who protest or testify with respect to employment discrimination are protected against retaliation.

· *Self-organization.* Employees are protected in their rights to self-organize, to form unions, to bargain collectively, and to strike to secure better working conditions. Employers may not discharge employees for union activity.

Any employer who

- makes payments or loans to any labor organization;
- makes payments to or reimburses the expenses of any employee to cause him to influence other employees with respect to their right to organize;

- makes expenditures with the intent of interfering with employees' rights or to obtain information concerning organizational activities, *except* for use in conjunction with certain proceedings; or
- hires a labor-relations consultant to persuade employees with respect to their organization and bargaining rights, *except* in conjunction with certain proceedings,

must report to the Secretary of Labor.

Employees have the right to engage in, or refrain from concerted activities vis-à-vis their employer.

Employers may not

- discharge employees because the employees urged other employees to join a union;
- refuse to reinstate employees in job openings they are qualified for because they took part in a union's lawful strike;
- demote employees because they circulated a union petition;
- refuse to hire qualified applicants for jobs because they belong to a union;
- interfere with employee rights by threats or promises;
- dominate a union by financial support.

- *Fair treatment:* A number of federal and state laws, such as the

  - Fair Labor Standards Act,
  - Employee Retirement Income Security Act,
  - Tax Equity and Fiscal Responsibility Act, and
  - Worker's-compensation laws,

protect employees' rights to fair treatment.

Employers may not act against any employee who exercises any right guaranteed by these acts or laws.

- *Notification of plant closing* (Worker Adjustment and Retraining Notification Act): Beginning in February 1989, employers must provide 60 days' advance notice of any closing or layoff that affects 50 or more employees at any one plant. The law requires written notification.

Employers who violate the law may have to pay laid-off employees back pay and benefits.

The plant-closing law covers all segments of the private business sector, including the termination of operational units, the hiring of contractors to provide services once performed in-house, or a temporary shutdown of a single site of employment. Also covered are all employers with more than 100 full-time employees or with 100 or more employees who work at least 4,000 regular hours per week.

Layoffs of six months or less and reductions of 50 percent or less in work hours aren't covered.

Businesses that face closings or mass layoffs caused by "business circumstances that were not reasonably foreseeable" and closings or mass layoffs due to "any form of a natural disaster such as flood, earthquake or drought" aren't covered.

CASES

Case 1: Union

The management of a large union ordered their business agent to testify in certain ways before a legislative committee, even if he had to lie. He didn't. The union fired him. He appealed the firing in court. Who will win?

Case 2: Salesperson

Joanne Mitchell had been promoted to senior sales representative. As a result, she was entitled to a 7 rather than a 5 percent commission on all sales.

The day after she closed a $5 million-dollar order, she was demoted.

Joanne protested the demotion, stating that it was done to save the company the 2 percent additional commission.

If the case goes to court, who will win?

Case 3: Toxic

When Jon Dunn, manager of Insight Plastic, entered the employee lunchroom, he discovered that Matthew Turner was soliciting signatures for a petition against companies that use toxic substances in the workplace.

Jon told Matthew to stop soliciting, as soliciting was against company rules. Matthew replied that the company let other employees solicit for charities, the United Way, and various other events. Jon told Matthew to stop the petition immediately.

The next day, Jon learned that Matthew was again soliciting during his lunchtime. He gave Matthew a written reprimand. Matthew protested the discipline. Who was in the right?

Case 4: Annette Murton

Annette Murton brought suit against her employer, stating that the employer drove by her house and peeked in her window to determine if she was really ill on her sick days. The employer denied this.

On what grounds did Annette base her suit? Who will win?

Case 5: Sheila Matts

Jim Burnette felt it his supervisory duty to talk to Sheila Matts, one of his top sales reps. She was dating the senior manager of his top competitor. The conversation did not go well. Sheila became offended and told Jim that her personal life was none of his business. After the conversation, Jim began to monitor Sheila closely; he kept a written log of her observations. Sheila found out about it.

Sheila resigned and sued, contending that Jim's close monitoring constituted harassment and made it difficult to do her job properly. She stated that the consistency of the monitoring indicated it would be only a matter of time until she was terminated.

Under cross-examination, her supervisor would admit to no reason for initiating the monitoring on Sheila, and could show no proof that he similarly monitored other employees. The monitoring began after the conversation concerning her dating of a competitor's employee. Jim admitted to having the conversation.

What were the grounds for Sheila's suit? Who will win?

Decisions

In *Union,* the business agent would win. In a similar case, *Peterman v. International Brotherhood of Teamsters,* the California appeals court said it "would be obnoxious to the interests of the state and contrary to public policy and sound morality to allow an employer to discharge an employee on the ground that the employee declined to commit perjury."

In *Salesperson,* Joanne would probably win. In a similar case, *Fortune v. National Cash Register* (Massachusetts, 1977), the courts ruled that enough evidence existed to show that the company's actions were motivated by a desire to reduce its obligation in paying commissions. The employer thus violated its obligation to act in good faith.

In *Toxic,* the person most clearly in the wrong was the supervisor. A written reprimand was incorrect, considering that the no-solicitation rule had not been previously enforced. The supervisor's actions were directed against an employee protesting toxic wastes on his lunchtime, which was his right.

In an actual case involving an electronics firm, two employees were given oral warnings, although the firm had allowed charitable and other solicitation. When the employees protested, the National Labor Relations Board held that the no-solicitation rule had been inconsistently enforced and was therefore discriminatory.

Jon would have been more correct had he checked into the enforcement of the no-solicitation rule and then let all employees know that it would be enforced consistently in the future.

Annette bases her suit on the right to privacy. If she can prove her allegations, she will win. However, she has the burden of proof.

Sheila will probably win. Given the evidence that Jim monitored only Sheila, that she had been a top sales representative, and that the monitoring began after the conversation about her dating, the monitoring appears to be harassment due to Jim's fears concerning Sheila's personal life.

Sheila has the right to privacy. Jim retaliated when she protected her right. Her suit could be based on the rights to privacy and fair treatment. In a similar case, IBM fired Virginia Rulon-Miller for dating an employee of a competitor's firm (1984). Ms. Rulon-Miller won $300,000 because her manager told her to decide between her boyfriend and her job. The manager subsequently made her decision himself, notifying Ms. Rubon-Miller that she was fired.

28

Employer Defenses: What You *Can* Do

YOU CAN DISCRIMINATE: IT'S LEGAL

Part of a manager's job is to make "discriminations" in terms of an employee's ability measured against the job's requirements. Without the freedom to discriminate on the basis of abilities and requirements, it would be impossible to make hiring, promotion, or disciplinary decisions. There are four other areas in which an employer is allowed to discriminate:

1. bona fide occupational qualifications,
2. business necessity,
3. job-relatedness,
4. no disparate impact.

These are employer defenses to employment-discrimination claims, for which the employer has the burden of proof. The courts interpret these defenses very strictly.

BONA FIDE OCCUPATIONAL QUALIFICATIONS (BFOQ)

An employer may use a BFOQ defense to justify an employment practice that would otherwise be unlawful because of its discriminatory impact. "BFOQ" means that a specific job requirement is a bona fide (true) qualification to do the job. An employer may select employees on the basis of sex, religion, or national origin when it is "reasonably" necessary to normal business operations.

Sex is a BFOQ where the position by its nature requires specific physical characteristics possessed by only one sex. This applies to actors and actresses, modeling jobs, and restroom attendants. A juvenile corrections facility might be able to require that individuals supervising young female prisoners be female. The BFOQ defense does not apply to situations in which the "customers prefer" one or the other sex. Thus, the airlines were not allowed to hire only women flight attendants. The BFOQ defense also does not apply to situations of sex stereotyping.

Religion is a BFOQ when the job involves the teachings of a particular religious organization. A church school might insist on its right to hire only the members of its religion as teachers. It cannot use the same defense in hiring secretaries. Why? Religion is not job-related for a clerical position.

National origin is a BFOQ in organizations whose principal activity is to promote the interests of a particular national group.

Race is never a BFOQ under the law.

Height may be a BFOQ. Airplane pilots must be at least 5 feet 5 inches in order to have easy access to all instruments and to see clearly over the front panel (see *Boyd v. Ozark Airlines,* 1977).

Practical BFOQ Situations

Which of these would hold up as a BFOQ?

1. Refusal to hire a woman as ship's crew member because it would involve providing facilities for her.
2. Refusal to hire a woman as a security guard because the job involves personal safety and customers might not feel as secure with a woman guard.
3. Refusal to hire a woman lifeguard at a hotel's swimming pool because most swimmers are men and the lifeguard has the additional duty of cleaning the men's locker room.
4. Replacing a man with a woman to care for female children at a workshop for training retarded children.

Situation 1 offers no defense. A washroom or bathroom can be made co-ed relatively easily. Situation 2 relies on two arguments. The first assumes that women cannot protect themselves. That barrier fell years ago when women police officers were recruited and performed successfully. The issue related to customer perception is similar to the one of the airlines used to keep all stewardesses female and single. The courts struck down that reasoning.

Situation 3 assumes that a woman would not have the strength to rescue a male swimmer. While it's permissible to give a strength test, it's not a good idea simply to assume that a female would not have the necessary physical ability. As for cleaning the restrooms, that could be arranged simply by a temporary sign suggesting that guests either wait 20 minutes or use another restroom. Situation 4 discriminates against males by assuming that men cannot care for female children.

Case

As a way of testing your understanding of the BFOQ defense, what would you decide in the following case?

The Alaska state troopers refused to hire women troopers, citing as a BFOQ that women could not pull 160 pounds of dead weight. They suggested that should a victim need to be pulled out of a burning car, a woman trooper would not be able to handle the situation. Is this a BFOQ?

Being a man in this case is not a BFOQ. A woman may be able to pull 160 pounds of dead weight, particularly in an emergency. A man may be unable to pull the same amount.

BUSINESS NECESSITY

An employment practice that has an adverse impact but that is demonstrated to be

- absolutely essential to the efficient and safe operation of the business or
- absolutely essential to the economic survival of the business (and for which no less-adversely impacting alternative can be found)

is a business necessity.

An example of a business necessity might be the requirement that bus drivers, who are responsible for the safety of a number of passengers, be under the age of 60. For some jobs, security checks or medical examinations are a business necessity.

Business "necessity" is not business "convenience" or the avoidance of minor expense or annoyance. For example, the expense of processing garnishment orders doesn't justify firing employees who have had their wages garnished. A good rule of thumb is that the reasons for granting the business-necessity defense must outweigh the human hardship of the discrimination involved. Business necessity must always be related to job-performance issues.

JOB-RELATEDNESS

To use the defense of job-relatedness, a company must prove that the apparently discriminatory job requirement is absolutely job-related. For example, if a prehire test is challenged, the company would need to prove either that an entry employee needs to know all the items on the test or that a high-scoring applicant would outperform a low-scoring applicant. To use the ability of pulling 160 pounds of dead weight as a job requirement, a company would need to prove that this ability is absolutely necessary to perform the job adequately.

NO DISPARATE IMPACT

A challenge to a job requirement as discriminatory may be defended if the company can prove that the requirement eliminates as many male as female candidates or as many nonminority as minority candidates. "No disparate impact" means that the requirement does not unfairly discriminate against any category of applicants or employees. For example, a minority applicant may appeal an employment test because it seems unfair to minorities. If minorities generally do as well as nonminorities on the test, it has no disparity, or unfair impact.

29

Developing an Affirmative-Action Plan

"Affirmative action" requires employers to do more than ensure equal employment opportunity. To comply with affirmative-action guidelines, an employer must make additional efforts to recruit, hire, and promote members of groups that have been discriminated against in the past. These groups include minorities (blacks, Hispanics, Asians or Pacific Islanders, American Indians, Alaskan natives), women, the handicapped, and veterans of the Vietnam era.

The company does not have to be guilty of past discrimination to be required to take affirmative-action steps. Any company that has a federal contract of $10,000 or more is required to be an affirmative-action employer. All companies that have 250 or more employees and $100,000 or more in federal contracts must have a written affirmative-action plan. In some cases, courts may impose the requirement of a formal affirmative-action plan on an organization found guilty of discrimination.

THE LEGAL BASIS

The Supreme Court has consistently supported affirmative action. Court rulings have stated that

- special job preference should be extended to all members of protected categories, not just to the actual victims of discrimination;
- goals giving protected categories preference may be lawful.

In a 1986 Supreme Court ruling, Justice William Brennan stated, "A court may have to resort to race-conscious affirmative action when confronted with an employer or labor union that has engaged in persistent or egregious discrimination. Or such relief may be necessary to dissipate the lingering effects of pervasive discrimination."

In a 1987 ruling, a court stated that an employer may promote a woman over a more qualified man to help get women into higher-ranking jobs (*Santa Clara County Transportation Agency*). The court stated that the promotion of more women is legitimate to overcome "a conspicuous imbalance in traditionally segregated job categories."

In *Higgins v. City of Vallejo* (1987), the court stated that the city "has established that manifest imbalance in its work force warranted adoption of an affirmative action plan pursuant to which it promoted [a] black firefighter over [a] white firefighter with a higher test score."

Smaller companies benefit from following basic affirmative-action practices since doing so provides an excellent means to achieve equal employment opportunity and a potential good-faith defense in case of a discrimination complaint.

AA ≠ EEO

Being an affirmative-action employer requires a company to take certain steps to help it reach real equal employment opportunity. For example, normal recruitment practices don't always bring in minority applicants. In many cases, minorities don't apply for jobs because they believe the company will discriminate against them. In other instances, word-of-mouth recruiting works against minorities because they don't have many friends in the company's current work force and thus don't hear of job openings.

Equal opportunity is thus not enough. Special efforts are needed. An affirmative-action employer actively recruits qualified women, minority, handicapped, and veteran employees by advertising in special-interest newspapers, making contacts with potential referral sources such as minority and women's organizations, and publicly stating their commitment to equal employment opportunity.

In many cases, women, minorities, the handicapped, and veterans are at a disadvantage in the hiring process. Due to past discrimination, they don't have the depth and breadth of work experience to make them the *most* qualified candidate for a job. An affirmative-action employer takes this into consideration in the hiring process. In some cases, an employer will hire these applicants anyway, as long as they have all the *necessary* qualifications.

Formerly, circular reasoning worked against minorities and women. For example, individuals in these categories were discouraged from entering some training and college programs because "companies would never hire them." Companies then stated they'd hire a qualified woman or minority applicant, but none had the training. As a result, many affirmative-action employers have created special trainee or intern programs to bring minority, female, handicapped, and veteran employees into their companies at an entry level, giving them the chance to prove themselves.

Past and present circumstances determine whether affirmative-action efforts are needed or lawful. For example, in *Johnson v. Transportation Agency* (1987), the court upheld the use of sex as a factor in promoting a female rather than a male employee into a job category in which females were conspicuously underrepresented. A company-union agreement giving minorities preference in a steel industry's training program was legal because of the industry's past pattern of discrimination (*United Steelworkers of America v. Weber,* 1979).

In 1986, the Supreme Court upheld a federal court ruling establishing a 29 percent minority membership goal for a New York sheet-metal worker's union that had long excluded nonwhites. However, in *Wygant v. Jackson Board of Education* (1986), a minority-preference clause was struck down because of the absence of a pattern of past discrimination.

Normally, affirmative-action programs include goals set voluntarily by the organization.

Finally, realize that good intentions are not enough if they are not matched by results.

AA Plan Basics

The basics of an affirmative-action plan

1. recognizing and removing barriers to equal employment;
2. identifying persons who have been held back as unfairly excluded;
3. training programs and other measures enabling them to compete more equally for jobs;
4. other efforts to remedy identified problems.

An affirmative-action plan must be real and not simply a document written then forgotten. Employers who must have a written affirmative-action plan can meet their obligations in nine steps.

Step 1: Develop an Overview of the Company

In step 1, a company writes a description of itself:

- name and geographical location;
- brief history of itself and its products or services;
- the present and anticipated economic picture of the company's geographic area;
- the amount of government business done by the company;
- planned changes in management personnel or other major reorganizations;
- statement of the company's progress in meeting the prior year's affirmative-action goals.

Step 2: Issue a Written Equal-Employment Policy and Affirmative-Action Commitment Statement

In step 2, the company issues a policy statement

- confirming the chief executive's positive attitude toward equal employment opportunity;
- stating that the company will recruit, hire, train, and promote persons in all job classifications without regard to race, color, age, sex, religion, or national origin;
- stating that all employment decisions will be designed to further the principle of equal employment opportunity;
- stating that the company will use only valid job requirements for hiring and promotion;
- stating that all decisions in personnel areas such as
  - compensation, benefits;
  - transfers, layoffs; and
  - company-sponsored training, social, and recreational programs

will be made according to equal-employment-opportunity principles.

Step 3: Appoint a Top Official with Responsibility and Authority to Direct and Implement Your Program

In this step, one person is appointed and given the authority necessary to coordinate the company's equal-employment-opportunity and affirmative-action programs.

Step 4: Publicize the Company's Affirmative-Action Commitment

In this step, the company publicizes its commitment to its managers, supervisors, employees, and unions. This includes making sure that all managers and supervisors understand their legal responsibilities. Many companies use formal one- or two-day training programs to give their managers a real understanding of their accountability.

The company publicizes its policy to all potential recruitment and referral sources for women and minority employees, as well as to the community at large.

Step 5: Survey the Number of Women and Minorities in the Company

A written plan requires an organization to review and analyze all its employment practices, including selection, promotion, and compensation, and then to address any discrimination with specific remedies.

At this point, the company needs clear information about its current progress in hiring and recruiting women and minority employees. To obtain this, the company must develop a work-force profile in which it collects information on the number of women and minority employees in each department and job in the company. This information is collected on the largest local population groups; for example, blacks, Alaskan natives, Asian Americans and Orientals, Spanish-speaking and Spanish-surnamed, women, and white males. Handicapped workers and veterans, though part of the affirmative-action program, are not usually one of the groups numerically analyzed in the work-force profile.

The company then looks at the labor force available to it for each job type. For many entry-level jobs, the available labor force is the state's population. The company then compares the proportion of women and minorities in the available labor force with those in the company's entry-level jobs. Let's assume the company employs 100 entry-level employees who need little qualifying experience. If 50 percent of the local labor force are males and 50 percent are females and if half of both the male and female labor force are minorities, this means that about 50 percent of the employees in entry-level jobs should be men and that about 50 percent should be women. Approximately half of both the male and female employees should be minorities.

The labor pool for different occupations changes on the basis of where the company recruits. The labor pool for engineers may be all the engineers available nationally if the company recruits nationally.

Once the company compares the percentages of women and minorities in its work force with the available labor pool, it determines "underutilization." Underutilization occurs when the number of women or minority employees in the work force is less than would be expected, given the labor force. The company does this analysis department by department and occupation by occupation, so that it develops a clear picture of where minority and female employees are and are not being utilized.

Step 6: Analysis of Problems

In step 6, the company analyzes all of its procedures to determine where there are barriers to the hiring, training, and promoting of minority, female, handicapped, and veteran employees. Company officials

- reevaluate job requirements to decide whether they reflect actual job needs or whether they ask for unnecessary education and work experience, and thus rule out potential applicants;
- review all hiring, selection, and employment procedures to determine if any have a discriminatory effect;
- analyze all the methods, sources, and procedures used in recruitment, from "help wanted" ads to application forms, from pre-employment inquiries to the employment agencies and referral sources used; and
- review all training programs, promotions, and wage and salary schedules.

Step 7: Set Goals and Make Plans

Goals and timetables are the focus of most affirmative-action plans.

At this point, the company has the information it needs to develop plans to increase the number of women and minority applicants in each area of the company's work force. The company makes plans for the kinds of procedural and policy changes it will make and sets goals and target dates for increasing the number of minority and female employees in the areas in which they are underutilized.

These goals are not quotas. Goals are *voluntary* commitments. For example, a company may decide that in one year's time, two out of ten positions in one job type will be filled by minority employees. If 11 months from now, only one minority has been hired, it does not mean that the company has to hire a nonqualified minority as a token. The company will need only to document its efforts and the reasons why meeting the goal was not possible.

Goals should be specific, attainable, and measurable. They should reference each area of underutilization, and should have target dates. Every manager and supervisor is responsible and accountable for efforts to meet the goals.

If the goal is not met for a number of years, the company may have to increase its efforts or create a trainee position, so that it can get the kind of minority employee it needs. On the other hand, the company may be able to show that its initial goals were not realistic. It is only through a court order, as the result of having been proven guilty of discrimination, that the company will have fixed quotas imposed on it.

Goals should include efforts such as (a) reevaluating job descriptions and hiring criteria to ensure they reflect actual job needs, (b) recruiting efforts, and (c) revision of all discriminatory employment practices.

Step 8: Regularly Measure Progress

During this step, the company will set up systems to regularly assess how successful its efforts are.

Step 9: Develop Supportive In-house and Community Programs

In this final step, the company will arrange programs to support its affirmative-action efforts. Many companies have both in-house training programs for supervisors and community-relations programs to increase the company's profile as an affirmative-action employer.

30

The Small Business's Perspective

YOU ARE COVERED

One equal-employment-opportunity myth is that small businesses can discriminate because they're too small to be covered by regulations or investigated. It is true that small businesses, except for those with federal contracts, need not file affirmative-action plans. It is true that Title VII of the Civil Rights Act covers only employers of 15 or more employees and that the Age Discrimination Act covers only employers of 20 or more employees.

However, many small-business owners have learned to their surprise that though they escape coverage under federal laws, they are covered by state or municipal guidelines. In many states, state or municipal equal rights commissions will take complaints from employees of the smallest of businesses. Small-business owners should call their state and municipal equal rights commission before they decide that they're immune from discrimination legislation.

Many states (Alaska and California are two examples) have discrimination laws that are far more extensive than the federal legislation.

GOOD BUSINESS SENSE

Beyond legality, it is good business sense for a small business to comply with discrimination legislation. First, the most vital business resource is people. If you follow the guidelines that prevent you from discriminating against categories of applicants, you open yourself up to hiring very productive workers. Many organizations have found that handicapped or older workers, groups that are often discriminated against, are their most hardworking employees. Also, when supervisors learn to base every employment decision on an individual's abilities, the job's requirements, and clear and objective performance standards, they achieve a payoff in increased morale among all employees.

Second, it's to a small business's advantage to operate according to the standards of a larger business. An employer who discriminates not only cuts his business off from potential federal contracts but also comes from behind once his company grows past 14 employees. Then the business must make immediate changes in its practices to avoid being caught in discrimination.

Finally, equal employment opportunity is good public relations. Customers come in many sexes, races, ages, and other categories, and tend not to do business with organizations that clearly discriminate against them.

31

Smoking and Nonsmokers' Rights

Do smokers have the right to smoke at work? Do nonsmokers have the right to a smoke-free workplace? Many employers feel caught in the middle. Balancing the rights of smoking and nonsmoking employees is a delicate task made particularly difficult by the intensity of the emotions involved.

In the past, employers commonly left the decision of how to divide airspace to their employees. Smokers smoked, and nonsmoking employees negotiated with smokers or fended for themselves.

Recent court decisions, however, are forcing most employers to make decisions. In a landmark case in 1986, the Washington Court of Appeals ruled that an employee with a debilitating lung disease could sue her employer for negligence for having exposed her to cigarette smoke at work. In 1987, two California workers with lung conditions aggravated by secondhand smoke were awarded damages.

A number of states—including Alaska, Arkansas, California, Connecticut, Florida, Hawaii, Iowa, Maine, Minnesota, Montana, Nebraska, Nevada, New Hampshire, New Jersey, New Mexico, Oregon, Utah, Washington, and Wisconsin—control smoking in governmental offices.

The legal issues involved result from an increasing body of research documenting the dangers of secondhand smoke. According to Joseph Califano, former U.S. Secretary of Health, Education, and Welfare, smoking, formerly seen as "slow-motion suicide," is now seen as "slow-motion murder." Consequently, an employee who is forced to resign from a smoky office because of a sensitivity to cigarette smoke may be entitled to compensation.

In addition to the legal issues, there are bottom-line productivity benefits to enforcing a smoke-free workplace. According to recent studies, an employee who smokes costs a company more than $4,000 yearly in property damage and maintenance, absenteeism, medical care for smokers and nonsmokers, wasted work time, and premature death. Because of these costs and associated legal issues, 54 percent of the 623 companies surveyed in late 1987 by the American Society of Personnel Administration now restrict cigarette smoking.

GUIDELINES

· As a minimum, a manager, supervisor, or organization should take a nonsmoker's complaint seriously and attempt to resolve the problem in-house.

· In some jurisdictions, employees who are medically sensitive to cigarettes and are forced to work in smoke-filled offices may be entitled to benefits from employers who allow smoking.

The Washington Court of Appeals ruled in *McCarthy v. State of Washington Department of Social and Health Services* that an employee with a lung disease could sue an employer for negligence in exposing her to cigarette smoke in the workplace.

Many states and municipalities are banning smoking in governmental offices. For instance, a regulation in New York forbids smoking at work unless the smoking is done in an enclosed area used *only* by smokers.

· Enforcement of a nonsmoking policy is tricky. Most smokers are willing to limit smoking but resent having to give up cigarettes completely.

To avoid costly litigation and morale problems resulting from smoking restrictions, employers should make the legal and financial reasons for a smoking ban clear. There are innovative approaches to restricting smoking, such as limiting smoking areas and upgrading ventilation systems.

· If your company plans to ban smoking, try to give employees 3 to 6 months' notice, along with guidelines on how to locate resources for learning not to smoke.

· Disciplinary action and other policies can backfire on an employer. An employee fired or given a poor performance evaluation due to smoking may be able to allege that as a nicotine addict he is entitled to protection under handicap-discrimination legislation.

· Another trap for employers is the perception or reality of favoritism. Workers may complain that executives with private offices are allowed to smoke, while workers cannot. Nonsmokers may complain that smokers take longer and more frequent breaks to accommodate their habit.

· Union contracts create another wrinkle. The National Labor Relations Act requires that employers negotiate changes in working conditions with representative bargaining units. Unless there are specific contractual waivers, most employers must at least notify union officials of the development and implementation of any smoking ban.

SAMPLE POLICY

A sample smoking policy follows. Before instituting *any* policy, you may want to consult an attorney.

Smoking Policy

Effective on [date], our company is implementing a Smoking Policy as the result of numerous employee requests and an increasing body of knowledge on the effects of secondhand smoke.

The policy is issued for use by all company, contractor, and consultant personnel. The policy is intended to establish guidelines and provide direction to smokers and nonsmokers alike. It is our policy to provide reasonable guidelines for regulating smoking at all company facilities.

The following general regulations will apply:

1. Smoking is not permitted in public areas: conference rooms, hallways, stairwells, and restrooms.
2. Smoking is not permitted in company aircraft outside of a designated smoking area or in company vehicles unless all passengers give their consent.
3. Smoking is not permitted in areas prohibited by municipal or state law, such as eating areas and elevators.
4. Employees may designate their immediate work area as a smoking or nonsmoking area and may post appropriate smoking or nonsmoking signs.

Disputes that occur between smokers and nonsmokers will be resolved by their immediate supervisors. The company reserves the right to designate further any work area as a smoking or nonsmoking area, depending on operational requirements.

CASE

Joan Bronson

Joan Bronson loved her job as accounting assistant. She liked her supervisor, Bill Martin, although he was difficult to work with.

The only habit of Bill's she hadn't learned to live with was his chain-smoking. Joan had been asthmatic since birth. Whenever she entered Bill's office, she had an asthma attack. Occasionally, coughing or breathing problems would occur when he came into her office. She asked Bill to compromise, and he agreed to crack open a window; however, he refused to smoke less.

Finally, Joan's doctor told her to quit her job or get her supervisor to change. He told her he'd done as much as he could do.

Given the medical issues, Joan felt that it would be reasonable for Bill to make a greater effort to change. The relationship between the two of them deteriorated. Finally, Joan resigned and complained to the state's Fair Employment Commission. What will the outcome be?

Decision

In a similar case, Danyse Brooks and Camillo Capo received $70,000 for pain and emotional suffering from California's Fair Employment and Housing Commission (1987).

Brooks was also asthmatic and suffered from attacks when in her supervisor's office. Brooks was also diagnosed as having ulcers and heart problems related to the asthma and the amount of medication she had to take to quell the attacks.

The commission said that the employer had not adequately protected handicapped employees.

In other states, employers have had to pay unemployment compensation when nonsmoking workers have quit jobs because of smoky work environments.

32

An Evolving Area: Dealing with Drugs

Drug and alcohol abuse is epidemic. Federal authorities estimate 10 to 23 percent of U.S. workers abuse drugs. A University of Michigan study quoted in the *Wall Street Journal* found that 10 to 15 percent of the nation's construction workers abuse drugs or alcohol.[1] The University of Michigan study estimates that 19 percent of all absenteeism and 15 percent of all job-related injuries relate to alcohol or drug abuse. Other studies indicate that drug abusers are three times more likely to injure themselves or others on the job. The estimated cost to U.S. employers is more than $60 billion per year.

The legal issues related to employee drug and alcohol abuse are complex. To a great extent, the courts are still developing the legal principles as cases are tried.

GUIDELINES

· The only federal statute applicable to alcohol and drug abuse, the Vocational Rehabilitation Act of 1973, protects handicapped persons from employment discrimination.

However, coverage of this act does not extend to any individual whose current use of alcohol or drugs prevents the individual from performing the duties of the job in question or whose employment, by reason of such alcohol or drug use, would constitute a direct threat to the property or safety of others.

Interpretation of this act varies. For example, an Illinois court found that a teacher who claimed his poor performance evaluations and

[1] *Wall Street Journal,* December 6, 1988.

discharge were due to his admitting to alcoholism had valid grounds under the Vocational Rehabilitation Act for challenging his discharge (*Athanas v. Board of Education of School District III, Highwood-Highland Park,* Illinois, 1980). In *Whitaker v. Board of Higher Education of the City of New York,* a court extended coverage of the act to a college professor denied tenure because of alcoholism (1978). In *Davis v. Buscher,* (1978), the court ruled that the city of Philadelphia violated the act by its policy against hiring current and former drug abusers.

The above decisions suggest that substance abusers may be protected by the federal Vocational Rehabilitation Act if they are qualified for jobs, perform satisfactorily, and do not pose a threat to property or the safety of others. To the extent substance abusers are thus protected, employers must reasonably accommodate them as they do other handicapped individuals.

State laws often protect individuals with physical or mental handicaps. Individuals who abuse alcohol and other drugs may be within these protected groups, with the result that accommodation would also be necessary under state laws.

· Employment policies concerning the hiring and firing of drug abusers fall in a gray area.

· Employee rights, including the fourth amendment right to be free from unreasonable search and the right to privacy, also affect the drug-abuse area. The legal questions for employers confronted with drug-abusing employees include

- How does the employer's need to know about suspected drug use balance with the employee's right to privacy?
- If an employer discusses suspected drug use, does that constitute defamation, libel, or slander?
- Do supervisors and co-workers have the right to receive information about suspected co-worker drug abuse if the abuse affects job performance and workplace safety?

In many states, including Washington and Oregon, employers may have liability if they publicize otherwise private matters in an offensive manner when the issue is not of legitimate concern to the public (*Washington State Human Rights Commission v. City of Seattle,* 1980).

For example, a jury awarded $450,000 to a discharged employee who sued on grounds of defamation, privacy invasion, and false statements concerning suspected drug abuse (*O'Brient v. Papa Gino's of America,* 1986).

· Employers should follow due-process guidelines, including adherence to just cause in any situation involving suspected alcohol or drug abuse.

For example, if an employer detains an employee against his wish, the employer may be guilty of false imprisonment or false arrest. If a manager makes a false report to the authorities, the manager may be liable for malicious prosecution, libel, or slander. However, if a manager makes a good-faith report to the police, based upon reasonable suspicion that an employee is engaged in illegal activity, any arrest is then a police decision.

· Issues of public safety, work performance, business necessity, and employer rights must be balanced against employee rights to privacy, confidentiality, and due process.

· As a general rule, managers have the complete right to insist that employees meet legitimate work-performance standards.

In most cases, if an employee's work performance is substandard, it is permissible to use performance reviews, oral and written counseling, and disciplinary procedures to motivate the employee to correct the problem. Corrective procedures must be consistent with progressive discipline. By handling drug-abuse symptoms as performance issues, you're treating all employees consistently. You're making no intrusions into any employee's private life.

In some instances, however, an employer may need to accommodate lower work performance. The most frequent accommodation would be weathering a period of lowered performance to give an employee with a previously good performance record a chance to "get back to normal."

· In general, supervisors confronted by extreme situations involving drug-abusing employees can best handle them by referring the employees to counseling or other resources rather than by attempting to counsel or diagnose a drug problem. This is because the only area in which an employer has a legitimate right to approach an employee with personal troubles is when the trouble interferes with how the employee performs on the job.

· If you suspect a drug-abuse problem, contact the person designated in your organization to advise you concerning employees with problems. This may be your personnel officer or manager. If you are the designated person, you may want to contact an attorney.

Do not ignore the problem. Not only will you suffer from performance problems, but you may be sued by others or the employee for negligence if the worker accidentally injures herself or others. An employer may have liability in such a case if it can be shown that responsible management knew of the problem but took no action.

Keep a record of the employee's work performance. List good and bad specific performance examples. You might note issues such as missed deadlines, customer complaints, or decreased productivity. However, do not engage in excessive monitoring. If a manager unfairly singles out a particular employee by unusually intense monitoring, this constitutes untenable job stress and can backfire.

Let your employee know that if a health or personal problem is causing difficulties affecting work, you can provide a referral. However, keep your disciplinary measures focused on specific work issues, and let the employee know that using a referral is voluntary. Also, avoid telling the employee that he has a drug or alcohol problem; if you're mistaken, it could provide the basis for a defamation lawsuit.

· *If the employee shows up intoxicated or under the influence of drugs,* don't ignore the problem. You need to protect your company, the employee, and others from accidents.

Don't assume or diagnose: The symptoms you observe could be the sign of an illness or a factor other than alcohol or drug abuse.

Don't allow a person to perform a dangerous job, and don't send him home driving his own car. While you cannot forcibly detain him, you can arrange for a cab or other ride or encourage him to wait. If you are keeping the employee in your office or arranging for another employee to drive him home, act with judgment. You don't want to place another person at risk.

Arrange for another member of management to witness the employee's behavior, so that you'll have corroboration of your observations. Be careful not to defame, slander, or libel the employee.

Record your observations specifically and objectively, then date your memo. Record symptoms, not conclusions or judgments. A good statement of symptoms might note "bloodshot eyes, slurred speech, shaking hands, the smell of beer"; a poor statement of conclusions: "He was stoned or drunk."

· *Drug Testing:* The growing drug-abuse problem in this country has prompted increasing numbers of employers to test for drug abuse. Forty-nine percent of *Fortune* 500 companies surveyed in 1988 by the Interface Group test job applicants for drug abuse. In addition to screening applicants, other employers have attempted to subject existing employees to random drug testing. However, drug testing is currently subject to legal challenge in nearly every state and federal jurisdiction.

In 1988, a federal judge blocked the Justice Department from forcing its employees to submit to random urine testing, ruling that the tests infringed on the constitutional rights of "trusted and apparently law-abiding employees," without being justified by an evident drug problem. The suit is one of a series of challenges to the Reagan administration's plan to ensure a "drug free federal workplace."

The suit was brought by 42 Justice Department lawyers and other employees, who stated that their constitutional rights against unreasonable search and seizure were violated by the plan to require those in "sensitive positions" to submit to random drug testing. However, the Justice Department is contending that random testing is necessary to ensure that employees are fit for duty, to deter illegal drug use, to protect sensitive information including grand-jury secrets, and to promote public confidence in the department's integrity.

The court decision equated random urinalysis drug testing with such privacy invasions as searching an employee's home, tapping his telephone, or censoring his mail. This decision illustrates the difficulty both public and private employers may encounter in conducting random drug tests.

In March 1989 the U.S. Supreme Court, in its first decision on workplace testing for alcohol and drug abuse, ruled that some workers in sensitive government jobs or entrusted with public safety may be forced to undergo mandatory blood and urine tests. The court's decision included railroad workers involved in accidents and U.S. Customs Service employees seeking drug enforcement jobs.

A number of states, including California, Minnesota, Rhode Island, Montana, Maine, Vermont, and Iowa, have laws restricting and regulating employee and applicant drug testing.

The area of drug testing is multifaceted and in a state of rapid flux. Because of this, any employer contemplating drug testing is urged to seek competent legal assistance.

· *Should you decide to initiate tests for drug use,* the following minimum guidelines should be kept in mind:

- Make sure you have a valid business reason for requiring the tests.
- Limit your testing to persons in special situations, such as employees whose jobs involve a significant safety risk to others.
- Test only when there is strong evidence of suspected abuse.
- Advise the employee that he is being tested specifically for drugs.
- Keep findings confidential.
- Confirm positive results through a secondary test. Drug testing is not fail-safe and may turn up a false positive.

· *Potential employer liability:* Employers may be held liable for the actions of drunk or drug-affected employees. Increasingly, when drunk employees cause traffic accidents after leaving work or company functions, their employers are being sued. The victims may hold the employers responsible.

In *D'Amico v. Christie,* a company was sued when an employee was fired due to drunkenness and had an accident on the way home. The company denied liability, stating that the employee no longer worked for it. The New York Court of Appeals found for the employer.

However, in *Otis Engineering Corp. v. Clark,* the Texas Supreme Court held an employer liable for sending home a drunk employee who caused a fatal accident en route. The court ruled that the employer had a duty to prevent the employee from being an unreasonable risk to others.

In 1988, the Oregon Supreme Court overruled the trial court's dismissal of a case where a construction worker, sent to a customer's home to do a routine remodeling job, first recharged himself by taking a hallucinogenic drug. He raped a woman who then sued the company. The court reinstated the case because the employee allegedly "ingested the drug to enable him to perform work for the corporation."

Given this potential liability, you may want to allow an intoxicated employee to sit in the supervisor's office or be driven home in a cab. If you serve alcohol at a company function, you may want to limit the amount served and serve food with the alcohol.

SIGNS OF EMPLOYEE DRUG ABUSE

There are clues, often overlooked or misunderstood by managers, indicating employee drug abuse. However, any one clue or combination of clues may indicate something else—often disease or emotional upset.

A clue is only that, a clue. Beware of broadcasting or acting on your assumptions; they could be wrong. If you choose to investigate, check with your personnel officer or attorney.

Many drugs lead to changes and swings in mood. A person may go from being especially happy and gregarious to irritable and depressed. A person may become unusually angry, suspicious, argumentative, or withdrawn. These mood changes may also be caused by emotional or personality issues or extreme stress. You may notice a poor memory, hallucinations, or a disregard for rules. Memory loss is also closely associated with stress and emotional problems.

Work-performance problems, from absenteeism to accidents and mistakes to lack of concentration and interest, can be caused by drug abuse. However, many work-performance problems stem from attitudinal, morale, and personal problems that have nothing to do with drugs.

Drug use can lead to extreme inconsistency in work quality, missing deadlines, and increasingly difficult relations with co-workers. Periods of hyperactivity are common with amphetamines and other stimulants; periods of lethargy are associated with marijuana, alcohol, and sedatives. Again, there may be a number of nondrug explanations for these performance problems.

Often, the physical signs of drug use are more definitive; however, these signs can also result from illness or medications. These include

- slurred or garbled speech;
- shortness of breath or breath odor;
- red and watery eyes;
- a runny nose;
- a lack of coordination or an unsteady, staggering walk;
- weaving or slowed motions or clumsiness;
- severe agitation, shaking, or tremors;
- nausea, vomiting, or sweating;
- needlemarks.

A sudden change in weight, while frequent among people with eating problems, may result from marijuana, alcohol, or other drug use.

Drug use may distort a person's sense of time and risk. For example, a person may think a minute has passed in 10 seconds or may be casual about taking a needless risk. As a result, there are significant safety problems associated with drug abuse.

Often, drug abuse shows up in an employee's absenteeism patterns, particularly in a consistent absenteeism on Mondays or after holidays. Absences may occur with no warning, and the employee will later excuse them with a story about an unexpected emergency.

CASES

Case 1: Doug Masters

When Doug's supervisor, Becky Smith, said, "Hey, I think you've had too much to drink; I'll need to send you home," Doug got belligerent and began shoving her. Becky asked another manager to help her and asked him to notice Doug's behavior. When she called the other manager, she worded the call carefully, asking, "Could you come over here for a few moments, Joe?"

When Joe Biggs arrived, Doug said Becky "had it in for him," and that he'd only taken some drug medication. Joe and Becky apologized to Doug for upsetting him and said they'd be glad to compensate him by 3 hours off with pay. Doug liked that idea and left the plant.

What did the two supervisors do well, and what could they have done differently and better?

Case 2: Peggy Newby

When Michael Broyan learned that Peggy Newby had applied for the senior account executive job for his radio station, he was pleased yet concerned.

He knew Peggy and thought her a terrific salesperson. Landing someone with her skills would be a real coup. At the same time, he'd heard rumors that she used cocaine, and the drug aspect concerned him.

Michael interviewed Peggy but ultimately hired Jim Jeffries, a less experienced salesperson. Peggy saw Michael in a restaurant three weeks later and jokingly said she'd sue him for sex discrimination, since Jim and all of Michael's other account executives were male. Michael realized Peggy was teasing but upset. He wondered what would happen if she did sue, and he had to admit that his reason for choosing Jim was Peggy's drug abuse.

How would a lawsuit like this turn out?

Decisions

In *Doug Masters,* Becky was wise not to ignore a problem. She was also correct to call Joe over and to use words to Joe that did not "defame" Doug.

Joe and Becky then handled a potentially messy situation smoothly by apologizing and a generous offer.

Becky could have approached Doug more smoothly with words that would have caused less defensiveness, such as "Are you feeling well?" or "You look like you're not feeling well."

Joe and Becky potentially exposed the company to liability by letting Doug drive home alone. When an employee is drunk, there are no easy options. He might have turned down a cab, and he might have caused a problem if another employee drove him home. Letting him drive himself, however, poses many risks.

Finally, follow-up is crucial. Becky's goal will be to ensure that Doug's behavior is not repeated and, if it is, to follow disciplinary procedures.

If *Peggy Newby* sued and discovered that the reason was her alleged drug abuse, she'd have potential grounds for damages. Depending on the state, she might be covered by state laws protecting individuals with mental or physical handicaps, and she might be protected by the federal law.

Michael could defend on grounds of "poor public image" and potentially erratic work performance, but his defense would be weak because he operated on the basis of hearsay and speculation.

Next time, Michael should consult with his company's personnel officer or possibly an attorney. In this increasingly litigious work world, you need strong reasons for hiring or firing decisions.

33

An Evolving Area: AIDS

With more than 48,000 diagnosed AIDS cases in the United States and speculation that more than 1.5 million have been infected with the virus, AIDS is now a statistical possibility for every employer.

GUIDELINES

· Currently, if you fire an employee with AIDS, you've discriminated against a person protected by legislation. In a precedent-setting case, the Massachusetts Supreme Court ruled that discharge of an AIDS victim due to his medical condition was illegal discrimination (*Cronan v. New England Telephone,* 1986).

In 1988, the Justice Department issued a legal opinion supporting federal policies that ban discriminating against AIDS victims. The Rehabilitation Act of 1973 and many state laws[1] forbid discrimination against handicapped persons who are otherwise qualified. A number of courts have ruled that AIDS, like tuberculosis or hepatitis, can be classified as a disability (*Chalk v. District Court,* 1987).

Also, the U.S. Supreme Court has ruled that a person with a contagious disease is "handicapped." Finally, a bill currently pending in Congress specifically includes AIDS victims as a category protected by federal discrimination laws.

Managers should deal with performance shortcomings of an employee with AIDS as they would with any employee. However, the risk of *future* inability to perform and concerns about high health-insurance costs

[1]States include Alaska, California, Minnesota, and Washington.

are generally *not* reasons to deny employment. Also, as with other handicapped employees, accommodation may be necessary.

· Employers can ask an employee who has AIDS to take a medical leave of absence *if* the employee is physically unable to perform job duties. Employers cannot require a leave unless they are certain that the employee can no longer handle the job.

A handicapped preson may be excluded from a job if reasonable medical judgment finds that significant risk of contagion or potential harm to others causes the person to be "otherwise unqualified." However, the current medical knowledge about AIDS is that it is not contagious in normal workplace settings.

The Defense Department has determined to remove military personnel infected with AIDS from sensitive and stressful jobs because of evidence that the virus can impair mental functions, even in people who show no overt symptoms of the disease. According to the Defense Department, there is no way to decide reliably which AIDS sufferers will and which won't have mental impairment.

Some AIDS victims suffer from memory loss, problems in attentiveness and concentration, and difficulties with hand-eye coordination. AIDS victims with these symptoms might be excluded from jobs for bona fide public-safety reasons.

Dr. Anthony Fauci, one of the government's leading experts on AIDS, has stated that not enough information on AIDS's neurological effects exists to suggest that civilian employers should follow the military's example.

· If your first inclination is to isolate the AIDS victim, you may run into trouble since current medical wisdom is that AIDS is not communicable in normal workplace settings. A U.S. court of appeals recently reinstated a teacher removed from the classroom because of AIDS for this reason.

The U.S. Surgeon General has said that employees with AIDS should be permitted to work as long as they are physically able, provided they do not endanger themselves or others.

Also, employees who refuse to work with an employee who has AIDS are not protected by federal law and can be ordered back to work. While the National Labor Relations Act allows employees to protect themselves from workplace hazards, there is insufficient or no evidence that normal workplace exposure to victims presents medical risks.

· In some states, it may be legal to test for AIDS; however, you cannot *use* the results of those tests to make hiring or firing decisions. At least three states—California, Colorado, and Wisconsin—have passed laws forbidding testing employees and applicants for AIDS.

· One clear-cut area is confidentiality. Disclosure of AIDS test results to other employees violates the AIDS victim's right to privacy and is actionable in court. Further, if you speculate verbally about whether or not a person has AIDS, you may be liable for defamation.

The Massachusetts Civil Liberties Union filed a lawsuit on behalf of a New England Telephone Company employee who said that a supervisor forced the employee to admit being treated for AIDS. According to the suit, when the information was released to co-workers, it became impossible for the employee to continue working there.

Several states, including California and Missouri, have newly enacted regulations specifically requiring that the results of *all* employment-related physical exams be kept completely confidential.

· If you discover that an employee has AIDS, you might want to make your first call to an attorney. The laws in this complex area are rapidly changing.

CASE

John Mondt

John Mondt, a gynecologist and a partner in a medical clinic, was barred by his two partners from treating patients after telling the partners he had AIDS. He is suing for breach of contract and discrimination.

John says he wants to work for financial reasons and that his condition poses no risk to patients or staff. Will John win?

Decision

This case is similar to a 1989 case (*James Gordon v. Women's Medical Group,* California) and others. A study released in September 1988 documented that 356 physicians and 2,826 other health-care workers had AIDS (U.S. Center for Disease Control).

The U.S. Center for Disease Control states that the question whether an AIDS-infected physician should be allowed to perform certain procedures (ones in which bleeding occurs) can be answered only on a case-by-case basis.

The issues involved include discrimination, confidentiality, breach of contract, and liability for another's infection and potential death. Many courts are recommending using the doctrine of informed patient consent ("what a reasonable patient would want to know") rather than the doctrine of "what a reasonable physician would disclose." The American Medical Association has suggested that doctors "should consult colleagues as to which activities the physician can pursue without creating a risk to patients." Some physicians have suggested that infected physicians be barred from all surgical proceedings.

John's case is too close to call. It will depend on the type of procedures he would be practicing and the extent to which his partners can reasonably accommodate him. In the one case whose outcome is known, *Alan Bouffard v. Cook County Hospital* (1988), the Chicago federal court ordered Bouffard reinstated. Bouffard, a neurologist, had been barred from performing invasive or surgical procedures.

34

An Evolving Area: Dress Codes

What rights does an employer have concerning employee dress? Can an employer require "professional" appearance? Can an employer insist that employees wear dresses and suits? Can an employer set standards for hair length and grooming?

GUIDELINES

· Before establishing a dress or appearance code, make sure there are no state or municipal laws contrary to your regulations. If you have a code currently in effect, you'll want to check with your state and municipal regulatory agencies (such as the Department of Labor, Human Rights Commission), so that your disciplinary actions will be upheld.

· Dress, appearance, and hair-grooming codes must have a sound business basis. Arbitrary codes may be discriminatory. Business reasons often include safety and hygiene or sanitation and may include favorable company image and customer perception. An occasionally used but questionable factor would be the need to reduce the "distraction" of outlandish or revealing clothes. In one case, when an employer disciplined a female worker for wearing "distracting" clothes, she sued and won on sex-discrimination grounds.

· Employers can set different standards for different job positions as long as the standards are nondiscriminatory and based on sound business reasons. For example, employers may set a stricter standard for employees who have regular business contacts with customers. In *Southern Bell Telephone and Telegraph Company,* an arbitrator upheld a rule that prohibited telephone collectors from wearing shorts (1980).

· Your code gives employees a general standard. You must make exceptions for genuine religious, ethnic, or cultural practices to avoid discrimination. You cannot set a standard that would conflict with an unchangeable characteristic of either sex or a racial, ethnic, or religious group. For example, because 25 percent of black males suffer from a skin disorder adversely affected by shaving, a no-beard policy may be discriminatory. The EEOC also has stated than an employer's hair standards must take into consideration the difference in hair texture between Negro and Caucasian hair (Decision 71-2444).

· Organizations such as police or fire departments may require stricter grooming standards.

· Most dress-code disputes are based on claims of sex, racial, or ethnic discrimination. While court decisions have varied from state to state, most (not all) courts have allowed employers to set different standards for men and women as long as they are not disproportionately burdensome for either sex. As an example, men may be required to have shorter hair than women if women must also meet hair-grooming standards (*Fagan v. National Cash Register*). A code requiring neckties for men might require women to wear business suits. At least one court has said that if male employees can wear slacks, female employees should also be allowed that privilege. However, another court has upheld an employer's ban on female employees' wearing pants in the executive office (*Lanigan v. Bartlett and Company Grain*).

· If you provide or require uniforms for male or female employees, you must provide or require them for both sexes. A bank that required only women to wear uniforms was found liable for sex discrimination.

CASES

Case 1: Store Clerks

A major retail outlet required that female clerks wear smocks and that male clerks wear ties. The women protested, saying that the smocks made them appear less professional in appearance than the men. What would a court decide?

Case 2: KTMM-TV

When Rhonda Masters was first hired by KTMM-TV as a receptionist, she dressed professionally. As a result of her professionalism and performance, she was promoted to secretary to the finance director, a job with less customer contact. Once in this new position, her appearance changed. She no longer wore suits and dresses with blazers but now wore slacks and sweaters.

Bonnie Brandom, the personnel officer, met with Rhonda at the request of the finance director and showed Rhonda KTMM-TV's dress code, which called for professional dress at all times by all employees. The interview did not go well. Rhonda felt insulted by Bonnie's tone and challenged Bonnie concerning the meaning of "professional."

After their meeting, Rhonda occasionally wore dresses and generally brought a suit jacket to wear over her sweaters and slacks. However, the jacket remained slung over the back of her chair.

Although Rhonda's work was good, the personnel director felt that Rhonda was setting a poor example for other staff, who questioned why they had to wear suits and dresses when Rhonda did not. The finance director also wanted Rhonda to change her appearance, saying that while customer contact was less in finance, customers still came in, and a highly professional appearance was important.

Bonnie issued Rhonda a written reprimand. Rhonda said that if she was discharged for her attire, she would sue.

If KTMM-TV discharges Rhonda and she sues, who will prevail?

Decisions

In *Store Clerks,* the female clerks may prevail. In a similar case, a federal court ruled that a code requiring smocks for women and ties for men "perpetuated sexual stereotypes." In another, a court stated that requiring uniforms for female employees demeaned them if male employees wore business suits. According to the court, employees who wear uniforms are generally seen as subordinate to those who do not (*Carroll v. Talman Federal Savings and Loan Association*).

KTMM-TV can present a strong case for professional appearance by all staff. TV stations sell "glamour." The question is what is "professional"? Sometimes this is difficult to spell out. In situations like this, employee agreement is an important factor.

When codes aren't specific and it can be awkward to make a dress code specific, supervisory diplomacy is crucial. Rhonda's situation became disciplinary in nature when she felt insulted, not persuaded.

35

When a Discrimination Claim Is Filed Against You

If a charge or lawsuit is filed against you, your first action should be to contact your company's personnel, labor relations, or equal-employment officer or attorney. If you are unsure about whom to talk to within your company, contact your manager.

You don't want to take any action until you can do so calmly and with some knowledge of the potential consequences. Supervisors who react too quickly may make potentially damaging statements or decisions and thus open themselves to charges of retaliation.

DISCRIMINATION COMPLAINTS

After a discrimination charge is filed with an equal rights commission, the agency's investigative staff analyzes the case. The law requires that the staff gather facts from the person filing the complaint and the company that has been cited. The staff is required by law to be impartial in weighing the evidence.

After the staff investigator talks with the person filing the complaint, she will ask both the company and the complainant to provide information. For example, if the person who filed the complaint was fired, the investigator will ask the company to provide fairly specific information concerning how people of different races and sexes are treated in similar disciplinary situations, the company's personnel policies, and documentation related to the termination.

If the complaint is filed at the federal level with the Equal Employment Opportunity Commission, the commission staff will first analyze the information and decide if there is reasonable cause for proceeding with the complaint. Upon a "reasonable cause" determination, it will arrange a conciliation meeting with both parties. State and municipal commissions also tend to hold resolution conferences with both parties. Resolution conferences are not hearings but a method most commissions use to resolve complaints informally. In some states, more than 90 percent of the complaints filed are settled informally before the hearing stage.

If the conciliation meeting fails to resolve the problem and the EEOC staff still believes there is a reasonable cause for the complaint, the EEOC will file suit in federal court against the employer. If the two parties at a state commission's informal conference don't reach an agreement, the commission staff investigates the complaint in more detail. If the staff determines there is no substantial evidence to support the complaint, the agency will then issue a determination order dismissing the administrative complaint, with the complainant generally free to pursue her own private action in state court.

If the staff decides that substantial evidence supports the complaint, the staff attempts to reach a conciliation agreement with the two parties. If an agreement is reached, the case is closed. If an agreement is not reached, the commission then convenes a public hearing conducted by an attorney "examiner," who makes a recommendation to the commissioners. Both parties have the right to be represented by an attorney at the hearing, to call witnesses, to present evidence, and to file objections to the "examiner's" recommendation. Under many states' procedural rules, as with EEOC proceedings, the complaining employee is represented by agency attorneys. In other words, if the case gets this far, it can become very expensive for the employer, and the employee may rely solely on the expert legal assistance of an agency lawyer.

At the conclusion of the hearing, the hearing officer will make a recommendation for the full commission. Either party may file objections before the full commission rules. Finally, the commission's final order, as a general rule, can be appealed by either the agency or the employer to a state court.

Figure 35.1 (page 228) illustrates the complaint-processing stages in most states.

EMPLOYEE LAWSUIT

If an employee files a lawsuit against you or your company, your first step should be alerting your manager and seeking legal advice on behalf of your organization.

While it may seem logical to first conduct an immediate internal investigation into all the facts related to the situation, that commonsense action could be dangerous. If the lawsuit proceeds, the other attorney may be able to learn, in "discovery," all the information you uncover in your

FIGURE 35.1 Complaint-Processing Stages

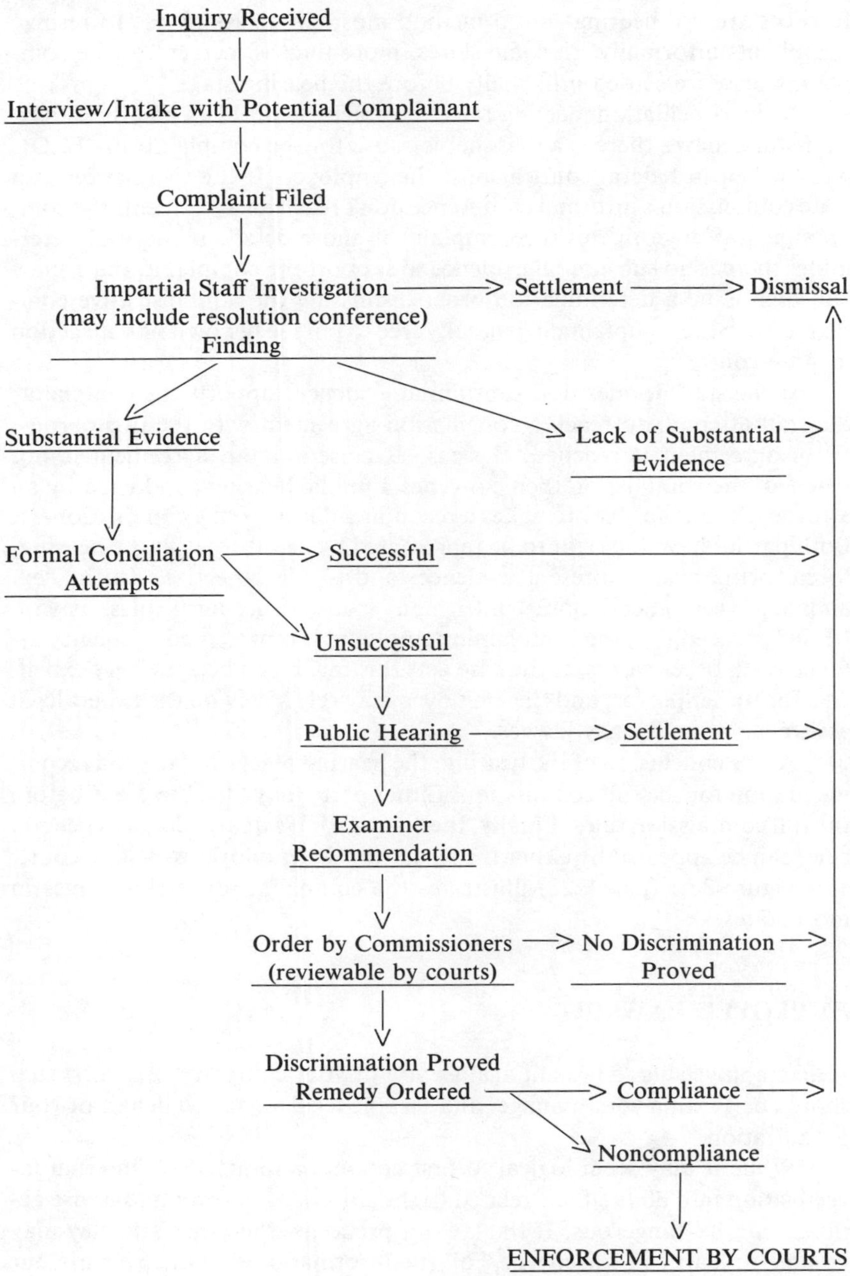

informal investigation. You'll then need to explain every memo or comment on every scrap of paper you uncover, including potentially damaging notes or memos written by someone who thought what was said would be forever confidential. However, if you've first contacted an attorney and the attorney requests that you conduct the investigation and supervises it, the information you uncover *may* be protected by the "attorney-client" privilege.

Discovery is one of the first stages in a lawsuit. During discovery, each side, through its attorneys, may formally request information from the other side by means of written *interrogatories* (questions) and requests for production of written records. "Discovery" can often be a fishing trip where the employee's attorney seeks all kinds of information about the company and its personnel practices in hopes that helpful evidence will shake out.

Another early discovery stage involves *depositions*. Parties and nonparties may be summoned by *subpoena* to testify in a deposition. Being "deposed" means being asked a series of questions by the other party's attorney in the presence of your attorney. Your deposition is recorded by a court reporter or stenographer. During the deposition, you're under oath.

In a deposition, the rules are different than a trial's. Judges are not present, and the other attorney can ask almost any kind of question in the interest of discovering information. During a trial, your attorney may raise objections to dangerous questions; in a deposition, most objections are only "for the record." Most questions are allowable, and in most cases, the rules require that you answer.

Preparation of key company representatives, usually the employee's supervisors and the personnel manager, is critical to the successful defense of a lawsuit. The company's attorney should spend time analyzing with each witness the questions that may be asked and decide how best to handle each question.

You may not want to research certain issues ahead of time because that information may be subject to disclosure to the other party during the discovery process. This is an area you will want to discuss with your attorney.

The deposition is not a game show. You will not get points for answering quickly. You protect yourself best by pausing and reflecting on each question, making sure that you understand exactly what the question asks. By doing so, you'll avoid a careless answer or giving more information than was needed to respond to the question. If the other attorney rushes you, you might say, "Counsel, excuse me, I haven't finished answering." Take your time.

Keep your answers short and honest. Short answers are easier to keep accurate and run less risk of adding information you'll later wish you'd left unsaid.

It is especially important not to guess or lie. Your guesses can be used against you, and a lie in a deposition can be used to *impeach* your testimony (question your credibility). A lie made under oath is a serious crime. "I don't know" is an acceptable answer when you truly cannot remember an event. It is equally acceptable, and perhaps better in some circumstances, to respond "My best recollection of that event is . . ." when your memory is hazy on precise details, but you have general recall of an event. A blanket "I don't know" response when you have some recall may be used by the other side to prevent or limit your testimony at trial about those subjects you did "not know" during your deposition.

If you are asked a question you don't understand, say so. If a question is too broad, vague, unclear, or ambiguous, you can ask to have it explained. In any of these situations, you can instead say, "I'm not sure I understand the question. Could you restate it?"

If the question contains an assumption—"Do you still beat your husband?"—you can answer, "I'm not sure I understand the question. I do not beat my husband."

Don't take the questioning process personally. Many honest witnesses become defensive or belligerent during the questioning process. Keeping your temper and your balance is important. In a deposition, your truthfulness, memory, perceptions, and bias may be challenged. While you may feel attacked, the other attorney is simply playing her part. If you let yourself react, you'll lose your ability to think clearly.

If the case goes to trial, your demeanor and dress will be important. You're on display while you're sitting at the defense table. Keep a low profile. Despite the stress of the trial, get plenty of sleep. You'll handle the situation better if you're rested.

As in a deposition, it's important that you tell the truth. You'll want to be polite, even if the other attorney is belligerent or insulting.

In a trial situation, it is even more important to pause if you're asked a difficult question. While you're pausing, you not only have time to consider your response but your attorney has time to raise any appropriate objections. Even if an objection is overruled, the objection itself may give you a clue about handling the question. For example, if your attorney's objection is "the question is too broad," you can say, "Could you restate the question. I'm not sure I understand." Be sure to take cues from your attorney and to listen to your attorney; her objectivity may save you from becoming emotionally clouded.

If you realize that you answered a question incorrectly, you can tell the other attorney, "I need to correct something I said earlier." Chances are, your attorney will want to clear up the error later during his questioning of you. It is better to correct a mistake or hastily offered remark than to let the opposing attorney use it against you later.

Finally, keep in mind that in employee-lawsuit situations, you as a management representative are still in charge. Don't weaken the company's position by lack of preparation or by forgetting that you can handle yourself and the process.

36

Cases Created from Actual Court Cases

Each of the following cases is fabricated from an actual court case (and all names have been changed). After you've read each of the cases, you'll have an idea of the types of cases that have been tried. Since the cases have been simplified, the names of the plaintiffs and the companies have been altered. In each of the cases, decide (1) Which guidelines apply. (2) What the court decision will be. Special questions follow some cases.

After you've made your decisions, turn to the back of the chapter to read a simplified summary of how the courts treated the cases.

Case 1

Harry Fallon joined Bishop Associates as its marketing manager. Two and a half years later, his supervisor, Pierce, left Bishop and formed Oasis, a competing company. Pierce contacted Fallon to see if Fallon would leave Bishop and join Oasis. Fallon said yes, provided he was given adequate insurance benefits.

Fallon continued to work for Bishop; however, he gave Oasis business advice and participated in discussions concerning Oasis' capital structure. He also met with potential investors for Oasis and told them he would join Oasis.

Several months later, Bishop management learned of Fallon's actions and confronted him. Fallon denied working for Oasis and refused to give Bishop managers any information, saying he had an obligation to Pierce. Bishop then asked Fallon to sign an addendum to his confidentiality agreement with Bishop. When Fallon refused, Bishop management told him he could not return to work until he signed. Two months later, Fallon signed.

In the interim, Bishop had replaced Fallon and was satisfied with his replacement's work performance. They told Fallon that he couldn't have his former position back but that he could have a comparable position in either Los Angeles or Phoenix.

One and a half months later, Fallon resigned and went to work for another company. Bishop paid Fallon full salary and benefits up to the date of his resignation.

Fallon then sued Bishop for wrongful discharge, breach of contract, and intentional infliction of emotional distress. He stated that his resignation was a "constructive termination."

What guidelines apply? What do you think the court decision will be?

Case 2

ABC Corporation discharged Edward Jones, a black man, because his wages had been garnisheed several times in violation of a written company rule that stated, "Conduct your personal finances in such a way that garnishments will not be made on your wages."

Jones had been given several warnings that garnishments would not be tolerated. Jones brought a complaint under Title VII alleging race discrimination, arguing that blacks are more frequently subject to garnishment than whites.

The company responded that its policy was justified because garnishments generated additional paperwork and employees whose wages were being garnisheed were less motivated to do good work.

Which guidelines apply? What do you think the court decision will be?

Case 3

ABC Corporation employs security guards. It imposes an absolute requirement that applicants be at least 5 feet 5 inches tall and weigh at least 130 pounds. The company imposes these requirements because a certain degree of strength is essential to good job performance.

Mary Small, an otherwise qualified applicant, was rejected because she failed to meet the minimum weight requirements. She brought a suit for discrimination under Title VII.

Which guidelines apply? What further evidence must Mary Small present in order to prevail? How will the company defend against Mary Small's claim, and what changes could it make in its employment practices to make its position stronger? As the situation now stands, what will the court decide?

Case 4

Big Company was involved in an ongoing dispute with Joe Hernandez with respect to its racial policies. Joe Hernandez was suspended for fighting and brought a discrimination complaint, charging that this suspension was motivated by racial hatred. The Equal Employment Opportunity Commission dismissed the complaint but advised Joe that he could seek a rehearing. Joe responded at length in a letter that contained both new information and totally unfounded charges that the employer had bribed the commission officials in order to obtain the ruling.

The letter was forwarded to the company, and Joe Hernandez was discharged on the basis that he made false and malicious statements about the employer. Joe protested his firing under Title VII.

Which guidelines apply? What do you think the court decision will be?

Case 5

Bank A had a standing order with a local employment agency for females between the ages of 21 and 25 for teller positions. It employed many women in this age group. It didn't employ any tellers over the age of 40. Mrs. Olds, 45, applied for a job with Bank A.

The bank manager stated that he thought continuous standing would be a problem for Mrs. Olds in a teller job. Mrs. Olds stated that she would accept his decision. The bank manager wrote in his interview notes: "too old for a teller position." The bank's opinion was that an older person couldn't stand on her feet all day.

Mrs. Olds had no experience, but some women in their twenties had been hired without experience. During an investigation, the Department of Labor discovered this practice. Mrs. Olds brought suit.

Which guidelines apply? What do you think the legal decision will be?

Case 6

Becky Smith, a black woman, was employed as a clerical worker. She was not an ideal employee; she was frequently absent or tardy, took excessive breaks, and used the telephone and copier for personal purposes. Nevertheless, in nine months of employment, she received one promotion.

She was formally reprimanded for her absenteeism and tardiness, and brought a charge with the Equal Employment Opportunity Commission, alleging that she had been denied promotion opportunities because of her race. Her department was not a very tight ship; most of the other employees were also frequently absent and tardy, and used the telephone for personal reasons.

Her supervisors were upset about the charge and felt the reprimand had been amply justified by Ms. Smith's poor working habits. They were also concerned that a successful charge might reflect badly on them. Therefore, they instituted a program carefully documenting the plaintiff's work habits. They kept written records of her times of arrival at work and the length of breaks she took. They also questioned other employees about her activities and kept records of other persons with whom she associated. They were very careful to reprimand her for every breach of company policy. They gave her special instructions concerning personal use of the telephone and reprimanded and suspended her for violation of those instructions.

Ms. Smith became increasingly difficult and upset as a result of this special attention. Ms. Smith was finally discharged. During this time, the other employees were treated as always.

Was Ms. Smith discriminated against? If so, how? Was the conduct of her supervisors proper? If not, what actions could they have properly taken to protect the company's interest? What do you think the court decision will be?

Case 7

Employer X has a staff for janitorial work. This staff is divided into cleaning women and maintenance men. The cleaning women dust, empty waste baskets, clean walls and floors, damp-mop, vacuum, and do other cleaning chores. The maintenance men also do cleaning chores. In addition, they move heavy loads of trash and scrub floors using large metal containers that weigh 400 pounds when full of water. They also do dusting in high places, which requires the use of scaffolds and ladders. They perform minor repairs and replace light bulbs.

One of the maintenance men is hit by a truck, and Employer X asks Flossie to fill in for him until he can come back to work. Flossie's job classification is not changed. Cleaning women are paid less than maintenance men. Flossie and her friends Ann, Marie, and Joan bring an action under the Equal Pay Act.

What factors will the court consider in reaching the result? Which guildelines apply? What do you think the court decision will be?

Case 8

Employer Y uses both men and women for a series of clerical jobs, including shipping and receiving, data processing, billing, and so forth. It describes the male employees as sales trainees and rotates them through the jobs with the express understanding that the males will be promoted to positions in sales. The trainees are promoted into sales positions as they become open.

The company does not employ females in sales positions because the positions require travel. The male sales trainees are paid more than the female clerical workers.

The women sued, basing their suit on the Equal Pay Act. In court, the company argued that the wage differential was justified, even though the men and women are doing the same work, because the males were involved in a training program that was a "factor other than sex" that justified the wage differential.

Which guidelines apply? What do you think the decision will be?

Case 9

Company Z is a drilling company which operates "work-over rigs" used to revive oil wells with declining production. Company Z operates with four-man crews headed by "pushers." The work is dangerous and difficult, and requires perfect communication between the workers to avoid safety problems. Joe Blow is a pusher. He imposes, on his own, a policy forbidding the use of any language but English on the job. Jim Able, an Alaskan native, is employed on the drilling crew. He was hired by Joe Blow and informed orally that he should not "talk native" on the job.

Jim Able, during a lull in the driller operation, brought some materials to a fellow native worker and asked him in Inupiat where they should be placed. The fellow worker replied in English, and Jim Able turned to leave. Joe Blow, infuriated, ordered Jim Able off the job site and told him never to come back. The other worker objected to this action, and Joe Blow knocked him down.

The entire incident was observed by a company supervisor. Joe Blow was retained because good pushers are hard to find. The supervisor acquiesced in the discharge of Jim Able. Jim Able brought an action under Title VII for discrimination on the basis of race or national origin.

Which guidelines apply? What actions could the company have taken before the incident to protect its interests? What actions could the company have taken after the incident to protect its interests? What do you think the court decision will be?

Case 10

Company A requires all job applicants except general laborers to make a certain minimum score on a generalized test of intelligence. In addition, all applicants for management positions are required to undergo a rigorous and extensive training program. Applicants can be admitted to the training only if they obtain a certain minimum score on a specially designed test of analytical and communication skills developed for the company by an expert.

The test has been used for five years, and follow-up studies conducted by the experts indicate a high correlation between success on the management-training test and successful completion of the program and good job performance. Four times as many blacks as whites fail to make the requisite score on the general intelligence test. Six times as many blacks as whites fail to make the requisite score on the mangement-trainee test. Rejected black applicants bring a Title VII action.

The black applicants challenge both the general employment practices of the company and the management employment practices of the company.

How will the company defend against the discrimination charge? Which guidelines apply? Under the facts given, what do you think the court will decide?

Case 11

John Smith suffers from cerebral palsy. In spite of his handicap, he obtained employment with the ABC Corporation. Over the course of 20 years, he worked his way up to a Grade 9 electronics-technician position. He analyzed electronic systems, performed routine checks on equipment, and made repairs. He was an employee of average competence in this job assignment. During a period of recession, reduction of the work force was necessary. The company did not need as many electronics technicians as it had; in line with company policy and seniority arrangements, John Smith was transferred to a related job assignment of the same grade.

This job assignment required certified soldering and other tasks that John Smith, because of his handicap, was unable to perform. Negative letters were placed in his personnel file. His supervisor did not want to fire John and asked John if he would accept a downgrading to his original job assignment of 20 years ago. John Smith reluctantly agreed to the demotion and protested to a higher supervisor.

In response to this, the supervisor circulated Smith's personnel file among all the company supervisors in an attempt to find him an equal-grade position in the company. Partly because of the negative letters, which by then were included in the file, an equal-grade job assignment was not offered. John Smith was demoted and brought an action under state law for job discrimination on the basis of handicap. The company maintains that John Smith was treated like anyone else.

Which guidelines apply? What do you think the court decision will be?

Case 12

The ABC Corporation employs a number of helicopter pilots. The work demands long shifts and involves substantial danger, both to the helicopter operator and to his fellow employees in the helicopter. The employer refuses to hire helicopter pilots over 40 years of age. A rejected applicant who is 41 and otherwise qualified brings suit under the Age Discrimination Employment Act.

Which guidelines apply? What do you think the court decision will be?

Case 13

An instructor at a juvenile detention center was fired for violating an unwritten dress code that required a "conservative, Brooks Brothers look." She sued, stating that the code had a negative impact on women and was thus sex-discriminative. She pointed out that no male had ever been discharged because of appearance.

Her employer, a judge, stated that the code related to "business needs," that the public's confidence depended on government employees' professionalism.

Which guidelines apply? What do you think the court decision will be?

Case 14

Many union issues are decided, as this one was, by a labor-management arbitrator, not a court. What do you think the outcome was?

The Bearings Company's contract with union employees authorized 62 minutes daily for breaktime. When company management learned that the average employee spent 95 to 97 minutes daily on break, they decided the more than half hour of daily time lost was an issue worth resolving.

Management decided to schedule breaks that had formerly been at the employees' discretion. They posted a schedule on a central bulletin board and sent all employees a memo.

When a supervisor later saw an employee taking a break at an unscheduled time, he told the employee not to do it again or face a written reprimand. Two hours later, the employee again took an unscheduled break and was fired.

The management felt the employee was intentionally disobeying an order and thus insubordinate. The union argued that the employee had been warned about a written reprimand, not a discharge.

What guidelines apply? How do you think the arbitrator will decide?

Case 15*

In 1981, Jones Food Stores switched to computerized scanners at their checkout stands. After that, their Naperville store issued a policy requiring that all clerks check groceries with their right hand. A left-handed checker, Chris Neese, resigned.

Although store policy required right-handed checking and Neese signed a form stating that she would always check with her right hand, she said she could work easier and faster with her left hand. Neese told newspaper columnist Bob Greene, "It was driving me crazy."

Neese, a store employee for one and a half years, stated that she quit in frustration after repeated arguments with the store manager. Neese sued, and the case went to a jury.

What guidelines apply? How do you think the jury decided?

*Based on an actual court case involving Jewel Food Stores.

Case 16*

In 1981, Lawson, an XRT employee in a lower-level job, dated an employee of a competitor. Her supervisor ordered her to stop the dating, stating that he feared she would release confidential information.

Lawson's supervisor then fired her before she could decide whether to stop dating the competitor's employee.

Lawson stated that a former chair of the XRT board had issued a memo ensuring employees that their personal lives were private. The supervisor said that no such policy existed.

What guidelines apply? What do you think the court will decide?

*Fabricated from a case involving IBM.

Case 17

Jim Straight, a devout Seventh-Day Adventist, works for ABC Corporation. ABC has a contract with XYZ Union that contains a "closed-shop" provision.

Jim Straight's religious beliefs forbid union membership. The union and ABC management have attempted to resolve this conflict by offering to allow Jim Straight to continue to work without union membership, provided he pays union dues.

Jim Straight, believing that unions act contrary to biblical precepts concerning obedience to employers, refused to pay the $5-a-month union dues. Straight offered instead to pay the dues to a nonreligious charity. The union stated that this would impose hardship on it and leave the door open to others who would take advantage of union benefits without finanically supporting the union. Jim Straight was the only Seventh Day Adventist employee of the corporation. The union forced ABC to discharge Straight. Jim Straight filed suit.

What guidelines apply? What do you think the court will decide?

Case 18

Avenue Terrace Cooperative hired Maxie Smith as the resident manager, giving her a written employment agreement. This agreement contained provisions related to termination but did not promise employment for a period of time. It did say that "if the resident manager . . . should have to be discharged for cause . . ."

When Avenue fired Maxie, she sued for breach of employment agreement, contending that she was fired without just cause.

Case 19

The city manager of Flat River, Missouri, terminated a policeman in 1983, based on the police chief's recommendatin. The chief felt the policeman had used excessive force in obtaining a sack of fireworks from a citizen.

The policeman petitioned the circuit court, stating that "excessive force" was not listed as a reason for discharge in the city's personnel manual.

Decisions

Case 1. The trial court granted Bishop summary judgment and entered a judgment of dismissal, resolving the case. Fallon appealed.

The court of appeals affirmed the trial court's decision. They stated that Bishop had good cause to terminate Fallon for breach of duty on the loyalty issue. Therefore, they found no wrongful discharge.

While Fallon had argued that his actions were permissible to seek other employment or be prepared to compete after resigning, the court ruled that Fallon had acted to further Oasis' and not his employer's interests.

The court denied that Fallon's discharge was punishment for seeking other work, stating that no public policy authorized an employee to assist an employer's competitor. If the discharge had been punishment for seeking other employment, it might have been a violation of public policy.

The court rejected Fallon's claim of emotional distress and held that Bishop's accusations of disloyalty were not outrageous but accurate.

Case 2. Ed Jones prevailed. Even though the policy of firing employees whose wages are garnisheed is superficially neutral, the policy may have a disproportionate impact on black people because they are more frequently subject to wage garnishment.

The court rejected the employer's argument that wage garnishment justified dismissal because it created inconvenience in paperwork. This argument was rejected because tangential inconvenience is not enough to justify a practice with discriminatory effect. It is necessary that there be a job-related reason for the burdensome policy.

The court believed that the argument that a worker whose wages were garnisheed would be less motivated was entitled to some consideration, in that it stated a job-related reason for the policy, but rejected the argument because the same result could be obtained by the less drastic means of dismissing unproductive workers on the basis of their lack of productivity.

The court approved a stipulation of the parties that ordered $3,173.32 to Jones in back wages and paid his attorney's fees and costs.

The company was also enjoined against discharging employees because of the garnishment of their wages. This case was based on *Johnson v. Pike Corp. of America,* 332 F.Supp. 490 (CD Cal. 1971).

Case 3. To prove her case, Mary Small must show that the height and weight requirements have a disparate impact on women and that a higher percentage of women are excluded from the potential applicant pool by the requirements.

She may do this by presenting evidence that a substantial percentage of women are excluded from the pool of potential applicants by these requirements, whereas an insignificant number of men are excluded. Statistical evidence may be used to show the percentage of women who fail to meet the height and weight requirements.

If she demonstrates this, the company must defend its policy on the basis of job-relatedness. The company will be in a stronger position if it has adopted and validated tests that measure strength directly. This case was based on *Dothard v. Rawlinson,* 433 U.S. 321 (1977), a Supreme Court case involving the employment of prison guards.

Case 4. The court held for Hernandez in spite of the fact that the charges of bribery were unsupported.

The court held that even after the defamatory material was deleted from the letter, the letter was sufficient to state a claim under the act and was therefore privileged under section 704(a) of the act (42 U.S.C. sec. 2000(e)-3).

The court held that Hernandez had to be reinstated and given back pay. This case is based on *Pettway v. American Cast Iron Pipe Co.,* 411 F.2d 988 (5th Cir. 1969).

Case 5. The court decision was that this was a clear-cut case of discrimination under the Age Discrimination in Employment Act. The court issued an injunction prohibiting further discrimination by this employer.

According to the court, the applicant's lack of experience was not a justification for refusing to hire her because younger applicants lacking experience were hired for the position. Also, regardless of age, an older person may be able to fulfill all the duties of a teller. An older person may be able to stand on her feet all day, and a younger person may not.

Furthermore, the decision stated, the applicant's agreement to abide by the bank manager's decision about her ability to perform the job was not an admission that she was unfit for the job.

An interviewer should use open-ended questions rather than stating assumptions about the ability of older people, women, or handicapped people. This case was based on *Hodgson v. First Federal Savings & Loan Association of Broward County,* 455 F.2d 818 (5th Cir. 1972). A similar Alaska case is *Simpson v. Alaska State Human Rights Commission,* 433 F.Supp. 552 (D. Alaska 1976).

Case 6. The court stated that Ms. Smith was not discriminated against on the basis of race.

The court found that her work habits were atrocious and that her treatment before the filing of the EEOC complaint had been evenhanded.

However, the court found that she had been subject to retaliation, in violation of 42 U.S.C. sec. 2000(e)-3, as a result of her original EEOC complaint and that she was entitled to back wages, reinstatement in her position, attorney's fees, costs, and a protective injunction to prevent further harassment. Retaliation may be found to have occurred when a legitimate rule is not evenly applied. The court stated that management singled Ms. Smith out after she brought her initial discrimination charge. Once she filed her charge, she became "protected" from harassment.

The company would have been okay had it instituted a program dealing with all employees. The company would have had a stronger position if it had prior written documentation of the problem. The company's excessive record keeping, combined with the fact that many other employees had similarly poor work habits, lost it the case.

42 U.S.C. sec. 2000(e)-3 provides that it is unlawful to discriminate against an employee because of a charge filed with the EEOC under Title VII.

According to the court, the company had a legitimate interest in being able to defend against EEOC charges. This interest could best have been served by a policy of keeping written documentation of work habits and making formal reprimands and suspensions.

The time to document a case is before, not after, an EEOC charge is filed.

Ms. Smith's supervisors should have been sensitive to the necessity of evenhanded treatment of all employees after Ms. Smith's charge. If they felt that absenteeism, tardiness, or personal phone use constituted a problem in that department, they should have instituted a program that applied equally to all employees. This case was based on *Francis v. American Telephone & Telegraph Company,* 55 F.R.D. 202 (C.D. Cal. 1972).

Case 7. In an equal-pay case such as this one brought in 1978, the court will consider the skill, responsibility, and effort involved in the two job categories to determine whether they involve equal work.

If there are extra duties in the "maintenance men" category, the court will investigate to see if they occupy a substantial portion of the workers' time. As a general guideline, the extra work done by the higher-paid employees must involve a substantial amount of the employees' time to justify the higher pay.

In this case, the difference in duties justified the maintenance men's higher pay. Flossie was entitled to the higher pay rate, with interest, for the time she had the maintenance job.

While the company prevailed, this is a case that might prompt further investigation of the company because all the maintenance personnel are men and all the cleaning personnel are women. If this company is investigated and a pattern of discrimination is found (i.e., the male-female staffing is the result of a discriminatory hiring policy and not the abilities of each applicant), the company would probably lose.

This case is based on *Marshall v. Building Maintenance Corp.,* 397 F.2d 716 (2d Cir. 1978); *Marshall v. School Board, Heritage School District,* 599 F.2d 1220 (3d Cir. 1979).

Case 8. This case, based on a 1973 case involving a drug company, is a good example of the problems relating to training programs. A bona fide training program allows employers to pay higher wages to trainees than to other workers, even though they perform the same work as regularly assigned workers.

The employer lost in this case, however, because of two deficiencies in its program.

First, the complete absence of females from the program made it suspect. Second, there was no definite time for promotion out of the training program and into a sales position. The "training" ended only when a sales position was available.

The employer could have prevailed if its training program had been open to women, even though male-dominated, and if the program had lasted a definite period, with promotion into sales at the end of that time.

The employer would have done better in screening applicants for the "sales training program" by making individual inquiries into their ability to perform the travel duties of the sales positions. It is a sexual stereotype to assume that women are not capable of travel. This case is based on *Hodgson v. Behrens Drug Co.,* 475 F.2d 1041 (5th Cir. 1973).

Case 9. Jim Able won his case in the original suit brought in 1969. The company rule forbidding employees to talk among themselves in their own language is discriminatory against native workers and employees of other national origins. However, a company can insist that employees speak only English when they are involved in dangerous operations. Business necessity would then justify the rule. However, Joe Blow applied the English-only policy in a nondangerous situation.

The company might have protected its position before the incident by informing all employees of an English-only policy in drilling situations and then evenhandedly handling discipline. Such a rule might be justified by safety considerations. It would be important for the policy to state that discharge would be the consequence of a policy violation.

The finding of discrimination against the company was also supported by the fact that it did not discipline Joe Blow for his even more serious violation of company policy—assault on a fellow worker. Even after the incident, the company could have protected itself against a discrimination claim by appropriately disciplining Joe Blow, reviewing Jim Able's dismissal, and reinstating him when it appeared the rule had not been effectively communicated to him. This case was based on *Saucedo v. Brothers Well Service,* 464 F.Supp. 919 (S.D. Tex. 1979).

Jim Able won back wages, interest, and attorney's fees.

Case 10. The company's case rests on the idea of business necessity. According to the company, the tests are job-related in that they predict job success and are related to work behavior needed for the job. The complainants' claim is that the tests are not job-related and that the tests, while apparently neutral, weed out more minority than nonminority applicants.

Because the company uses business necessity as a defense, it needs to demonstrate that the tests are job-related or that the tests predict success in a job.

The company will probably fail with respect to the generalized intelligence test, which is not related to any particular job. Some jobs may not involve significant communications skills, reading ability, mathematical ability, or other abilities tested by a general intelligence test.

The company will probably prevail with respect to the test for the management training. Because of the expense of training, the company has a legitimate interest in screening out applicants who are unlikely to complete the training program successfully.

Further, the management test addresses specific skills, communications ability and analytical ability, that are related both to the training program and to the ultimate management position.

The company's position is also supported by the fact that the test was designed to measure the skills necessary for the completion of the training program and successful job performance and that the test has been validated by follow-up studies. This case is based on two similar cases: *Griggs v. Duke Power,* 401 U.S. 424 (1971) and *Washington v. Davis,* 426 U.S. 229 (1976).

In these two similar cases, the complainants won on the general test. It was not sufficiently job-related to justify its discriminatory impact. The company won on the management-trainee test. This test was specifically designed to assess managerial communication and analytical skills and was validated as a predictor of success. Further, the company's expense in the cost of the training program justified the use of the test as a screening device.

Case 11. The court considered this a very close case. It found that the company failed to make reasonable accommodation to John Smith's handicap.

The court acknowledged that John Smith was not treated any differently than any other employee would have been under the circumstances. It pointed out that because John Smith was different from other employees, identical treatment in his case was a source of discrimination.

The employer was obliged to make reasonable accommodation to the physical limitations of its handicapped employee.

It could have and should have placed John Smith in a job where he was not destined to fail. By following its internal procedures and placing him in a job where he was doomed to fail and then demoting him, the company failed reasonably to accommodate his handicap.

John Smith recovered attorney fees, actual damages, and costs. This case is based on *Holland v. Boeing Co.,* 583 P.2d 621 (Wash. 1978).

Case 12. Although this is a clear case of age discrimination, the company will probably win. The applicant was rejected solely on the basis of age.

The company raised the defense of business necessity. First, it demonstrated that the age requirement is related to a business purpose. It was able to do this by showing that degenerative changes as a result of aging increase the risk of pilot error and that this risk is clearly related to the company's business.

The pilot argued that although the safe running of helicopters is related to the employer's business, the age qualification was not justified because ability testing could screen out unqualified applicants.

The company showed that such a test is not readily available and that degenerative changes that could not be detected by such a test were likely to cause pilot error in the rigorous circumstances of the job.

On these facts, the company prevailed, particularly because this job involves safety considerations. However, before a company imposes an age limitation, it should be satisfied that no less burdensome tests can be applied.

The courts are much more willing to uphold age limitations if they involve safety factors rather than mere considerations of efficiency.

An older employee who is inefficient could be fired on that basis, but the consequences of an accident cannot be reversed. This case is based on *Hodgson v. Greyhound Lines,* 499 F.2d 859 (7th Cir. 1974).

Case 13. In *Wislocki-Goin v. Mears* (7th Cir. 1988), the court upheld the dress-and-grooming code. The court ruled that the code was reasonably related to "business needs."

In the court's opinion, the code did not adversely affect women. The court noted that a number of the more senior managers at the detention center were female and that no evidence showed that male employees were treated differently.

While it was not an issue that the court considered in this case, the instructor might have a valid complaint based on the right to fair treatment in that she was discharged for violating an "unwritten" policy.

Case 14. Arbitrators base their decisions on the history and facts of a case, the labor-management contract, the testimony of all involved, and other evidence.

In this case, the arbitrator ruled in Barney's favor, reinstating him with full back pay. The primary issue was that the company violated its own rules of progressive discipline by moving directly from verbal warning to termination. The arbitrator considered the second incident of unscheduled breaktime a rule violation and not insubordination.

While arbitrators do not follow precedent, this case does give you an indication of how one arbitrator analyzes a situation.

Case 15. An all-right-handed jury awarded Neese $136,700: $18,323 in lost wages and $118,377 in punitive damages. They based their decision on the fact that Neese "was an excellent checker" and was "forced to do something unreasonable and arbitrary." The legal concept is "intentional interference with an advantageous relationship."

Case 16. This case was based on *Rulon-Miller v. IBM* in which the trial court awarded Lawson (Rulon-Miller) $100,000 in compensatory damages and $200,000 in punitive damages. The punitive damages resulted partly from the fact that the supervisor fired Rulon-Miller before she could decide whether to stop dating the competitor's employee. IBM appealed. The California Court of Appeals upheld the award (*Rulon-Miller v. IBM,* 1981).

Case 17. According to the court, both the union and the employer have a duty to make reasonable accommodation to Jim Straight's religious beliefs.

The court rejected the argument that complying with Jim Straight's suggestion that he pay the dues to a nonreligious charitable organization would impose an undue hardship on the union. The court stated that under other circumstances, the diversion of money might involve such great sums as to impair the union's function but that this was not the situation in this case. According to the court, if the circumstances had been different, the union and employer might have successfully argued undue hardship. This case was based on Wondzell v. Alaska Wood Products, 601 P.2d 584 (Alaska 1979).

Case 18. This case was based on *Dixie Streckfus v. Gardenside Terrace Cooperative and Triangle Associates,* 481 N.E.2d 423 (Ind.App. 1985), in which the trial court entered summary judgment for the employer. In the actual case, Dixie (Maxie) appealed the decision. The court of appeals upheld it, stating that even if Dixie had been promised that she would be discharged only for cause, she was an "employee at will" because there was no valid promise of permanent employment.

This case is an extremely close one, and courts in other states might rule differently.

Case 19. This case was based on *City of Flat River v. Lester Short,* 694 S.W.2nd. 767, Mo.App. 1985, in which the circuit court agreed with the policeman and ordered him reinstated with back pay. When the city appealed, however, the Missouri Court of Appeals reversed the decision and found for the city.

According to the appellate court, the city's personnel manual didn't grant tenure to the employee, who was thus an "employee at will." Also, the introduction to the manual stated, "This is a suggested guide only, and it is not the intent of the city to grant any employee any contractual commitment, express or implied, by its adoption." The decision also stated that it would be impossible for a manual to define every possible act of misconduct that might provide "good cause" for discharge.

Glossary

This glossary defines terms used in this book and terms that the reader may encounter in related reading. This glossary is thus a handy reference to technical and legal terms that the reader may encounter in legal and other situations.

Accessibility. A barrier-free environment in which the physically handicapped can move unaffected by external forces (such as architectural design and physical barriers).

Adverse Impact. An employment practice that negatively affects one group of employees or applicants but not another, such as a management test that most minority candidates flunk but most nonminority candidates pass, and has an adverse (negative) impact (effect) on one group.

Whether or not the test users or designers intend the test to be discriminatory, it in fact discriminates against the group it negatively affects.

If the employer can demonstrate that the job requirement or other employment practice is reasonably necessary for the successful performance of the job, the requirement or practice is allowed. If not, the employer must give it up because of its adverse impact.

Affected Class. Any employee group that has suffered and continues to suffer the effects of unlawful discrimination (the term generally refers to women and minorities).

Affirmative Action, Affirmative-Action Plan. Affirmative action is the set of procedures and the plan by which a company reaches equal employment opportunity.

Affirmative action means that qualified minorities and women must be sought out, recruited, and fully considered on the basis of their qualifications. Also, handicapped individuals and veterans must be fully considered.

Affirmative action is necessary because

1. employers continue to recruit employees by word-of-mouth, which works to the advantage of the acquaintances of most employers' primarily white male work forces;

2. past discrimination, whether intentional or not, means that there are fewer minority employees to promote into higher positions; and
3. an employer's discriminatory reputation may keep minorities from applying for jobs.

Affirmative action does not mean that a person who is not qualified for a job must be given a job. Affirmative action means that qualified or qualifiable minorities must be actively recruited and fully considered on the basis of their qualifications.

In its company affirmative-action plan, management identifies and eliminates discriminatory barriers to employment and promotion.

The management takes a look at how many minorities, women, and handicapped are employed relative to how many of those categories of workers there are in the work force.

The management takes steps to provide employment opportunities to people who have been discriminated against.

Workers who belong to a category that may have suffered effects of discrimination in the past are given a chance to "catch up."

The plan provides measurable, yearly goals or improvements in hiring, training, and promoting minorities and females. The plan's effectiveness is measured by the results it achieves. A written AAP is required of all federal contractors with contracts of $50,000 or more and involving 50 or more employees.

American Indian, Alaskan Native. A person born to and maintaining cultural identification through tribal affiliation or community recognition with any American Indian or Alaskan native group.

Applicant Flow Record. A written, objective measure used to monitor the recruiting efforts of an organization's affirmative-action plan. This record shows each job applicant's name, race, national origin, sex, referral source, date of application, position applied for, and results of the interview.

Asian, Pacific Islander. An individual born to any of the original peoples of the Far East, Southeast Asia, the Indian subcontinent or the Pacific Islands.

Availability. The number of women and minorities "ready, willing and able to work" in a geographic region. This figure is used in setting goals and determining underutilization for affirmative-action plans. Measures of availability include occupational parity, labor-force parity, and population parity.

Black. A person born to any of the black racial groups.

Bona Fide Occupations Qualification (BFOQ). An employer can use an employment practice that would otherwise be discriminatory if it is a bona fide occupational qualification reasonably necessary for the normal operation of business.

An employer may select employees on the basis of sex, religion, or national origin where it is "reasonably" necessary to normal business operations.

The burden of proof is on the employer who claims as a defense to charges of discrimination the exception of BFOQ.

Race is never a BFOQ under the law.

Sex is a BFOQ where the position by its nature requires specific physical characteristics possessed by one sex. This applies to actors and actresses, modeling jobs, and restroom attendants. This does not apply to situations in which the "customers prefer" one sex. It does not apply to situations of sex stereotyping.

Religion is a BFOQ when the job involves the teachings of a particular religious organization. This is strictly interpreted. For example, a religious school could claim that it needs to hire only teachers of a certain religious faith as a BFOQ. It could not make the same claim for its receptionist.

National origin is a BFOQ in organizations in which the principal activity is to promote the interests of a particular national group. A BFOQ for an airline pilot may be that the pilot must be at least 5′ 5″ in order to have easy access to all instruments and to see clearly over the front panel.

Business Necessity. An employment practice that has an adverse impact, but is demonstrated to be

1. absolutely essential to the efficient and safe operation of the business, and
2. absolutely essential to the economic survival of the business, for which no less adversely impacting alternative can be found, is allowed as a business necessity. Business necessity is not business convenience. The employer must prove that the practice is necessary.

An example of a business necessity might be the requirement that airplane pilots, who are responsible for the safety of a number of passengers, be under the age of 60.

Chilling Effect. If an employer has a work environment or uses employment practices that discourage minorities or women from seeking employment or promotion, a "chilling effect" exists.

Class Action. A class action is a lawsuit brought by one or more persons on behalf of "all others similarly situated." If successful, the legal remedies won will not only eliminate the discrimination that has occurred against an individual and compensate him for the effects of that discrimination but will also compensate all others in similar categories who have suffered as a result of the same practices. This means that the employer may wind up paying wages and damages not only to the suing party but to all other members of similar categories of applicants or employees.

Complainant. A person who files a discrimination complaint.

Complaint. A statement filed with a municipal, state, or federal equal-employment-opportunity regulatory agency or commission claiming that an employer has discriminated.

Compliance. The requirement that federal contractors carry out (comply with) the affirmative-action plan or nondiscrimination clause in their contracts.

Defamation. When a person is held up to ridicule, disdain, or contempt in the community by injury to reputation, goodwill, or esteem or by inciting unfavorable, harmful, or unpleasant opinions about the person, defamation occurs. Defamation includes both libel and slander.

Defendant. A person against whom a lawsuit or a discrimination complaint is filed.

Disabled Veteran. A person whose discharge or release from active duty was related to a disability that occurred or was aggravated by conditions occurring in the line of duty and who is entitled to a 30 percent disability compensation under the regulations administered by the Veteran's Administration.

Discrimination. Discrimination means denying certain classes of people equal opportunities.

Discrimination may be done by people who actively intend to discriminate or by people who deny opportunities due to stereotypes.

Discrimination happens whenever a distinctly different treatment is given to a group of people. It is any employment practice that tends to have an unequal and unfavorable impact on protected classes unless such a practice is justified by "business necessity."

To prove discrimination, a person need not prove that the employer was prejudiced. It is the *effect* of the employment practice that counts.

Not all discrimination is against the law. For instance, you may be able to discriminate against people who smoke cigars.

You may not discriminate against individuals in certain "protected categories" because they are members of that category or because of characteristics related to that category. These categories include:

race or color;
national origin;
sex;
age;
physical handicap;
religion;
pregnancy;
Vietnam era veterans.

In certain states and jurisdictions, other categories such as parenthood, marital status and changes in marital status become "protected."

Finally, discrimination is not always conscious. You may be unaware of some of the stereotypes you hold.

Disparate Effect. The definition for disparate effect is the same as the definition of "adverse impact."

Employee Rights. Employee rights include rights in these areas:

privacy;
off the job associations;
access to information that concerns themselves;
free expression;
protesting and investigation of unsafe work conditions;
protesting discrimination;
self-organization and forming of unions;
fair treatment;
filing of worker's-compensation claims; and
pursuit of wage-and-labor claims.

Employer Information Report EEO-1. This is a report due annually that shows the representation of female and minority employees in an employer's total work force. This report, which is also called Standard Form 100, also shows work-force "groupings" (i.e., office/manager, professional, technical, sales, clerical, and so forth).

Employment at Will. An employment situation in which an employee can resign at any time and employers can terminate employees at any time, even without notice.

Equal Employment Opportunity (EEO). Equal employment opportunity refers to laws intended to eliminate discrimination in every aspect of employment.

EEO means that each employee should be treated equally in all job-related matters and that all decisions should be based on the abilities of the individual and the requirements of the job.

EEO means that each individual has a right to be fully considered for any job for which she is qualified. It does not mean that a person who is not qualified for a job must be given a job.

Equal Employment Opportunity Commission (EEOC). The EEOC administers Title VII of the Civil Rights Act of 1964, which ensures equal treatment in employment.

Goals and Timetables. The "goals and timetables" concept was developed by the Office of Federal Contract Compliance Program as a major element in affirmative-action programs required by government contractors. According to the OFCCP, goals and timetables are numerical targets for hiring and promoting minorities and women who are underrepresented in specific *job groups.* Despite some opinions to the contrary, the OFCCP has always maintained that goals and timetables are not the same as *quotas.*

Good Faith. When an employer takes real actions to implement affirmative action, this is good faith.

Guidelines. Federal EEO agencies issue guidelines to explain and interpret the laws and executive orders they enforce. Although guidelines don't have the force of law, they have more clout than the name would indicate. They can be legally enforced by their sponsoring agencies unless the courts overturn them, and courts usually give them great deference.

Handicap. A physical or mental impairment that substantially limits one or more major life activities.

Handicapped Individual. The legal definition of a handicapped person grew out of the need to identify those who are protected from job discrimination by the Rehabilitation Act of 1973. Section 503 of that law requires government contractors to take affirmative action to employ and promote handicapped people; Section 504 forbids discrimination against the handicapped by recipients of federal funds.

The definition protects those who (1) have a physical or mental impairment that substantially limits one or more major life activities, (2) have a record of such impairment, or (3) are regarded as having such an impairment.

A handicap is substantially limiting if it is likely to cause difficulty in securing, retaining, or advancing in employment.

Hispanic. A person of Mexican, Puerto Rican, Cuban, South American, or other Spanish culture or origin.

Impact vs. Intent, Intent vs. Effect. Discrimination does not have to be intentional to be illegal. Disparate treatment refers to employment practices in which the employer denies opportunities to women, minorities, and the handicapped by treating them differently than nonminority, male, and nonhandicapped employees or applicants. These practices are illegal.

Disparate treatment refers to situations in which employment practices have discriminatory impact in that they prevent a disproportionately higher number of protected class (minority, women, or handicapped) than nonprotected class (white males) applicants from employment opportunities. For example, the requirement of a high school diploma may screen out more minority applicants than white applicants, and yet may not be necessary for good job performance.

Employers don't necessarily intend to discriminate when they treat some employees or applicants differently; however, accidental discrimination denies employment rights as fully as intentional discrimination.

An example of practices that are fair but might have discriminatory effects include height and weight requirements (discrimination against many women and minority applicants), credit checks, high school diploma requirements and questions about arrest records (discrimination against many minority groups).

If a job requirement is reasonably necessary for the successful performance of the job for which it is used (job-related), it is lawful; if it is discriminatory in effect and not job-related, it is unlawful.

Job Categories. These are the categories of employees that are listed in a company's affirmative-action report. Examples of these categories: officials and managers; professionals; technicians; sales workers; office and clerical; craft workers (skilled); operatives (semiskilled); laborers (unskilled); and service workers.

Job Group. This term refers to the basic work unit that government contractors must use in determining if *underutilization* exists in their organization. As defined by the Office of Federal Contract Compliance Program, a job group consists of jobs with similar content, wage rates, and promotional opportunities. The jobs can cut across departmental lines (such as secretarial jobs). Job groups are refined versions of *job categories.*

Job-Group Analysis. In developing their affirmative-action programs, contractors must do a job-group analysis to determine the makeup of each job group in terms of minorities and women. This analysis will then be used to determine *underutilization* in each job group.

Job Qualifications. In EEO language, the term "job qualifications" has special meaning. An employer's qualifications for hiring and promoting must meet legal EEO requirements. Basically, this means that any job qualification that has the effect of screening out minorities or women at a greater rate than others must be validated—that is, proven by the employer to be actually related to job performance.

Job-relatedness. It is crucial that any criteria you use to decide if a person should be hired, fired, promoted, or transferred be directly related to the job content and to what is required for job performance. For example, if a prehire test is challenged, the company must prove that an employee needs to know all the items on the test and that a high-scoring applicant will outperform a low-scoring applicant.

Just Cause. Action taken—based on reasonable grounds, fairness, honesty, and good faith—that is sufficient to be justified under the law.

Labor-Force Parity. The percentage of women and minorities in the total local labor force.

Libel. Publication of defamatory statements or material by means of printed words, writing, pictures, or signs. (See *defamation.*)

Minorities. All persons classified as black, Hispanic, Asian or Pacific Islander, American Indian or Alaskan native.

No Disparate Impact. The company must prove that a job requirement or other employment practice eliminates as many male as female candidates, or as many nonminority candidates as minority candidates.

Noncompliance. This is a term used by the Office of Federal Contract Compliance Program to indicate that a government contractor is not abiding by equal-employment-opportunity and affirmative-action requirements of Executive Order 11246. Major noncompliance can eventually lead to a contractor losing present (and being denied future) government contracts.

Nondiscrimination. Nondiscrimination requires the elimination of all existing discriminatory practices and conditions. It differs from *affirmative action,* which requires special efforts to remedy the effects of past discrimination on minorities and women.

Occupational Parity. The representation of women and minorities in particular occupational categories in an employer's recruiting area. Occupational parity is accepted as the primary basis for defining affirmative-action goals and underutilization.

Office of Federal Contract Compliance Program (OFCCP). The OFCCP reviews and enforces the equal-employment and opportunity practices of all federal prime contractors.

Parity. In EEO language, parity means that minorities and women are being employed in each *job group* in approximately the same proportion as they are available in the *relevant labor market.* Federal law does not require parity, but any government contractor with job groups below parity must take *affirmative action* to try to achieve it. (See *relevant labor market* and *affirmative action.*)

Predictive Validation. Predictive validation means that a test used to determine who is hired or promoted predicts who will do best in the job. The test scores of all candidates are then later compared with their job performance. A test is seen as a valid predictor if the people who did best on the test do best on the job.

Prejudice. Prejudice refers to feelings of superiority or negative or biased feelings toward a group as a whole or toward an individual because she is a member of that group.

Present Effects of Past Practices. "Present effects of past practices" means that employers are liable today for events and decisions in the past. If past discriminatory practices prevented women and minorities from acquiring experience or skills, they are considered to be suffering the present effect of past discrimination.

Prima Facie Evidence. Evidence that doesn't need to be otherwise "proven" because it is sufficient on its face or appearance. For example, if all of a company's women employees are clerks and all its white male employees are supervisors, a compliance agency might consider this prima facie evidence of discrimination.

Protected Class/Category. A protected class is any group that is protected from job discrimination by EEO laws. The protected categories include race, color, religion, sex, national origin, handicap, age, and Vietnam era veterans.

Qualified. The minimum qualifications for a job should be no higher for members of a protected-class applicant than they have been for the least-qualified person who presently holds the job. Job qualifications should be carefully written so that they include only those skills needed to perform the job.

Qualified Handicapped Individual. This is the term for a *handicapped individual* who is capable of performing the essential functions of a particular job with *reasonable accommodation.* Government contractors must take *affirmative action* to hire and promote qualified handicapped individuals. (See *handicapped individual, reasonable accommodation, affirmative action.)*

Quotas. In EEO language, this means the hiring and promoting of specified numbers or ratios of minorities and women for positions from which they have been excluded. Most quotas are ordered by federal courts after a finding of discrimination; however, in 1979, the Supreme Court ruled in *Weber v. Kaiser Aluminum* that an employer could voluntarily use quotas under certain circumstances, even without a finding of discrimination. The Supreme Court has also ruled in *Fullilove v. Klutznick* that Congress can order affirmative-action quotas.

Racial Minority. A protected class, members of which have been defined by the Equal Employment Opportunity Commission as black, Hispanic, American Indian, Alaskan native, or Asian or Pacific Islander.

Reasonable Accommodation. This term is used when defining the job rights of handicapped persons and persons with unusual religious practices. Federal contractors must make alterations, adjustments, or changes in the job and the workplace that will enable an otherwise *qualified handicapped individual* to perform a specific job. All employers covered by Title VII must also accommodate employees whose religious practices may conflict with normal working schedules (such as a Saturday Sabbath).

Reasonable Cause. The EEOC uses this term when it investigates a discrimination charge and finds that there is reason to believe the charge is true.

Relevant Labor Market. This refers to the area from which an employer draws applicants for a specific *job group.* Local areas are usually relevant labor markets for the lower-skilled jobs. For higher-level jobs, the relevant labor market may be the whole country. An availability for hire analysis must be based on the relevant labor market. Sometimes the OFCCP may question the employer's choice of a relevant labor market if it tends to exclude large concentrations of minorities within "reasonable" commuting distance of the employer's facility.

Requisite Skills. Government contractors must determine the *availability* of minorities and women with requisite skills for each job group. These are the skills required to be able to compete as applicants for certain jobs.

Respondent. When a discrimination complaint is filed against an employer, the employer becomes the respondent.

Reverse Discrimination. Although this term has no legal meaning, it is commonly used to refer to claims by white males that they have suffered unfair discrimination because of favorable treatment for minorities or women.

Slander. Defamation in the form of oral expressions or gestures. (See *defamation.*)

Systematic Discrimination. This term refers to employment policies and practices that negatively affect large groups of employees. Thus, the discrimination is "systematic" or systemic rather than true only in isolated cases.

Timetable. The time frame (in years) set for attaining measurable goals in an employer's affirmative-action program.

Underutilization. This means that there is a smaller number of women, minorities, or handicapped in the work force than would reasonably be expected by their presence in the external work force.

Undue Hardship. In order for an employer legally to refuse to accommodate an applicant's or employee's handicap or religious beliefs, the employer must be able to show that such accommodation would place an unreasonably severe burden on the business.

Unlawful Employment Practice. Any policy or practice that has discriminatory intent or effect.

Utilization Analysis. Every government contractor is required to conduct a utilization analysis to determine if it is underutilizing minorities and/or women in any of its *job groups.* This is done by comparing the percentages of minorities and women in each job group with their percentages in the appropriate *relevant labor market.* If the comparison shows underutilization, the employer must develop *goals* and *timetables* for hiring and promoting more minorities and women into these job groups.

Validation. Validation involves showing that an employment test or any other selection procedure actually predicts job performance. Employers must validate any procedure that screens out minorities and/or women at a greater rate than other groups.

Veteran of the Vietnam Era. A person who served on active duty for a period of more than 180 days, any part of which occurred between August 5, 1964, and May 7, 1975. Nondisabled Veterans of the Vietnam era are a protected class for up to 4 years after discharge.

Work-force Analysis. All federal contractors must conduct this analysis. It involves listing each job title in the organization with the number of whites, blacks, Hispanics, and women in each title. The analysis must also show all normal limits of formal and informal job progression.

Bibliography

Affirmative Action Today: A Legal and Practical Analysis. A Special BNA Report. Bureau of National Affairs, 1986.

Anderson, Howard L. *Primer of Equal Employment Opportunity.* Bureau of National Affairs, 1978.

Baer, Walter E. *Discipline and Discharge Under the Labor Agreement.* American Management Association, 1972.

Bureau of Business Practice: Job Discrimination Handbook.

Connolly, W. W. *A Practical Guide to Equal Employment Opportunity: Law Principles, and Practices.* Vols. 1 and 2. Law Journal Press, 1975.

Coulson, R. *The Termination Handbook.* Free Press, 1981.

Dichter, M. S., Morikawa, D. J., Gross, A. J., and Sauntry, Susan S. *Employee Dismissal Law: Forms and Procedures.* Trial Practice Library Series. John Wiley, 1986.

Doeringer, P., ed. *Programs to Employ the Disadvantaged.* Prentice-Hall, 1969.

Downing, Paul L. *Present and Proposed Affirmative Action Regulations of the Office of Federal Contract Compliance Programs for Minorities and Women.* Congressional Research Service, The Library of Congress, 1981.

"EEO Today." *The Journal of Equal Employment Opportunity Management,* Vol. 5, No. 3/Autumn, 1978; Vol. 6, No. 1/Spring, 1979; Vol. 6, No. 2/Summer, 1979; Vol. 3, No. 4/Winter, 1976.

Equal Employment Opportunity: Unification of Functions. Archived Issue Brief, Congressional Research Service, The Library of Congress, 1980.

Equal Employment Opportunity Compliance Manual. Prentice-Hall.

Famularo, Joseph J. *Handbook of Human Resources Administration.* McGraw-Hill, 1986.

Farley, Lin. *Sexual Shakedown: The Sexual Harassment of Women on the Job.* McGraw-Hill, 1978.

Federal Register, Part II. Department of Labor, Office of Federal Contract Compliance Programs.

Goodman, Jill L. "Sexual Demands on the Job." *Civil Liberties Review,* Mar.–Apr., 1978.

Hill, Marvin, Jr., and Sinicropi, Anthony V. *Management Rights, A Legal and Arbitral Analysis.* The Bureau of National Affairs, 1986.

Idelson, E. *Conducting a Self-Audit to Identify and Voluntarily Remedy Systemic*

Discrimination in Personnel Practices. Discussion Outline for National Civil Service League, Equal Employment Opportunity Law Conference, San Francisco, and Washington, D.C., 1977.

Kelber, M. "Sexual Harassment: The UN's Dirty Little Secret." *Ms.,* November 1977.

Kingsley, Daniel. *How to Fire an Employee.* Facts on File Publ., 1984.

Larson, E. R., and McDonald, L. *The Rights of Racial Minorities.* Avon Books.

Lawrence, K. *Sex Discrimination in the Workplace.* Aspen Publications.

Lawson, Joseph, II. *How to Develop a Personnel Policy Manual.* Dartnell, 1984.

Lindsey, K. "Sexual Harassment on the Job and How to Stop It." *Ms.,* November 1977.

McCulloch, Kenneth J. *Selecting Employees Safely Under the Law.* Prentice-Hall, 1981.

Mead, Margaret. "A Proposal: We Need Taboos on Sex at Work." *Redbook,* April 1978.

Michal-Johnson, Paula. *Saying Goodbye, A Manager's Guide to Employee Dismissal.* Scott, Foresman, 1985.

Peres, R. *Dealing with Employment Discrimination.* McGraw-Hill, 1978.

Perritt, H. H. *Employee Dismissal Law.* 2d ed. (Trial Practice Library Series), John Wiley Publ., 1987.

Player, M. A. *Federal Law of Employment Discrimination in a Nutshell.* West, 1976.

Puckett, Sam, and Emery, Alan. *Managing AIDS in the Workplace.* Addison-Wesley, 1988.

Roberson, Cliff. *Staying Out of Court, A Manager's Guide to Employment Law.* Lexington Books, 1985.

Ross, J. J. *Equal Employment Opportunity Compliance: 1976.* Corporate Law and Practice Course Handbook Series Number 206. Practicing Law Institute.

Schmeltzer, Aptaker, and Sheppard (law firm). *Without Just Cause: An Employer's Practical and Legal Guide on Wrongful Discharge.* BNA Customer Service Center, 1988.

Seymour, William. "Sexual Harassment: Finding a Cause of Action Under Title VII." *Labor Law Journal,* March 1979.

Terminating the Employment Relationship—Under Increasing Restraints. Association of the Bar of the City of New York, April 1981.

U.S. Commission on Civil Rights. *A Guide to Federal Laws and Regulations Prohibiting Sex Discrimination.* Clearinghouse Pub. No. 46; July 1976 (revised).

Unjust Dismissal—ILR Report. Cornell University, Fall 1982.

Walker, James W., and Lazer, Harriet L. *The End of Mandatory Retirement, Implications for Management.* John Wiley, 1978.

Weatherspoon, Floyd D. *Equal Employment Opportunity and Affirmative Action, A Sourcebook.* Garland, 1985.

Weiner, Paul I. *Wrongful Termination and Its Prevention.* ALI-ABA Courts of Study on Advance Labor and Employment Law, July 1984.

White, Jane See. "Sexual Harassment: A Pivotal Issue." *The Washington Post,* 15 August 1978.

Index